A BYZANTINE JOURNEY

A BYZANTINE JOURNEY

JOHN ASH

RANDOM HOUSE NEW YORK

THIS BOOK IS DEDICATED TO

THE PEOPLE OF ANATOLIA

Library of Congress Cataloging-in-Publication Data
Ash, John
A Byzantine journey / John Ash.
p.   cm.
Includes bibliographical references.
ISBN 0-679-40934-3 : $20.00
1. Turkey—Antiquities, Byzantine. 2. Turkey—Description and
travel. 3. Byzantine Empire—History. I. Title.
DS155.A85 1995
915.6104´39—dc20   94-36159

Book Design by Lilly Langotsky

In the battles between truth and prejudice, waged on the field of history books, it must be confessed that the latter usually wins. . . . At the hands of such prejudice many historical epochs have suffered, and most of all the epoch known as the Later Roman or Byzantine Empire. Ever since our rough crusading forefathers first saw Constantinople and met, to their contemptuous disgust, a society where everyone read and wrote, ate food with forks and preferred diplomacy to war, it has been fashionable to pass the Byzantines by with scorn and to use their name as synonymous with decadence.

—STEVEN RUNCIMAN, *The Emperor Romanus Lecapenus and His Reign*

THE ORIGINS OF A JOURNEY

For many years I had wanted to write a book about Byzantium, but I did not know where to begin. How could a mere amateur attempt a description of a civilization that had endured for more than a thousand years? The few Byzantinists I spoke to were clearly alarmed at the thought of me trampling through their scholarly vineyards. But the idea kept nagging at me, and over five years of life in New York this nagging intensified. A passage in Mark Girouard's *Cities and People* seemed to cast some light on my growing obsession. The passage describes the impression Constantinople made on visitors arriving from the West in the ninth and tenth centuries: "When the first view of Constantinople exploded on their vision, it must have filled them with the same kind of awe and amazement as filled immigrants from Europe when they approached Manhattan from the sea."

I began to think of Constantinople-Byzantium as a medieval Manhattan and Manhattan as a modern Byzantium. Although the analogy is, no doubt, a dubious one from a scholarly point of view, the word "Byzantine" was frequently bandied about in the salons and newspapers of New York. It soon became clear, however, that the term was extremely mutable and uncertain. Sometimes it seemed to evoke vague ideas of mystery and exoticism, perhaps influenced by Yeats' hypnotically musical "Byzantium" poems, but most often it meant something needlessly complex and involuted, and was frequently applied to worlds of bureaucracy and diplomacy. This was perhaps a dim, collective historical memory of a time before the rise of the West and the "discovery" of America, when Byzantium was the only Christian state with a well-organized and highly educated class of civil servants, but over time the term "Byzantine" had also acquired subtle (and not so subtle) pejorative connotations to do with duplicity, corruption and decadence. As early as 968 Bishop Liutprand of Cremona, the western envoy, described the Byzantines as "idle liars of neither gender," while in the eighteenth century the magisterial Gibbon dismissed the whole of Byzantine history as "a tedious and uniform tale of weakness and misery." Even in the early years of our own century historians routinely slandered all things Byzantine.

Liutprand's outburst has something in common with fundamentalist fulminations against Sodom-on-the-Hudson, but when New Yorkers described their city as "Byzantine" they were being rather more positive: if New York was decadent, it was *glamorously* decadent; it might be crime-ridden, squalid and corrupt, but it was also one of the world's preeminent centers of civilization. The much-resented arrogance of New Yorkers is distinctly Byzantine: for most of their long history the people of Byzantium remained convinced—with some justification—that their city and its civilization were infinitely superior to anything to be found farther to the West.

My casual survey revealed that most of the people I spoke to were aware that the Byzantines had produced great art, but they were not clear who they were or which territories their empire had covered. It was generally understood that Byzantium-Constantinople-Istanbul were one and the same place, but it was not so generally known that the Byzantines spoke Greek and diligently preserved the traditions of Hellenism (albeit in a Christianized form), nor that their empire was the direct descendant of the Eastern Roman Empire and that, in consequence, every self-respecting Byzantine, between the fourth and the fifteenth centuries, considered himself to be "Roman," however "Greek" he might appear to his contemporaries in the West.

Such confusion was hardly shocking, but, given the enormous debt we owe the Byzantines, it was saddening. Although in certain respects they are very remote from us, their contribution to the character and destiny of European civilization is immense: without them the West might never have existed. Consider that of the 55,000 ancient Greek texts that have come down to us, we owe fully 40,000 to the repetitive labors of Byzantine scholars and scribes. Their empire provides an unbroken link between the culture of late antiquity and the beginnings of the modern age. And it was they who defended Europe's eastern approaches against Islam—from the seventh to the eleventh centuries against the Arabs, and from the eleventh to the fifteenth centuries against the Turks. One does not have to be hostile to Islam to appreciate the magnitude of this achievement.

There was good reason to believe not only that the general reader might like to hear more news of Byzantium, but that he or she actually needed to. The list of modern nations and states that once formed part of the empire, or were profoundly affected by their interactions with it, is impressive. It includes Italy, Greece and all the Balkan states, the Ukraine, Russia, Turkey, Cyprus, Georgia and Armenia. Since many of these nations are presently undergoing convulsive change or are the actual or potential sites of conflicts of extraordinary savagery, we clearly need to know more about their pasts, and woven in among these pasts is the gleaming and tarnished thread of Byzantium.

How is it possible to understand Russia without realizing that both its religion and its civilization were gifts of Byzantium? The Byzantines regarded Constantinople as the second Rome, but after that city had fallen to the Turks, the Russians came to regard Moscow as the third Rome, and their orthodox empire as the direct inheritor of Byzantine traditions. Similarly, the Serbs' genocidal determination to create a Greater Serbia becomes more comprehensible, if no less deplorable, when one bears in mind their memories of the Byzantinized empire they ruled briefly in the first half of the fourteenth century, when it looked as if a Serbian king might establish himself on the ancient throne of Constantine and Justinian.

The urgency of these considerations helped me overcome any remaining misgivings. What I had in mind was in the nature of a portrait or an evocation that would attract the reader who might be reluctant to embark on a three-volume history, however lively its style. My book would take the form of a travel memoir: episodes from Byzantine history and aspects of Byzantine art and society would be linked to places and monuments that I would visit and describe at first hand.

Having decided that a journey would determine the form of the book, I then had to decide on a route. Any Byzantine journey had to include Istanbul, but I did not want that already much-celebrated city to be the book's focus. My visit would have to take me into the Byzantine provinces, but these were very extensive and I soon realized that a journey beginning in Italy and ending in Syria would result in a book of nearly interminable length. I finally chose to confine myself to Anatolia (which is to say Asia Minor or Asiatic Turkey). From the time of the first Arab invasions of the seventh century until the virtual completion of the Turkish conquest in the early fourteenth, Anatolia was the empire's main source of wealth and manpower. It outweighed all the European provinces and functioned as a vast natural fortress, protecting Constantinople from any threat that might come from the east, and yet, with the exception of certain Cappadocian cave-churches, its Byzantine monuments had been largely ignored by the outside world. I considered it essential to keep a visual record, and so invited the photographer and filmmaker Andrew Moore to accompany me. He proved to be the ideal traveling companion, and it is his presence, not any grandiloquence on my part, that accounts for the frequent use of the first person plural in the main body of the book.

The project began to look viable, and I set about planning our route. I settled on a relatively modest and manageable itinerary that kept to the western and southern edges of the great central plateau. This route had certain obvious advantages, quite apart from its practicality: it would take me to Nicaea (modern Iznik) and Amorion, both of which had played dramatic roles in Byzantine history; it would pass close to the site of the decisive battle of Myriocephalon and would lead me to the two largest groups of mid-period Byzantine churches to be found anywhere—Binbir Kilise (or the Thousand and One Churches) and the frescoed cave-churches of Cappadocia. Furthermore, the route overlapped at several points with the passage of the First Crusade, and passed through three important early Turkish capitals—Bursa, Konya and Karaman.

But how much should I say about the *non*-Byzantine cultures that had left visible evidence of their existence along my route? Byzantium had to remain my primary focus, but it would be absurd to travel wearing blinkers. This was to be a book about a journey through Turkey, as well as a meditation on Byzantine civilization and history, so there was no reason to exclude mention of the monuments left by Phrygians, Greeks, Romans and Turks. In the case of the last-named, however, limits had to be set. An important part of the story I wanted to tell had to do with the transformation of central Anatolia from a region that was Greek-speaking and Christian to one that was predominantly Turkish and Muslim, but if I did not control my fascination with Turkish culture my central theme would be submerged. The obvious cutoff point was 1453, the year in which Mehmed the Conqueror rode into Constantinople, and Byzantium ceased to exist. The rule was impossible to observe strictly, however, and in Iznik, for example, I talk of the glories of Iznik ceramics, which postdate the conquest.

As it turned out, the latest date to be mentioned repeatedly in the book was 1923, the year in which the last Greek communities of Anatolia—many of them directly descended from the original Byzantine population—were expelled from their homeland. This was the much-delayed final act of the immensely long Byzantine tragedy. At nearly every stopping point on my journey I came upon the churches, houses and graffiti of these nineteenth- and twentieth-century people, now vanished and almost lost to history.

Enjoyment of the book should not require a detailed prior knowledge of Byzantine history, but the nonchronological manner in which events are narrated may initially prove confusing to readers unacquainted with the basic framework into which these events fit. Such readers are referred to the chronology on p. 311, but for the moment I think it is sufficient to mention the battle of Manzikert. This is not described in any detail in the body of my text, since I did not visit Manzikert (which lies on the eastern edge of Anatolia, to the north of Lake Van), but it is frequently referred to, and is without doubt one of the truly decisive battles of medieval history. It happened in 1071, and the reader should keep this date firmly in mind.

By 1071 the Turks had been raiding Anatolia for more than a decade, but the empire had previously survived nearly three centuries of Arab raids and emerged triumphant; no one imagined that these incursions marked the beginning of a process that would end with its fall. To the Turks, as to the Byzantines, the empire seemed eternal and immovable: it was difficult to conceive of a world without it. But all this was changed by the calamitous defeat of the Emperor Romanus IV Diogenes by the Seljuk Sultan Alp Arslan at Manzikert—a defeat that culminated in the capture of Romanus and the annihilation of the greater part of the imperial army. The complete collapse of Byzantine administrative and defensive systems that followed in the wake of the battle created a vacuum which nomadic Turkish tribes (the Turkmens) were more than happy to fill. The loss of Anatolia led the Byzantines to appeal to the West, and thus began the crusading movement that would eventually do more harm to Byzantium and the cause of Christendom than it ever did to the Turks and Islam. And without Manzikert there might be no such place as Turkey. The empire had been in steep decline for forty years before the battle, but if Romanus had defeated Alp Arslan—as he had good reason to believe he could, for his army was much larger—it is quite possible that the decline could have been reversed. Byzantium had proved its resilience many times before, and twice again it would be saved from apparently ineluctable disaster by the rise to power of men of outstanding courage and intelligence. But these men—the heroic emperors of the Comnenian and Lascarid dynasties—could only achieve partial restorations, since the heartland of their empire (central Anatolia) remained firmly in the possession of a people who were alien in language, culture and religion. Without Manzikert, Anatolia might now be, for better or worse, part of a Greek state. The Ottoman Empire would never have come into being, and there would be no Muslims in Bosnia for Serbs and Croats to slaughter. So this story, which begins in the fourth century and includes many digressions, has several endings: the first is 1453, the second 1923, the last is the date on which you, the reader, open your newspaper or turn on the radio.

CONTENTS

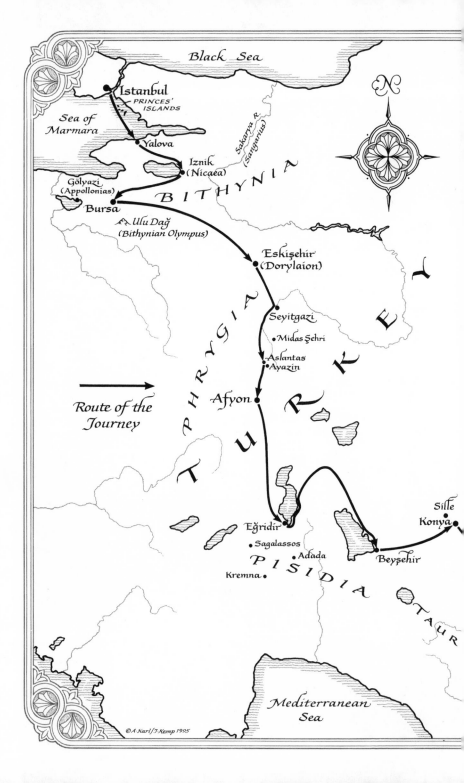

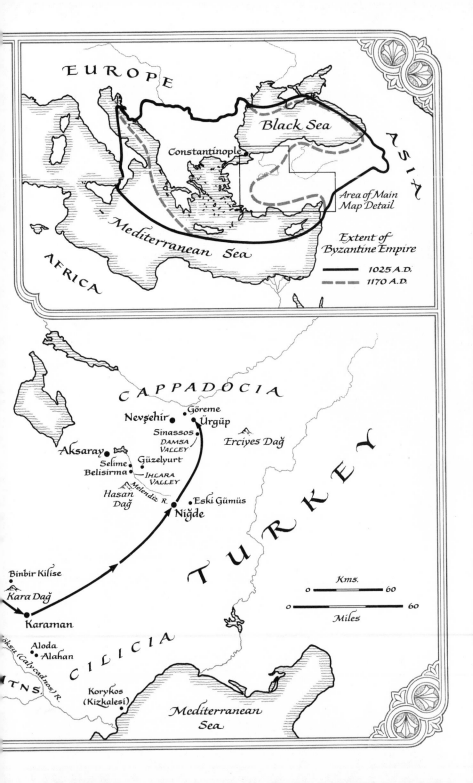

EUROPE

Black Sea

Constantinople

ASIA

Area of Main
Map Detail

Mediterranean Sea

AFRICA

*Extent of
Byzantine Empire*

—— 1025 A.D.
– – – 1170 A.D.

CAPPADOCIA

Nevşehir · Göreme
· Ürgüp

Sinassos ·
DAMSA
VALLEY

Erciyes Dağ

Aksaray ·

Selime · Güzelyurt
Belisirma ·
IHLARA
VALLEY

Melendiz R.

Hasan
Dağ

· Eski Gümüs
Niğde

TURKEY

Binbir Kilise
·
Kara Dağ

· Karaman

CILICIA

Aloda
· Alahan

Göksu (Calycadnos) R.

TNS

Korykos
(Kızkalesi)

Mediterranean
Sea

Kms.
0 ———— 60

0 ———— 60
Miles

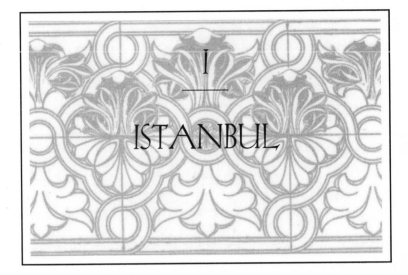

I

ISTANBUL

ARRIVAL

Flying east from Paris to Istanbul above dense layers of cloud, it occurred to me that it was almost thirty years since I had first encountered Byzantium. It happened on a dull afternoon in school. I had been reading a condensed history of the Roman Empire and was astonished to discover, from a brief final paragraph, that an empire still calling itself Roman, with its capital at Constantinople, had continued to exist until the improbably late date of 1453. I soon learnt that, in some quarters, this empire had a very bad reputation. It was synonymous with decadence and decline. Even at this early stage it struck me as unlikely that a civilization could have declined continuously for over a thousand years. Such longevity surely suggested a people and a culture possessed, at the very least, of great reserves of tenacity and vigor. My curiosity was aroused. Hours spent in the echoing rotunda of Manchester's Central Library acquainted me with the art and architecture of Byzantium. What I saw was not "decadence" but an unparalleled fusion of spiritual refinement and overwhelming material splendor. Here was something great and mysterious, something also neglected and slandered, something that seemed to demand my sympathy and understanding.

On visits to Greece in the 1960s I sought out Byzantine monuments and art—the monasteries of Daphni and Hosios Loukas, the citadel of Monemvasia and the ruined town of Mistra (its red-roofed churches clustered among cypresses below the forbidding mass of the Taygetus Mountains). At the University of Birmingham my interest was encouraged by Professor Anthony Bryer—a short, rubicund gentleman whose collars and ties were in a state of perpetual wild disarray, a state I found somehow romantic, since it suggested that his enthusiasm for his subject was so intense that he resented the slightest distraction from it. I aspired to a similar intensity, and he responded with great sympathy and kindness to my lengthy poem "The Fall of 1453" (although he could not resist pointing out certain inaccuracies). It was thanks to the power of Professor Bryer's name among fellow Byzantinists that I was able to see the frescoes of Lagoudera—high in the Troodos Mountains of Cyprus—while they were still being restored. As I climbed up into the restorer's scaffolding I came, quite literally, face-to-face with the angels, saints and courtiers of Byzantium. I remember a procession of handmaidens holding votive candles, but, due to a flaw in the pigment, the candles had been reduced to mere smudges or had vanished altogether, while the hands that once held them, the faces of the figures and their vivid robes of red and blue, remained as clear as they must have been some eight hundred years before, in the time of the Comnenian emperors.

And in 1968 I visited Constantinople itself, traveling the length of Europe in trains that seemed to get progressively slower the nearer I approached my goal. Periodically we would come to a complete halt in a valley carved out by a large muddy river, and there would be nothing to look at except endless fields of sunflowers, which obediently turned westward as the sun set. As the train looped maddeningly back and forth across the desolate province of eastern Thrace I could barely contain my impatience, but the first sight of the great land walls of the city descending toward the Sea of Marmara was compensation enough for all the trials of the journey: I had arrived in the place the Emperor Michael VIII Palaeologus once described as "the Acropolis of the Universe." Now, more than twenty years later, I had graduated to air travel and my goal lay far beyond Istanbul. Jet lag permitting, I intended to leave the city the next day and embark on a five-week journey that would take me from Yalova on the southern shore of the Sea of Marmara to Cappadocia in the center of the Anatolian plateau. The plane dipped through clouds. A wintry expanse of sea opened beneath us, and within minutes we had landed.

BLACK RAIN AND
THE BLACHERNAE

It should not rain in Turkey in May, or it should not rain much, but the entire country had just endured its worst and wettest spring in decades. Huddled under ragged banners of weeping cloud, the city presented its most melancholy aspect, but melancholy in any weather may be the keynote to Istanbul: it is visible in the blank phalanxes of apartment blocks marching through the outer suburbs, in the yellowed and blackened tanneries pressing up against the Theodosian walls, in the ominous convoys of tankers encumbering the Sea of Marmara, and in the eyes of the handsome carpet dealer, who asks, "How are you today?" and answers himself with a laugh, "I'm not feeling so good myself."

Everywhere people seemed to be gazing heavenward and murmuring apologies. It had been raining for three weeks almost without a break. Hoteliers, café owners and tourist touts were dismayed, and only a few mud-splattered tour buses from Romania or Bulgaria were in evidence at the great church of Hagia Sophia, disgorging sorry crowds who did not seem overeager to inspect the places from which so much culture and religion—and so many centuries of political oppression—had once been disseminated. If their eyes revealed anything, it was the desire to fall quietly asleep in the sun, but a cold, relentless rain continued to pound the gravel of the tea gardens, and only government officials and meteorologists (who perhaps did not want to think the unthinkable) had any doubt that all of this was linked somehow to the fires still burning in Kuwait. Black rain was said to have fallen in the southeast.

I had envisaged our crossing into Asia many times. It was to take place as soon as possible after our arrival, and sunlight would pour down on the calm waters of the Sea of Marmara. Obviously we would have to wait until reality conformed to reasonable expectation. Blustery showers continued to sweep across the city, and it seemed the perfect day to visit the sad remnants of the Blachernae Palace, which are to be found in the extreme northwest angle of the old city walls, in the dilapidated, half-rustic district now known as Balat. A taxi dropped us in the narrow street that led up to the Ivas Effendi Mosque and beyond the mosque we found the Tower of Isaac Angelus. Shoddily built and surmounted by a pavilion patched together from materials robbed from earlier structures, the tower seemed an appropriate monument to the memory of an undistinguished emperor who had been deposed and blinded by his even more worthless brother. Between mosque and tower a broad flight of garbage-strewn concrete steps led down into the substructures of the palace, once a place so luxurious it was the envy of the world.

Although guidebooks will often tell you that the Blachernae was built in the eleventh or twelfth century, there was a palace on the site as early as the sixth century. It contained three great halls, but for centuries remained overshadowed by the Great Palace that stood at the opposite end of the city on the ground that slopes down from the Hippodrome and Hagia Sophia to the Sea of Marmara. Its period of greatest glory coincides with the rule of the Comnenus dynasty (1081–1185), when it was the preferred residence of a succession of remarkably vigorous and intelligent emperors—Alexius I, John II and Manuel I. The last of these paid particular attention to the embellishment of the Blachernae, and it was here, in the declining years of the twelfth century, that emperors and courtiers were able to enjoy, for the last time, a life of festivities and ceremonies unrestricted by ideas of economy or responsibility. Walls and ceilings were covered with mosaics depicting scenes from the *Iliad*, the Greek tragedies or the triumphs of Alexander. Western visitors were often left nearly speechless with amazement. The twelfth-century Jewish traveler Benjamin of Tudela, for example, was convinced that the precious stones in the great crown suspended over the throne of Manuel I Comnenus emitted so much light that no lamps were needed at night. The testimony of the twelfth-century French monk Odo de Deuil is particularly impressive, since he is often scathingly critical of Byzantium and the Byzantines. Of the Blachernae he declares breathlessly: "Its exterior is of almost matchless beauty, but its interior surpasses anything that I can say about it. Throughout it is decorated elaborately with gold and a great variety of colours, and the floor is marble, paved with cunning workmanship; and I do not know whether the exquisite art or the exceedingly valuable stuffs endow it with the more beauty or value."

Of this beauty almost nothing remains. The great red towers built to defend the western flank of the palace are its most impressive surviving feature, but the substructures behind the Ivas Effendi Mosque present a dismal prospect of bare brick vaults like the segments of a broken skull. In 1195, somewhere in these cheerless spaces, Isaac Angelus was imprisoned and blinded, dragged from his arched pavilion with its view of the woods and hills beyond the city walls.

Close by the Blachernae an amiable old man in a gray felt cap emerged from a wooden mansion largely hidden by planes and fruit trees, to bid us welcome to Turkey and tell us how much he loved America and President Bush. Unsure how to respond to this effusion, I thanked him without conviction and remarked on the beauty of the trees in his garden. Yes, he replied, they were very beautiful, but the fruit was never allowed to ripen. The local children would strip them bare as soon as the first green plums appeared. He said this without rancor: the taste of children for unripe fruit was something to be accepted.

We went on our way down the steep slope of the Blachernae hill, hoping to find the site of the Church of the Virgin of the Blachernae that Justinian had built to house the magically fragrant robe of the Virgin and a miraculous portrait of her said to have been painted by Saint Luke. Many stories were told of the church and its relics: on Fridays, it was said, the curtains that concealed the icon would part on their own accord; during sieges, the image was paraded along the walls to stiffen the resolve of the defenders and overawe the barbarians, and reliable witnesses would often testify that they had seen the Virgin herself pacing along the battlements dressed in shining robes. It was not until the calamity of the Fourth Crusade that anyone seriously questioned the idea that the city enjoyed divine protection. How else could it have survived the malice of its enemies for eight centuries? The common Byzantine view of the matter is expressed in *The Life of*

Saint Andrew the Fool, whose eschatological musings were immensely popular. When Epiphanius, his eager disciple, asked the saint, "Tell me, how will the end of this world come about? How will this City, the New Jerusalem, pass away?" Andrew replied unhesitatingly: "Concerning our City, you should know that until the end of time it shall not fear any enemy. No one shall capture it—far from it. For it has been entrusted to the Mother of God and no one shall snatch it away from Her hands. Many nations shall smite its walls, but they shall break their horns and depart in shame, while we gain much wealth from them."

But the Virgin was unable to protect her city from the fires that repeatedly afflicted it and, in 1434, her own church at Blachernae was burnt. By this time the empire had become so impoverished that funds for the restoration of the church could not be found and this, perhaps, is an even sadder indication of decline than the fake gems used at the coronation of John Cantacuzenus almost a century earlier—those little pieces of red and blue and green glass that struck the poet C. P. Cavafy as "a sorrowful protest" against "the unjust wretchedness" of those who had been crowned.

At the time of the Turkish conquest, the Church of the Blachernae was a charred shell, but the site retained its holiness thanks to a sacred spring, which continued to issue from the ground long after the Virgin's icon and her sweet-smelling robe had vanished. As we wandered in the crooked streets of Balat we had no clear idea of what we were looking for. What would remain? I knew, however, that the Turks call a sacred spring an *ayazma*—a word they have borrowed from the Greeks—and before long I caught sight of the word carved on the arch of a gate surmounted by a cross. Beyond the gate was a rose garden in full bloom, fed by sacred waters and decorated here and there with finely carved capitals and fragments of entablatures. At the end of the garden, beneath the brow of a wooded precipice, was the present-day church of Blachernae—a low rambling structure, painted pink and looking more like a summerhouse than a church. There was an odd gaiety about the place, a feeling that was enhanced when an invisible person began to throw log after log over the garden wall. This is what I will remember of the Blachernae: roses and the clack and clatter of falling logs.

THE CITY AT THE END OF TIME

The sky remained a menacing gray but the rain held off, so we decided to walk from Blachernae-Balat to the Church of Saint Polyeuctus, which lies at the center of the old city in the district known as Aksaray. This proved to be a severe test of my powers of orientation. The districts we had to pass through are politely termed "undeveloped," which means that the people are poor and the layout of the streets is so chaotic that no reliable maps exist. You are on your own. First-time visitors to Istanbul who happen to wander from the prescribed tourist track are often dismayed by the squalor, confusion and sheer dreariness of its poorer districts. This is only to be expected: two sacks, the first accompanied by devastating fires, have ensured that little or nothing remains of Byzantine domestic architecture, although you will sometimes pass locked and sadly neglected churches of the twelfth and fourteenth centuries—churches that must once have resembled reliquaries or jewel boxes. Even the charming Ottoman houses are fast disappearing, and the few that remain seem to lean together as if grieving over a common loss, while the more recent buildings are of such wretched quality that many of them are already on the verge of collapse. But although we tend to think of medieval Byzantium as a city of noble mansions and colonnaded streets, this would be something of an exaggeration.

When Justinian came to the throne in 527, Byzantium still preserved the broad, rational outlines of a classical city. It covered an area of eight square miles and must have contained at least half a million people, but in 542 the bubonic plague, arriving from Ethiopia by way of Egypt, made its first appearance. It raged for four months, and according to contemporary accounts between five and ten thousand people died each day. The plague or other unidentified epidemics recurred no fewer than six times before the century's end. Even allowing for rhetorical exaggeration—to which the Byzantines were especially prone—this must mean that the population was reduced by at least two-thirds. The plague returned with renewed virulence in 747, producing another sharp reduction, and by that date the city must have been melancholy and oppressive. The main axial road (the Mese) remained in place, as did the many splendid public squares, but vast areas of the city were given over to fields, cemeteries and orchards, and great public buildings fell into ruin. None of its inhabitants could escape the knowledge that there had once been better times; they succumbed to an incurable nostalgia and their literature came to be written in forms of Greek that no one had spoken for hundreds of years.

Even when there was no external threat to its existence from Arab armadas or barbarian armies, the city was an uneasy place. Astrologers and soothsayers were much in demand, but those who could not afford their services simply looked at the many ancient sculptures in the city and interpreted them as they saw fit. The fact that the triumphal arches and commemorative columns were crowded with scenes of war and captivity tended to encourage the gloomiest prognostications. According to Saint Andrew the Fool, on the Last Day the Lord in His anger would seize a scythe and cut the earth from under the city, and all the waters of the earth would crash in upon it, and it would rise up on a great wave and spin around like a millstone before being plunged into the abyss. The fact that this event was not due to occur until the end of time was not as reassuring as it might seem, since the Byzantines were convinced that time was in strictly limited supply. On the basis of scripture, the end was confidently expected in the sixth century and again in the seventh. It was later calculated that the end had to come sometime before 1324, since it was believed that the city could not attain the age of a thousand years. When that date passed without cataclysm, they recalculated and came up with the interesting date of 1492.

During the hard times of the seventh and eighth centuries the idea of the end must sometimes have figured as a source of consolation, but by the middle of the ninth century life was improving. Arab power was in decline; the plague had mysteriously disappeared and the population and the economy were expanding rapidly. New churches and dwellings soon began to rise. Despite imperial edicts governing the height of buildings, the placement of latrines and the organization of plumbing, this rebuilding followed a haphazard pattern. Some areas became intensely built up, and here the rich and the poor lived cheek by jowl, but others remained largely rural, with houses and monasteries scattered thinly among fields and vineyards. The number of foreigners increased dramatically. By 1028 there were enough Muslims to necessitate the construction of a mosque, but they were soon outnumbered by westerners, especially Italians, whose wealth and arrogance became the focus of a popular resentment that issued in riots and the occasional massacre.

Military disasters in the eleventh and twelfth centuries did little to diminish Constantinople's preeminence: in the whole of Europe there was no city that could rival it in size, wealth or beauty. Estimates of its population during this period vary widely, but even if we opt for the very conservative figure of 300,000—as against 800,000 to a million—this would still mean that it was three times the size of Venice, the largest city in the West at the time. When the fleet bearing the Fourth Crusade drew within sight of Constantinople, the unsophisticated knights of France and Germany could scarcely believe what they saw—so many palaces and towers and churches, and, most astonishing of all, such enormous numbers of people crowding the battlements. As the chronicler Geoffrey de Villehardouin put it: "They had never imagined that anywhere in the world there could be a city like this."

Constantinople was a place of paradox—the New Jerusalem and the New Babylon, the most Christian of cities and the mother of all iniquities, an object of desire and passionate hatred. Odo de Deuil remarked that "In every respect she exceeds moderation; for just as she surpasses other cities in wealth, so too does she surpass them in vice." The Constantinople of the twelfth century fore-shadows the unmanageable cities of the late twentieth century and, if we allow for a few transpositions, the complaining letters of the poet John Tzetzes (ca. 1110—ca. 1183) strike a note that will sound astonishingly familiar to thousands of beleaguered New Yorkers. Tzetzes lived on the second floor of a three-story apartment building in front of which monks from a nearby monastery kept digging up the road, so it was sometimes impossible for him to get in or out; heavy rain turned the streets of his neighborhood into quagmires; his upstairs neighbor kept pigs and had twelve children, who together "urinated so much that they produced navigable rivers"; his ceiling had been damaged by a broken drainpipe; the landlord had been neglecting his duties and long grass had grown up around the building. This Tzetzes considered an obvious fire hazard: if he was not to be burnt alive, drowned in ordure or stunned by falling pigs, it was essential that the landlord cut the grass, fix the ceiling and evict the upstairs neighbor.

It should be said in fairness that Tzetzes also wrote exuberantly of his city, boasting that he knew how to greet all foreigners politely in their own languages, be they Russian, Arabic, Turkish, Latin or Hebrew. Nor was he obliged to spend all his time in his life-threatening apart-ment: his literary gifts made him a welcome guest at some of the city's most elegant soirees and salons, events that might even be presided over by members of the imperial family. Although he may have complained constantly, it is unlikely that he ever considered living anywhere else. Like any true Byzantine—or New Yorker for that matter—he believed that there was only *one* city.

PEACOCKS AND PILASTERS

Our progress toward Saint Polyeuctus was slow. Streets that began promisingly enough turned inexorably in quite the wrong direction or narrowed to alleyways that ran straight into blank walls. The people in the streets were not as friendly as Turks normally are, and seemed to regard us with suspicion. A gaunt, unshaven man with the look of a goatherd turned us brusquely away from the Church of the Virgin Pammakaristos. With its multiple domes and fanciful niches, it resembled a coronet made for an empress or the mistress of an emperor, but the women who passed in the street were dressed with puritanical drabness and an unusually large number were heavily veiled in black: clearly the neighborhood was not only poor but devout. Looming over it was the dull mass of the Mosque of the Conqueror, like an immense black tent pitched on the site of the former Church of the Holy Apostles. It was here, on the summit of a hill commanding views of the Golden Horn and the heart of the city, that many of the greatest emperors of Byzantium were buried. The church was shaped like a cross and stood amid fields and gardens. Its interior was covered with mosaics of such expressivity that the twelfth-century poet Nicholas Mesarites felt he could almost smell the decayed flesh of the risen Lazarus. The Venetians reproduced its plan when they built San Marco, but of the original church and the tombs of the emperors not a stone is visible today.

The Mosque of the Conqueror is not the most architecturally distinguished of Istanbul's mosques, but it provided me with a useful landmark. Beyond it, I knew, there were long flights of steps descending to the street that led from the Adrianople Gate to the center of the city, passing on its way the church that once enshrined the skull of Saint Polyeuctus. This third-century martyr is not much remembered today, but he inspired Corneille to write a play, and Gounod an opera. More important, he was the patron saint of the formidable and immensely wealthy Lady Anicia Juliana who, in the early years of the sixth century, decided to build a shrine to his memory that would surpass in luxury and exotic beauty all the other churches of the capital.

Excavation of the site began in 1960 after construction of a new road brought to light a fragment that scholars immediately recognized as part of the dedicatory inscription of Juliana's church. (Its full text had been copied down in the tenth century and preserved in the Palatine Anthology.) It consists of a floridly rhetorical poem of seventy-six lines that originally encircled the entire central space of the church; it praises Juliana's distinguished lineage (she could claim descent from the Emperor Theodosius I) and proclaims that "She alone has conquered time and surpassed the wisdom of renowned Solomon." This is not an entirely idle boast: the church had roughly the same dimensions as Solomon's temple as they are recorded in the Bible, and the excavators were astonished by the profuse and fantastically varied sculptural decoration that began to emerge from its buried rubble. There were tangles of vines executed with a delicate, classical naturalism, but there was also an entirely new vocabulary of highly stylized motifs that would not have looked out of place in the palace of a Persian king—palmettes and basket-work designs, extravagant unidentifiable flowers spilling out of vases, and broadleaved palms weighed down by heavy clusters of dates. At Saint Polyeuctus between 524 and 527 an artistic revolution was taking place. Juliana must have hired master craftsmen from Isauria, Syria or Mesopotamia, and, as a result, all the elements of the mature Byzantine hybrid are present for the first time. The synthesis is not complete, but here the classical and the Oriental are juxtaposed in a manner that revitalizes both traditions, and in this sense Anicia Juliana is the patron of all later Byzantine art. She cannot have foreseen this result, but that she fully intended to astound posterity is attested by the larger-than-life-size peacocks that adorned the niches on either side of the nave of Saint Polyeuctus: their opened fans, carved with an exquisite attention to detail, curved inward to canopy the niches; their necks and crested heads were carved boldly in the round, and—as if all of this was not already enough—they were also painted and gilded.

The peacocks, I feel sure, were Juliana's idea, since they were traditionally associated with empresses. And an empress, or at least the mother of an emperor, was what Juliana felt she was destined to be, but her family had been pushed aside by the family of Justinian, which was of extremely humble origins. Juliana's disgust was profound, and Saint Polyeuctus is as much the result of thwarted political ambition as of piety. It was completed in 527, the very year in which Justinian came to the throne. The new emperor visited Saint Polyeuctus on at least one occasion and must have read its dedicatory poem with mounting irritation—it might have been calculated to remind him of his family's lack of distinction—but he also took careful note of its innovative, centralized domed design and lavish decoration. When his own great church was completed, a mere ten years after Juliana's, he is said to have exclaimed, "Solomon, I have vanquished thee." If this is true, alert courtiers would have known how to interpret the remark: Justinian was making it clear that he had finally outdone the Solomon-imitating Juliana.

Posterity has not been kind to Anicia Juliana. Her church had fallen into ruin by the twelfth century, and today the site lies close to a major intersection, wreathed in the fumes of Istanbul's frequently stalled traffic. Apart from a few capitals scattered around the perimeter of the excavation, all that remains is an overgrown mass of brick substructures, pungently anointed by the local dogs. I had not gone far into the ruins before the stench drove me away. In Istanbul it is hard to escape a recurring sense of loss: no civilization fought harder than the Byzantine to preserve the past for future generations, yet so much that was great in its own art and archictecture has vanished.

It would be wrong, however, to think that succeeding generations failed to appreciate Juliana's achievement. They demonstrated their appreciation in the most brutally acquisitive fashion. As the excavations proceeded, certain newly unearthed capitals and fragments of pilaster seemed strangely familiar to the archaeologists. It soon became apparent that the church had been very thoroughly plundered by the Venetians, some time shortly after 1204. Palmette capitals from Saint Polyeuctus surmount columns on the façade of San Marco, and the two sumptuously decorated pilasters that stand nearby in the piazzetta, which for long were thought to have come from Acre, were undoubtedly part of the same parcel of loot: the match with the fragments discovered in Istanbul is exact. For centuries Venetians and visitors have admired the pilasters' intricate workmanship without knowing that they were the beneficiaries of the munificence and adventurous tastes of the Lady Anicia Juliana.

THE GREAT CHURCH

My second day in Istanbul did not begin well. I woke to the sound of torrential rain drumming on the vines and the fire escape. My neck was aching from a futile attempt to sleep on pillows that might have been used more appropriately as landfill. The Sea of Marmara was battleship gray and choppy. Clearly this was not the morning to catch the boat to Yalova. There was no choice but to take refuge in the largest covered space in the vicinity. Since this was Hagia Sophia, the Church of the Divine Wisdom, I could hardly complain of hardship. Besides, it would have made no sense to set out in search of churches,

monasteries and cities hidden away on Anatolian mountainsides without first visiting the incomparable edifice
that stood, symbolically and physically, at the center of the
Byzantine world.

Painted a disconcerting shade of deep rust-pink, the vast
external mass of Justinian's masterpiece can have a
crushing effect on the visitor. It is not graceful, it does not
soar toward the heavens: rather, it is as if the entire
burdensome weight of more than 1,400 years of history
has been rendered visible. It is a building I always
approach with a curious mixture of eagerness and reluctance. To pass beneath the dully glimmering vaults of the
narthex and the mosaic image of an emperor prostrating
himself at the feet of an enthroned Christ into the great
central space should be an overwhelming experience, but
I find myself unable to elude a mood close to despondency. As a westerner, I am aware that it was the soldiers
of the Fourth Crusade who first desecrated the church and
stripped it of its gold and silver furnishings, but the feeling
that overcomes me goes beyond consideration of crimes
that I might wish undone. Perhaps it comes down to the
fact that after over nine centuries as a church and nearly
five as a mosque, Hagia Sophia is no longer a place of
worship: it has been emptied of significance as if it were
merely the shell of an abandoned railway station or gargan-
tuan bathhouse.

The dimness of Hagia Sophia's interior tends to support
the popular idea that the highest aim of Byzantine church
builders was an atmosphere of mysterious murk amid
which gorgeous images glimmered faintly by candlelight.
In fact the Byzantine ideal was dazzling illumination.
Windows were larger and more numerous than they are
today, and since the sky of Constantinople was often overcast and services were held at night, the church could also

be lit by gilded lamps suspended from the ceiling. All of this light was given life by the mosaics that covered the entire surface of the upper walls and the vaults. Simple geometric designs suggestive of Oriental textiles alternated with curling garlands of vines and acanthus, but whatever the motif might be the ground was always gold. And gold, according to the theologians of Byzantium, symbolized truth and incorruptibility: it represented light in its most concentrated form. Plotinus had defined beauty as "symmetry irradiated by life," and the Byzantines, although sometimes reluctant to admit to the pagan Neoplatonic sources of their ideas, enthusiastically agreed. The ceaseless movement of light within the church was intended to render the entire structure insubstantial, as if barely tethered to the earth. The illusion was so perfect that the first worshipers to enter the building were alarmed. How did the dome keep from falling?

Anthemius of Tralles, principal architect of Hagia Sophia, was not an architect in the modern sense at all. He was a scientist, a mathematician and notable eccentric whose experiments included the production of a steam-powered artificial earthquake. His church is a pure experiment in three-dimensional geometry. Saint Polyeuctus may have provided him with some inspiration, but even so nothing quite like Hagia Sophia had been attempted before. Its dome is a hundred feet in diameter, suspended over a square by means of pendentives and buttressed, to east and west, by immense half-domes. There were severe problems during construction—walls bulged outward and arches threatened to collapse—and in 558, after the city had been shaken by a series of earthquakes, the dome came crashing down. It was immediately replaced, but there were partial collapses in 989 and 1346. On the face of it, it is surprising that Justinian should have supported such a radical project. He was the most conservative of emperors, in love with the idea of Rome, but like his great rival, Anicia Juliana, he was determined to hold posterity in thrall, and so devoted the resources of the empire to the construction of a monument that is both Greek and Oriental but not in the least Roman.

It is tempting to see in Hagia Sophia the form and sign of a glorious new beginning. It is and it is not. Long-lost provinces were reconquered, laws were codified, men, women and eunuchs behaved heroically, but the sixth century was also a time of riots, oppressive taxation, high inflation, plague and natural disasters. One of the reasons Justinian built so much is that there was so much to rebuild. Hagia Sophia itself was built to replace an earlier church that had burned down in the terrible Nika riots of 532, which claimed the lives of at least thirty thousand people. In sum, it would appear that this was a time when only the extremely wealthy and well-protected had much reason to give thanks for being alive. And yet there *was* a glory to the age, and, although later Byzantine architects never attempted to equal Anthemius' prodigious creation, the centrally planned, domed church became standard, as did the splendor of mosaic and polychromed marble ornament.

Over the centuries Hagia Sophia underwent many changes. From the late ninth century onward, new, figural mosaics were introduced, the most important surviving example of which is the exquisite Virgin and Child in the apse. This disproves the common notion that Byzantine art lacks humanity and is always characterized by extreme stylization. To be sure, there is some stylization in the way the artist has depicted the folds of the Virgin's dark-blue robe, but it is not so very far from the naturalism of classical drapery, and the softly modeled face, with its wide, luminous eyes, is fully human. When the learned Patriarch Photius delivered a sermon on the occasion of this mosaic's inauguration, on 29 March 867, he stressed its "lifelike" qualities, adding that "She looks as if she might speak if someone were to ask how she could be both virgin and mother, for the painting makes her lips seem of real flesh, pressed together and still as in the sacraments . . ." That such an effect could result from an arrangement of thousands of tiny colored cubes of glass and gold and stone is a miracle unique to Byzantine art.

Many of the mosaic figures in the main body of Hagia Sophia are difficult to appreciate, since they are relatively modest in scale and placed high on the walls, but in the south gallery there are mosaics that stand almost at eye level and can be examined closely. It was toward these that I now hurried, hoping to reach them before crowds obscured the view. The galleries are approached by a massive, darkly enclosed ramp from which it is a relief to escape into the harmoniously proportioned spaces beyond. It was under these broad cross-vaults that the Byzantine court would gather amidst a susurration of silks, and it is here that one comes closest to the heart of Byzantium. On the east wall of the south gallery the faces of emperors and empresses gaze out from two magnificent group portraits. One shows the Empress Zoë and her third husband, Constantine IX Monomachus (who ruled between 1042 and 1055) standing on either side of an enthroned Christ. By all accounts Zoë was a remarkably empty-headed woman. She had the childish habit of talking to her favorite icons, and in her later years devoted much of her time to the concoction of new perfumes. Nor do the duties of the imperial office seem to have weighed heavily on Monomachus. He was an amiable hedonist, fond of theatrics and practical jokes, who frequently appeared in public with his mistress. But it was not for Constantine's or Zoë's sake that I had come. Standing next to them are the haunting images of John II Comnenus and his wife, Irene the Hungarian.

Constantine IX was one of many ineffectual rulers who presided over the empire's precipitous eleventh-century decline, but between 1118 and 1143 John II struggled tirelessly to bring about a restoration. The Byzantine chroniclers are unanimous in their praise: John was neither extravagant nor cruel; he remained faithful to his wife; he was brave, he was pious and took a detailed interest in philanthropic works. This surfeit of virtues makes his character hard to grasp (for it is often the failings of the great that bring them alive for us), so it is an extraordinary stroke of luck that a portrait of such high quality should have survived. It is the only one of many mosaics commissioned by the Comnenian emperors that has come down to us. The red and gold imperial robes are dazzling, but it is the sadness and distinction of John's face that leaves the deepest impression: somewhat narrow, fine-boned and bearded, it might be the face of a philosopher or an ascetic, but it is also the face of a man who could lead armies into battle and win. John wears a crown like a dome. The Empress Irene's crown is like a jeweled fortress that seems to weigh on her oppressively. Her features are delicate, but her cheeks appear hollowed by illness or fatigue. She died some ten years before her husband.

My contemplation of the imperial portraits was rudely interrupted by a lusty outbreak of hammering and hollering. Most of the north side of the nave was obscured by scaffolding, and workmen had arrived to resume the task of cleaning the church's sumptuous marble paneling. For the first time in many centuries the lovely milky blues, soft reds and greens of the stone were reemerging. This was all to the good, but in places where the paneling had vanished, garish fake marble panels were daubed on the walls. Worse was to follow in the vestibule attached to the southern end of the narthex, which, until recently, did not seem to have changed much since the close of the tenth century. Now it was full of scaffolding, and its superb vine-carved cornice had been painted sky-blue and white. To clean and uncover is one thing, but to dispel Hagia Sophia's overwhelming sense of age with licks of new paint comes close to vandalism. It might be argued that the church's cornices and capitals were originally painted and gilded, but one could say the same of the Parthenon, and imagine the outcry if someone proposed applying coats of red, blue and yellow paint to the Elgin marbles.

The south vestibule is still a place to linger. In a lunette above a door is a perfectly preserved tenth-century mosaic, which shows Constantine presenting his city and Justinian his church to the enthroned Mother of God. Its colors are undimmed and the whole harmonious composition is perfectly adapted to the space it occupies. In it Steven Runciman saw "the triumph of the classical ideal." It sums up the central Byzantine myth in all its grandeur and mystery—the myth of a city, a church and an empire enjoying the special protection of Christ and His Mother, and therefore destined to endure until the last day of the world.

TO ASIA

A dramatic change had come about while we were exploring Hagia Sophia. The city lay under a dividing line. Clouds were shifting to the east, while from the west brilliant Aegean air poured down. The waters of the Sea of Marmara, the Bosphorus and the Golden Horn began to shimmer, and for the first time we could see that, despite everything it had suffered in the way of destruction and development, Istanbul was still one of the most beautiful places on earth. It was possible to recognize at least the outlines of the city that the twelfth-century poet Constantine Manasses hailed as "eye of the universe, ornament of the world, star shining afar, beacon of this lower world."

Sunlight meant departure. To catch the ferry to Yalova you must go to Kabataş on the Bosphorus. Not far beyond the dock, the Dolmbahçe Palace stretches out along the shore like a pale and too heavily bedecked Ingres odalisque. The work of the Balians, a remarkable Armenian family of architects, the Dolmbahçe is routinely dismissed by the experts as vulgar and preposterous—an Oriental misapprehension of Western ideas. But therein lies its considerable charm (the charm of "A Rhapsody on Baroque Themes" by Rimsky-Korsakov), and compared to the brutish glass and concrete towers that now rise from the hill behind it, the palace's swags, finials and heavy pediments look almost delicate.

Although delighted to catch a glimpse of the Ottoman Versailles, I was anxious to begin the crossing to Asia, and before long the boat obliged, pulling away from the dock with a shudder and a shrill hoot, while a gathering of cheerful *ragazzi* waved us off with fishing lines. The mouth of the Golden Horn was soon passed and, as the city receded behind us, the great domed masses of Hagia Sophia and the Blue Mosque came to resemble clouds pinned down by the enormous needles of their minarets. The boat turned toward the Princes' Islands and a man with a high childish voice began to advertise the virtues of a new kind of pen, demonstrating it in a bold hand on sheets of paper which he distributed to interested passengers. Waiters continued to serve tea, sour-cherry juice and Nescafé (Nescafé that was more expensive than the token that took you from Europe to Asia). Then, on cue—for despite the gloomy warnings of guidebooks that say it is not fit to swim in, the water appeared very clear and brilliant—a school of dolphins broke surface, arching in and out of the sea as if attempting to thread its waves together.

I had never seen dolphins before. Their sudden apparition was much more than the fulfillment of a vague hope, and it was impossible to think of it as a cliché. This was a moment of pure vitality, an unshadowed celebration of the physical world, a moment in which the centuries contracted like the folds of an accordion, for these delightful creatures were the lineal descendants of others we were to see many days later, carved on the doorjambs of a church perched on a ledge high above the immense blue chasm of the Calycadnos River.

The Princes' Islands are a suite of nine miniatures beginning with Proté. Like its more luxuriant sisters—Antigone, Chalke and Prinkipo—Proté has wooded hills and wooden mansions with verandas, gables and broad eaves. Somehow I was reminded of the Crimea, or of how I imagined the Crimea to have been in the years just before 1914. The islands looked like ideal places in which to write regretful memoirs or voluminous novels detailing the mores and morbidities of doomed aristocracies.

Throughout the long centuries of Byzantine rule, the Princes' Islands were places of political exile. High-ranking persons who were suspected of treason, or whose presence in the capital had simply become an embarrassment to those in power, were removed here. Sometimes they were deprived of their sight to make doubly sure they would cause no further trouble. This practice has been cited by Byzantophobic historians as evidence of the innate depravity of Byzantine society, but mutilations of various kinds (from nose-slitting and the cutting off of tongues to amputation and castration) were common forms of punishment throughout the medieval world, and there is no certain evidence of punitive blinding in Byzantium before the eighth century. Even after this date it was not uncommon for deposed emperors or disgraced politicians to suffer nothing worse than banishment or forced tonsure, and in this respect one could as easily claim that the Byzantines were considerably more humane than their western European contemporaries or their eastern neighbors, the 'Abbāsid caliphs of Baghdad and Samarra. Furthermore, blinding in Byzantium could be a serious liability for the perpetrator, provoking violent popular resentment and the enmity of the Church. The usurper

Michael VIII, who ordered the blinding of the legitimate heir to the throne, was one of the most unpopular sovereigns in the entire history of Byzantium, and, after his death in 1282, the practice was largely abandoned. Michael's son, Andronicus II Palaeologus, felt obliged to visit his father's victim and offer abject apologies.

At first glance the Princes' Islands might seem to have been the world's loveliest place of exile, yet there was an element of cruelty in the choice: those exiles who had retained their sight had only to walk down to the harbor or look from the windows of some hilltop monastery to see the alluring outline of the Queen of Cities floating on the horizon. Even at night they could not escape this torture, since we are told that the Church of the Divine Wisdom, lit by innumerable lamps, glowed like a beacon and was visible far out to sea.

After we left Prinkipo behind, there was nothing but open water between us and the hills of Asia—hills that many weeks of rain had covered with a mantle of brilliant green, fading to blue and violet in the distances that concealed the snows of Mount Olympus. When she was dying of cancer the Empress Theodora had sailed the same waters, seeking the cure that eluded her in the thermal springs of Bithynia, and her husband's nephew and successor, Justin II, had come this way too, hoping to soothe his depression and agitation in the palace he had built above Yalova. The one died in terrible pain, the other went mad, but my thoughts kept returning to Proté and its most distinguished exile, who in his last days had achieved a serenity that seemed in keeping with the radiance of the afternoon light falling on a calm sea and flowering hills.

THE BOOK OF SINS

The Basileus Romanus I Lecapenus, during whose reign the Bulgars were humbled and the rich city of Melitene was returned to the bosom of the empire, was nevertheless the son of an unlettered Armenian peasant who rejoiced in the name of Theophylact the Unbearable.

History, alas, does not record how Theophylact came by this unflattering name. His son was a usurper who rose to the world's highest eminence by the judicious exercise of treachery and mendacity, but it must be said that his good government did much to excuse his usurpation.

Nor was much blood spilt. Constantine VII, called Porphyrogenitus, the legitimate heir, was permitted to live and, indeed, was married to the daughter of Romanus, the lady Helena, a woman of unusual beauty and intelligence. She was to prove a loyal wife, and Constantine meanwhile was encouraged to retreat into the realms of literature and art. He is the only emperor we know who painted pictures with his own hands. According to the account of Bishop Liutprand of

Cremona they were excellent pictures, and the worst that can be said of Constantine is that he was a little too fond of wine.

The preeminence that should have been Constantine's was instead shared by Romanus' two sons. But Romanus was unlucky in them: they were arrogant, faithless and impolitic, and the common people soon grew to detest them. Their sister, Helena, also knew her brothers for what they were. It was said that when the famous Image of Edessa was paraded in triumph through the streets of the capital, the sons of Romanus glimpsed only a ghost or shadow, whereas the Porphyrogenitus could clearly distinguish the features of Our Lord and Savior.

By now—it was the winter of 943—Romanus was old and ill and had come to recognize the unworthiness of his sons. He began to succumb to wild fits of repentance, which issued in "acts of indiscriminate charity and intolerant piety."

Foreseeing that Romanus would bequeath the throne to their brother-in-law, his sons began to plot against him. Only Romanus did not see this. He was concerned with the fate of his soul, and surrounded himself with monks who understood little of politics. He was further distracted by the appearance in the city of twins who were joined at the hip, facing each other. There could be no doubt that their deformity portended evil.

On 20 December 944, during the midday hours when the Great Palace was closed to outsiders (anyone bearing petitions or other nuisances) the sons of Romanus trapped their father in his chambers, and bundled him summarily onto a boat bound for Proté, where he was confined to a monastery.

But the sons of Romanus had made a foolish mistake, and their sister knew it. Now was the time for her husband to assume power. *Agents were sent out into the streets and the squares. The people, in a fury, demanded to see their beloved Constantine, the purple-born grandson of the Emperor Basil the Macedonian. Notwithstanding, the Lecapeni brothers, in their madness, planned to kill Constantine at a breakfast party, but he did not attend and countered by arresting them at a dinner party on 27 January 945. In this way the sons of Romanus were sent to join their father on the island of Proté.*

Romanus, meanwhile, had lost neither his eyes nor his wits, and these are the words with which he greeted his sons:

> *Now may God bless the day*
> *Which has moved Your Imperial Highnesses*
> *To visit my humble retreat. It was,*
> *I make no doubt, that same piety*
> *Which expelled me from the palace*
> *That would not permit your longer sojourn there.*
> *But O! well done to have sent me on before you!*
> *For our brethren here, devoted as they are to the*
> *   divine*
> *Philosophy, would otherwise scarcely have known*
> *How to receive Your Majesties, unless I*
> *Had gone on ahead to show them the way.*
> *But look, we have prepared a banquet for you—*
> *Here is boiled water, cold as the Varangian*
> *   snows,*
> *Here are soft beans and leeks freshly plucked,*
> *And all manner of greens beside. If there is*
> *Illness here it is brought about by our frequent*
> *   fasts.*
> *We have no room for an extravagant company,*
> *But there are chambers here for Your Majesties*
> *Who have refused to desert their father in his old*
> *   age.*

How the sons of Romanus responded to this speech is not recorded. They died not long after in obscure places far from their tormentor.

A lesser man might have spent his remaining days in contemplation of his achievements, but Romanus' conscience still troubled him and he became prey to terrible dreams. In these dreams the mouth of hell gaped open and his sons were driven with whips toward it; he, Romanus, was to follow them, but at the last moment he always awoke or the Virgin Mary stretched out her hand to pull him back.

Romanus sought relief in writing. He wrote down all his sins in a book, and in front of a convocation of three hundred monks (some of whom had come from as far away as Rome) recited the sins he had written down, while a neophyte (a mere child) goaded and insulted him. In this way Romanus hoped to abase himself and achieve redemption.

The book of Romanus' sins was then sent to a monastery high on the slopes of the Bithynian Olympus, with the request that the monks pray for the soul of the former emperor. (A certain amount of money was also included.) The request was granted, and in the middle of the night the holiest of the monks heard a voice that cried out three times: "God's mercy has conquered." When he looked again at the book of Romanus' sins he found its pages blank.

Some two years later, on 15 June 948, death came peacefully to Romanus. His corpse was carried back to the city and the empty book was entombed with him in the Church of the Myrelaion.

II

BITHYNIA

ON THE ESPLANADE

On Yalova's bustling waterfront we ate pistachios and waited for the *dolmuş* to leave for Iznik. The word *dolmuş* derives from the same root as *dolmades*, and means essentially "stuffed" or "filled." A *dolmuş*, which may be a taxi but is usually a minibus, will wait at its stop until there are enough people on board to make the journey financially viable. The beauty of this system is that nobody has to consult timetables, which always involves great anxiety on all sides, and everyone gets to go where they want at approximately the right time. The area around the driver's seat on the Iznik *dolmuş* was festooned with good-luck charms and signs invoking the protection of Allah. We soon found out why.

The road from Yalova to Iznik was steep, winding and narrow, and its surface far gone in decay. None of these factors came near to inhibiting the natural exuberance of Turkish drivers, who regard brakes with profound disdain and are fond of overtaking two abreast. I attempted to focus my attention on the beauties of the passing landscape, but without much success. Then the road crossed a high pass in a sweeping curve like an impresario's extravagant gesture, disclosing the pale turquoise expanse of Lake Ascania, lying many hundreds of feet below, and I forgot my fears. At the far end of this lake lay Iznik, the ancient Nicaea, a city of councils and emperors, sultans and ceramics, a city ringed by one hundred and forty magnificent towers.

This was Asia, but the view from the pass revealed nothing Asiatic. There were olive groves, vines and poplars, and the outlines of the mountains were long and graceful. This was the landscape of the first lyric poets, and to most Byzantines it was the heartland of their realm. The art patron and high government official Theodore Metochites, writing in the early fourteenth century, when Anatolia was already all but lost to the empire, described it as infinitely richer and more beautiful than the Byzantine territories in Europe. It was a land of fertility and piety, of social grace and noble customs, and without it the empire was destitute. Driving toward Nicaea along the northern shore of Lake Ascania through olive groves and fields incandescent with poppies, with the lake always visible to our right through flickering poplars, it was not hard to appreciate Metochites' feelings.

We entered the city through a gash torn through its walls. To the left were the sunken arches of the Constantinople Gate, and two pillars surmounted by masks wreathed with snakes, their mouths gaping in what might have been horror or simple astonishment at what the centuries had done to them.

Evening found us in the garden of the Çamlik Hotel, eating catfish pulled from the lake and börek—a delicacy consisting of soft cheese and herbs wrapped in thin filo pastry that was known to the Byzantines of the sixth

century. The garden contained a shallow pool surrounded
by untidy rosebushes. One of Nicaea's massive towers rose
behind us, while before us a low sun was pouring liquid
fire across the lake. To the south, dense black clouds hung
over the mountains and an approaching storm grumbled
borborygmically; between storm clouds and sunset shifting
veils of saffron light were suspended. As it grew darker,
the young men of Nicaea came out to stroll back and forth
under the trees of the esplanade, talking in whispers, their
arms thrown around each other's shoulders. Scraps of song
drifted in and out of the gardens of cafés with charmingly
up-to-date names like Dallas and Lambada. The storm, for
all its ominous throat-clearing, never managed to deliver
itself of its pronouncement, and the few fat raindrops that
spattered into the garden were hardly enough to drive us
indoors, while to the west the sky had invented a hitherto
unrecorded color somewhere between burnt orange and
oleander pink. In the tree that canopied our table, an
unseen bird embarked on an ambitious baroque aria full of
rapid runs and intricate, languishing roulades. There is a
song about a bird that was sung at Byzantine banquets:

> O wild bird become tame,
> O golden bird come to my hand!
> If you dare to fly away, golden bird,
> The hunter will find you with his arrow,
> And your bright feathers will cover the fields.
> Wild bird, be safe from harm, alight on a branch
> Of the fruit tree in my garden, the flowering fruit tree,
> And I will feed you with cool water and musk.

THE BOATS
AND THE CAPTIVES

Since the sun rises behind the city, the dawn over Lake Ascania could not equal the chromatic drama of the sunset, but it had its own appeal. Sky and lake waters were equally pale and opalescent, and I looked for a long time trying to discern the line at which they met.

Early on a spring morning in 1097 the Turkish soldiers manning the towers along the lake shore were not much concerned with effects of light. Something dark was moving on the horizon, something that should not have been there. As the light became clearer they heard distant fanfares and the beating of drums, and saw a forest of pennants fluttering on the morning breeze. They realized to their horror that a flotilla of the Byzantine navy was advancing toward them. Since the armies of the First Crusade already surrounded the land walls, the city was now completely encircled. The Seljuk sultan (whose capital Nicaea had been since 1080) had attempted and failed to come to their rescue, and the defenders now began to lose hope. What they did not know was that the seemingly impressive flotilla out on the lake consisted only of light craft, lightly manned but abundantly supplied with trumpets, drums and pennants. The Emperor Alexius I Comnenus was a master of psychology and political theater.

By the time the crusaders arrived at the walls of Nicaea they had already sworn to return the city to its rightful lord, the emperor. Alexius for his part was prepared to cooperate fully (the boats on the lake were there at the request of the crusaders), but he also bore in mind the fact that Nicaea had been in Turkish hands for less than twenty years; consequently the majority of its inhabitants were still Greek Christians, whom it was his duty to protect. Nor did he wish to see one of the most beautiful cities of western Asia reduced to a smoking ruin. Although he admired their courage and fighting skill, he knew what savagery and discipline the "western barbarians" were capable of. (His daughter Anna remarks with horror that even their priests were "men of blood.") It was essential that the city should not be taken by force. Accordingly, as soon as he had gained control of the lake, Alexius opened negotiations with the garrison and the trapped members of the Turkish court. His terms of surrender were extremely generous, and so it turned out that on the very morning of a general assault the astonished crusaders heard voices proclaiming the emperor to the accompaniment of trumpets, and looked up to see the imperial standard flying from the towers of Nicaea.

It was the ideal outcome, and the work of a truly Christian emperor. Lives were saved on all sides. The city was both liberated and preserved, but the rank-and-file crusaders felt cheated of the heady pleasures of a sack. They had already amused themselves with a certain amount of idle killing and raping in nearby villages (all of which were Christian), but these were mere preliminaries. There were better things to look forward to. Then to their dismay they found that they would only be allowed into the city in small groups, closely supervised by the imperial police: in this way a conquering army hungry for blood, loot and women was efficiently broken up into parties of sightseers trudging around the principal churches.

The feudal lords had less to complain about, since they left their audiences with the emperor laden with gifts, but even they were shocked by Alexius' treatment of his Turkish captives, who hardly seemed captives at all. They watched in disbelief as these enemies of Christ were respectfully conducted across the lake, in boats loaded with all their movable possessions, to safety in the emperor's camp or capital. Some converted to Christianity and took service with the emperor. The sultana—the principle wife of the sultan—was treated to a formal reception in Constantinople, where she and her children resided in luxury befitting their rank until word came from her husband of where and when they might most conveniently be reunited with him. When the messenger arrived, no ransom was demanded.

None of this made any sense to the great mass of westerners crowded around the walls of Nicaea. The chronicler Raymond of Aguilers, who was present at the siege, denounces Alexius as "false and iniquitous," and thus from the first moment of victory the collaboration of eastern and western Christians was poisoned. The westerners could not be expected to understand the complexity of the situation in Anatolia, but nor was the emperor to blame. Alexius Comnenus was the greatest statesman of his day: as he sat in his purple tent at Pelecanum courteously receiving the dignitaries of the sultan's court, he was aware that many regions of Anatolia had been settled by Turks in such numbers that they could not possibly be driven out. It was therefore essential that relations between Turks and Byzantines, between Muslims and Christians should move beyond simple antagonism, and to a significant degree they had already done so. Since 1028 there had been a mosque in Constantinople; Turks fought in Alexius' armies, and the sultan himself had been awarded the title of *sebastos*, which in theory made him an honorary member of the imperial family. If Anatolia was to be Byzantine once again, co-option would be at least as important as outright conquest, and much depended on Turkish perceptions of the prestige and character of the emperor. Whether or not Alexius was, as Runciman claims, "a kindly man" (and there is some doubt), his superb magnanimity in 1097 was a political necessity. It was unfortunate that, to the Latins, so much subtlety and foresight seemed tantamount to a betrayal of the Christian cause. Why did the emperor not exact vengeance for the forty years in which the Turks had terrorized Christians and menaced the Holy Places?

The Byzantines, in turn, were convinced that these great hordes of unwashed and illiterate western barbarians could not really be interested in the conquest of Old Jerusalem—or would not long be satisfied with it—when they had seen Constantinople, the New Jerusalem and the richest and most beautiful city on earth. Anna Comnena is particularly emphatic on this point, and Alexius himself, in a work called *The Muses*, composed with painful care during his last illness, warns his son to "use all his ingenuity to turn aside the commotion coming from the West." Their concern was fully justified.

A DESIGN OF
BIRDS AND FLOWERS

What kind of place was Byzantine Nicaea? The question is surprisingly hard to answer. It is described as "wealthy and populous," but we have no figures for its population. It was famous for the beauty and regularity of its buildings, but most of them have vanished without trace. It was the capital of the *theme* (or military district) of the Opsikion, and was the headquarters for some six thousand troops. It contained colonies of Muslim and Jewish merchants. Silks and laudanum were manufactured, and the crustaceans of the Ascanian Lake were highly prized as a cure for paralysis. The city's patron was Saint Tryphon, whose church, close to the Constantinople Gate, attracted crowds of pilgrims who came each year to witness the miraculous blooming of lilies out of season. In one respect Nicaea was—and remains—remarkable: unlike most of the cities of Byzantine Anatolia, it retained the broad outlines of an antique city. Streets ran from north to south and from east to west along a strict Hippodamian grid plan without the superimposition of haphazard medieval entanglements, like a child's scrawl on graph paper.

The thirteenth-century philosopher and scholar Nice-phorus Blemmydes apostrophized Nicaea as "a city of wide streets, full of people, well-walled, proud of what it encloses." At the time Blemmydes wrote this, Nicaea was the capital of an empire. Today it is a town of roses, honeysuckle and poplars, with no ambitions to be a great city. Having played its part, it has turned its back on history and fallen into a pleasant slumber, yet in its walls and gates, in its ruined churches and the regular layout of its principal streets one can still glimpse at least the ghost of the city described by Blemmydes, and the place still has its pride: a genial, bearded old man whom we encountered close to the Nilüfer Hatun Imaret remarked, "Iznik is little but nice," and the motto of the Iznik municipality is "Clean city, green city."

They might, in addition, take for their mascot the stork. Storks seem to be everywhere in Iznik, moving about the town without any apparent fear of its inhabitants. Picking their way fastidiously among the marble capitals and sarcophagi in the grounds of the Iznik Archaeological Museum, they will pose very obligingly, with wings outstretched, for the camera. They are discriminating birds, naturally attracted to the oldest and most architec-turally distinguished buildings in town. Truncated minarets and early Ottoman domes are capped by the big, untidy turbans of their nests.

The low, ramshackle houses that line the sidestreets are brilliantly painted, as are those in most of Anatolia's old towns. On a single block there are houses that are aqua-marine, peacock blue, leaf green, rose pink, rust red, lilac and bright ocher. This flair for brilliant color, manifest in so many areas of Turkish life and culture, is obviously linked to the Turks' love of flowers, which they will grow in anything that comes to hand: if a garden is unavailable, a pot will do; if that cannot be found, an empty oil can is pressed into service. Walking along the straight street that runs from the lake to the Lefke Gate, I passed four-story apartment buildings almost hidden behind enormous art nouveau embroideries of climbing roses; purple fuchsia spilled from pots; orange lilies clustered around gateposts, and even the bus station had a carefully tended rose garden protected by a clipped hedge.

The Turkish devotion to the floral achieved its definitive expression in the sixteenth century, when Iznik contained more than three hundred workshops producing the superb ceramics (particularly ceramic tiles) we now know as Iznik ware. The varied motifs of Iznik ware include vines, lamps, cypresses, birds and Chinese-style clouds, but the dominant motifs are floral, and although the forms are stylized, the flowers can still be recognized for what they are— carnations or tulips, hyacinth or quince flowers—disposed in intricate designs of blue, turquoise, green, white and a startling tomato red. It was the addition of this lustrous red, which is unique to Iznik ware, that made the accurate depiction of so many flowers possible. As a result, any interior that is covered with Iznik tiles, be it a mosque, a palace or a tomb, becomes an image of paradise. A fourth-century A.D. tomb a little to the north of the city suggests that such things may have had a long history in the region of Nicaea-Iznik.

Approached through orchards and groves of poplars, the tomb is carved into a hillside that overlooks the city and the lake. It is a simple barrel vault, painted to resemble a kind of bower. The roof is covered with a lattice design filled with orderly patterns of leaves and flowers, and along the lateral walls are a series of panels in which lush sprays of foliage support bowls of fruit on which birds are perching. After the passage of sixteen hundred years the colors (mostly reds, greens and yellows) are still fresh, and one of the birds is unmistakably a partridge. Between lattice and panels is a curiously modern and playful abstract frieze that, from the vantage of the door, resolves itself into a trompe l'oeil impression of projecting beams. On the end wall two peacocks stand facing each other in a field of tall red flowers. A large area of the fresco between the peacocks has been lost, but it appears to have contained a vase; both birds are stretching one leg forward as if to grasp the handles of that invisible vase with their feet. It is a motif of Oriental, probably Persian origin.

Peacocks can be found pecking at grapes or sipping from fountains in churches built nearly a thousand years later, and this was only partly a matter of aesthetic preference— of the complementary iridescence of plumage and mosaic—for the peacock was a symbol of eternal life. And yet, as with the vertical garden of a tiled Ottoman tomb, nowhere does the decoration of this burial bower allude explicitly to religion or death. If the tomb were a little larger, it might be a room in which intimate friends were entertained with quietly bibulous suppers.

THE REPRISALS

To walk east from the lake shore to the Lefke Gate was a disconcerting experience. At first the houses and gardens that bordered the street appeared to be sinking. Between the houses, narrow tracks led down steeply from the road and lost themselves in neglected remnants of orchards, but a moment's thought told me that it was not the houses or the gardens that had sunk: in constant use for two thousand years, repaired and resurfaced again and again, the street had risen until it resembled a causeway cutting across a marsh.

This was most dramatically apparent at the crossroads in the center of the city, where the roofless church of Hagia Sophia (not to be confused with the church of the same name in Istanbul) brought to mind a half-submerged and rotting hulk. Its arches barely rose above street level and I almost expected it to list suddenly to one side, yet it was on this site, in 325, that Constantine the Great convoked the first church council: here the Nicene Creed was formulated and the Arian heresy condemned. What remains today is a confusing architectural palimpsest amid which one can find little trace of the church where Constantine made his conciliar entrance, clothed "in a garment which glittered as though radiant with light," thereby establishing the tradition of sartorial magnificence that was to earn the Byzantine emperors such an undeserved reputation for effeminacy in later centuries.

There are traces of an intricately patterned marble floor from a church of Justinian's day, the rest of which has largely disappeared under a third church built after an earthquake in 1065. By that time Turkish raiders were already ravaging Anatolia from end to end. When the Turks took permanent control in the fourteenth century, the church became a mosque; in order to correct its infidel orientation, a *mihrab* (prayer niche) had to be built in a corner of the southern aisle where it makes a distinctly awkward impression. After a final restoration, the structure, like the city that surrounds it, fell into a long decline that left it in its present roofless and abandoned state. The broad arches are blotched with crumbling plaster, and their dignity has been further reduced by successive rises in floor level. The three tall windows that once illuminated the spacious eastern apse were all bricked up years ago, with the result that it bears an uncanny resemblance to a band shell, if one can imagine a band shell with an air of tragic nobility. Below the blocked windows archaeologists have uncovered a remarkably well-preserved *synthronon*—a tiered semicircle of stone benches looking exactly like a miniature theater.

Sad though it is, Hagia Sophia's state of ruin is as nothing compared to that of the once-famous Church of the Dormition, which lies (or rather lay) nearby in the southeast quarter of the city. It is thought to have dated from the seventh or eighth centuries, which would make it very rare, since few churches were built during this troubled period. Its fame rested on the exceptional beauty of its mosaics. A photograph of the ninth-century mosaic in the conch of the apse shows a standing Virgin and Child on a plain gold ground; one side of the Virgin's robe is elaborately folded and edged with gold brocade and tassels; above her head the hand of God extends downward amid a burst of heavenly light that fans out in three broad rays across the surface of the conch.

The narthex was decorated with mosaics of the eleventh century, and the tympanum above the door that led into the main body of the church held another image of the Virgin "wearing a violet mantle edged with gold, and stretching out her arms as an orans." We must take it on trust that "she wore an expression of tender and simple gravity," since not a single cube of glass remains. The Church of the Dormition today is a deep hollow overgrown with grass and weeds, scattered here and there with fragments of white marble that can hardly be dignified with the term "ruins."

After 1919, with the connivance and encouragement of the Western Allies, who were then occupying Istanbul, the Greeks embarked on an invasion of western Anatolia. Perhaps they dreamt of restoring their medieval empire, but dreaming, when transposed into the actions of politicians and generals, usually ends in blood and ineradicable hatred. The Greeks spread out steadily from their base in Smyrna, and by 1920 they had occupied Nicaea and all the surrounding districts of Bithynia. This was a devastating blow to Turkish pride, which patriotic Turks were understandably eager to avenge. Before long they had their opportunity. The Greek army, overextended and abandoned by the Western Allies, was decisively defeated at the battle of Dumlupinar on 6 August 1922. The reprisals began at once. Turkish fury was directed not just against the surviving Greek communities in Anatolia, but against the monuments of Greek Christian art. The Church of the Dormition was packed with dynamite and blown to pieces. Now it is impossible to make out even the outline on the ground of the apse that protected the Virgin and her Child.

There are long-lost monuments and works of art beyond number whose passing one might mourn abstractly, but the destruction of the Church of the Dormition is not a subject for merely formal elegiacs. Somewhere there must be people still living who saw its mosaics, who as children, must have returned that gaze of "tender and simple gravity." There is another reason for particular regret, for the Dormition was the burial place of Theodore I Lascaris, emperor of Nicaea. He died in 1222, and if any medieval monarchs deserve a lasting memorial, it is Theodore and his successors of the house of Lascaris. Their story and the story of their empire begins in Constantinople, in another year blighted by the enmity and mutual incomprehension of nations.

WHY COULD NOT HELEN?

In 1204 Byzantium was burning. What Alexius I and his daughter Anna had feared had come to pass. The soldiers of the Fourth Crusade had broken through the city's defenses.

Since the siege of Nicaea, relations between Byzantium and the West had been tense, when not actively hostile. The ambitious monarchs of the West, especially the German emperors, were infuriated by the Byzantine emperor's exclusive claim to the title "Emperor of the Romans," and thus to divinely sanctioned hegemony over all Christendom. Humbler merchants and crusaders resented what they perceived as the arrogance and effeminacy of Byzantine aristocrats, and envied their enormous wealth. The Byzantines, for their part, could not shake the old habit of regarding all Latins as mere barbarians, and felt nothing but contempt for their greed, violent manners and shocking ignorance of classical Greek literature. Even the shared Christianity of East and West was not a unifying factor—in western eyes the schismatic Byzantines were little better than heretics.

There were more specific reasons for western hostility, chief among them the widespread but unfounded belief that the Emperor Manuel I Comnenus was responsible for the dismal failure of the Second Crusade. In the turbulent years that followed Manuel's death, tensions were exacerbated by acts of violence: in 1182 the Byzantian mob succumbed to anti-Latin hysteria and massacred Constantinople's large western colony; three years later the Normans of Sicily subjected Thessalonika to a sack of such thoroughgoing brutality that even the city's dogs and pack animals were slaughtered. But the most fateful dispute concerned trade.

Ever since Alexius I had granted the Venetians trading privileges in return for help against an earlier Norman invasion, they had assumed a dominant role in Byzantine commerce. As their wealth and confidence grew, they became increasingly resistant to imperial authority, and in 1171 Emperor Manuel's patience ran out: on 12 March of that year he ordered the arrest of every Venetian in the empire, and the confiscation of all their property. The Venetians responded immediately by raiding the islands of Lesbos and Chios, but they also began to think in terms of a more comprehensive solution to the Byzantine problem. In 1203 the simultaneous arrival in Italy of a pretender to the Byzantine throne and a crusader army entirely dependent on the Venetians for shipping gave the "Serene Republic" its chance. So it happened that an army that should have gone to the aid of the beleaguered crusader kingdoms of the Holy Land was diverted to an attack on the greatest city in Christendom.

For the Venetians the capture of Constantinople was a great commercial coup, but for civilization it was an unprecedented catastrophe. The crusaders were dazzled by their first sight of the city, but once it was within their power they killed, raped, burned and looted without compunction. The historian Nicetas Choniates could scarcely believe what was happening. The barbarity of the westerners surpassed his worst expectations. They seemed to have fallen into the grip of collective madness. How else could one explain the fact that these Soldiers of the Cross rode their horses through the doors of Hagia Sophia and placed a screeching prostitute on the patriarchal throne? But Nicetas was not aware of the wickedness of the crusading clergy, who had assured their credulous flock that the Greeks "were enemies of God and worse than the Jews."

As he watched his mansion burn to the ground, Nicetas grieved for the loss of his art collection. Throughout the city, libraries, palaces and churches were burning. The tesserae of mosaics fell in scorching showers, and in a few days Europe lost half its artistic heritage. Constantinople's streets and squares were full of the best works of Greek and Roman sculptors. Nicetas' sorrow over the loss of the statues is extraordinarily intense: for him they were symbols of civilization and continuity. He refers to a bronze Hercules created by Lysippus, the favorite sculptor of Alexander the Great. Its knees stood higher than a man's head, yet it was melted down for coin. He describes a marble statue of Helen, and asks, "Could not she, with her white arms and lovely form, soften the hearts of the barbarians?" She could not: her image was smashed to pieces.

Nicetas and his entire family took refuge in the home of a Venetian merchant whom he had earlier saved from the wrath of an anti-Latin mob, but as more and more of his friends arrived it soon became apparent that they could not all stay hidden for long. Accordingly these grandees of the imperial court dressed themselves in rags, smeared their faces with dirt and began to pick their way through the carnage that littered the streets, hoping to reach the comparative safety of the countryside unmolested, but before they had gone very far a drunken soldier snatched a young woman from their party. Since they were unarmed, it looked as if they would have to stand helplessly by while she was raped. To Nicetas this was beyond endurance, and at considerable risk to himself he accosted a passing group of soldiers, and by reminding them of their vows managed to shame them into rescuing the girl.

Once in the open country, insult followed injury. The disguises adopted by Nicetas and his friends cannot have been very convincing, since they had to endure the jeers of disaffected peasants who were delighted to see representatives of the class that had bled them dry reduced to misery. Nicetas remarks bitterly, "They had not yet had much to do with the beef-eating Latins and they did not know that they served a wine as pure and unmixed as unadulterated bile, nor that they would treat the Byzantines with utter contempt." For now there was nothing to do but continue, in tears or stunned silence, the long walk to Selymbria on the Marmaran shore, where they hoped to find a boat to take them to Asia.

THE IMPERIAL STATUE

"O happy Asia! O happy powers in the East! They do not fear the arms of their subjects nor dread the interference of the pontiffs." Thus wrote Frederick II, German emperor and king of Sicily, to John III Vatatzes, emperor of Nicaea—for, despite appearances, the world had not ended. Nicetas and his companions found their way safely from Selymbria to Nicaea, where the Byzantine resistance quickly established itself under the energetic leadership of Theodore Lascaris. Only four years later Nicetas had the honor of composing Theodore's enthronement speech. The brilliant Lascarid dynasty was founded, and Nicaea was suddenly the capital of a small but growing and gallant empire-in-exile.

The Byzantines had proved their resilience many times before, but never more astonishingly than in the aftermath of the ultimate, dumbfounding shock—the loss of the city to the barbarians. Possession of the city was fundamental to the Byzantine worldview and one might have expected them to succumb to paralyzing disorientation, but within the walls of Nicaea twenty-five years of societal decay and demoralization were reversed. Theodore set about driving back both Latins and Turks. In 1210, near Antioch in the Maeander valley, he challenged the Seljuk sultan to single combat, and defeated and killed him. His son-in-law and successor, John Vatatzes, continued his work, extending the empire's territory deep into Europe and capturing Thessalonika. New fortresses were built along the eastern frontier; the ancient cities of western Asia were restored; taxes were fairly administered (something all too rare in the later Byzantine period), and from the Maeander valley to Amastris on the Black Sea the land prospered.

Vatatzes' son, Theodore II Lascaris, composed a proud panegyric to the city of Nicaea: "Thou hast surpassed all the cities, since the Roman state, many times divided and crushed by foreign troops . . . has been founded, established and strengthened only in thee." For once Byzantine hyperbole spoke no more than the truth. Here Nicetas Choniates could settle down securely to finish his great history, the *Chronike Diegesis*, a work so humane and so deeply civilized that its author even attempts to understand, rather than merely denounce, the destroyers of Constantinople.

It is typical of the Lascarids that they should have recognized and rewarded Nicetas' talents. Their martial exploits were remarkable enough, but they also deserve to be honored as heroes of learning and literature. In addition to storehouses for weapons, libraries and schools were founded in the major cities and scientific expeditions were sent out into all the Greek lands to collect valuable books and manuscripts. What the western barbarians had dispersed the emperors would gather in. Scholars and poets, historians and philosophers were drawn irresistibly to their court, and chief among them was the remarkable polymath Nicephorus Blemmydes. Nicephorus had been a boy when he fled with his parents from the Latin occupation of Constantinople, and by traveling among the cities of the Nicaean Empire, seeking out different teachers, he was able to acquire such a commanding knowledge of poetics, rhetoric, philosophy, logic, natural sciences, medicine, geometry, physics and astronomy that his contemporaries were amazed.

Blemmydes was the author of a work known as *The Imperial Statue*, a portrait of the ideal ruler, which he dedicated to his most distinguished pupil, Theodore II, doubtless in the hope that he would be inspired to imitate the portrait. Blemmydes and the other Nicaean intellectuals (notably Georgios Akropolites) were convinced that "States will have rest from evils . . . when rulers become philosophers, philosophers rulers." Accordingly the young emperor studied Aristotle and Plato assiduously, and wrote many philosophical and religious treatises. He has also left us a collection of more than two hundred letters, in one of which he records the profound feelings of awe and sadness aroused in him by the ruins of Pergamum—its vertiginous theater, its red basilica under which a river flows, its altars carved with gods and titans. In the style and sentiments of this letter scholars have discerned a foreshadowing of Italian humanism.

A somewhat melancholy pride in the achievements of Hellenism set the tone of Theodore II's learned court. A protective shield of books was raised against the blunt fact of imperial decline. Exiled in western Asia, shut out from "the Acropolis of the Universe," Nicaean intellectuals discovered belatedly that they were as much Hellenes as Romans. By laying exclusive claim to the Hellenic inheritance—for how could a barbarian ever arrive at a proper appreciation of Homer and Hesiod?—they differentiated themselves from the hated Latins, and demonstrated, at least to their own satisfaction, the innate superiority of their culture and society.

Theodore II reigned for only four years. He had inherited his father's epilepsy in an aggravated form and in his last year the ravages of the disease affected his mental stability. He became increasingly moody, seeing enemies everywhere, and in 1258 died at the age of thirty-six, but while he lived his capital city was hailed as the new Athens. The exaggeration is pardonable. The Nicaeans maintained a very high standard of civilization in difficult circumstances. Their empire represents the last flowering of Hellenism in western Asia, and was thus the epilogue to a history stretching back to the Bronze Age. It may be true that the Nicaeans' devotion to the classical past, and the extreme archaicism of their literary diction left little room for original invention, but their achievement surely amounts to more than a collection of bombastic eulogies and dusty commentaries. They contributed to Byzantium's cultural resurgence in the early years of the fourteenth century, and since this, in turn, nourished the revival of Hellenism in Italy, perhaps we should accord Nicaea some of the respect we automatically extend to Florence and Venice. But Nicaea is different, of course: there is much less for the tourist to see.

THE WALLS OF NICAEA

Visible evidence of the enlightened rule of the Lascarids is scant. Of their palaces and the mansions of their nobles there is nothing, and not a single church has remained intact. It has sometimes been said that they were too busy with warfare and too thrifty in their economic policies to pay much attention to the arts, but this would have been a break with the best Byzantine traditions which the Nicaean emperors would not have countenanced. Art, like learning, was an essential adjunct to the imperial image, and it is reasonable to assume that many of Constantinople's best painters, mosaicists and architects would have found refuge in Nicaea after 1204. The fact that we are ignorant of their names and their works does not argue that they never existed, or that the emperors failed to make use of their talents. John Vatatzes, in particular, was an energetic builder, founding hospitals, almshouses and churches throughout his territories. The foundations of one of these churches have come to light at Sardis. It is small, but its plan is of the most elegant and sophisticated

Constantinopolitan type. Such churches would have been richly decorated with frescoes and, more rarely, with mosaics.

The disappearance of Nicaean fresco painting is a source of frustration and sorrow to art historians, since it must have provided the link between the mannerism and pathos of Comnenian painting, and the dramatic intensity of the great anastasis in the Church of St. Savior in Chora in Constantinople. The picturesque elements in the Chora mosaics (the fanciful architecture with its strange awnings, the birds and fountains, the little boys playing with hoops), which seem to hark back to Hellenistic genre painting, may be the fruit of classicizing tendencies in Nicaea. Certainly the appearance of work of such superlative quality in Constantinople in the early years of the fourteenth century must mean that Byzantine techniques and traditions had been kept alive in exile during the thirteenth.

On either side of the apse of the Nicaean Hagia Sophia there are tall, domed chambers dating from the Lascarid period, and in one of these there are extensive traces of frescoes, too blackened for their subjects to be legible. Perhaps if they were cleaned and restored we could move beyond conjecture, but for now the most substantial evidence of Lascarid rule is the line of outer walls that was raised around the city in the reign of Theodore I.

At the Constantinople Gate a fragment of Roman bas-relief has been pressed into service in the construction of the outer gate. It shows a procession of robed figures, weathered or defaced almost beyond recognition, and is most likely a panel from a sarcophagus. It demonstrates how insecure the times were in the early thirteenth century, and with what haste the outer walls were built as Theodore sought to defend his remnant of empire against predatory Latins and Turks. He must have felt that the city's magnificent third- and fourth-century walls were no longer enough and yet these walls remain one of the wonders of Anatolia.

Guidebooks give details of the sunken triumphal arches at the Constantinople and Lefke gates, but finding the Saray Kapi or Palace Gate was, for us, very much a matter of accident. Heading south from Hagia Sophia and following the signs for the Roman theater, we soon found ourselves amid fields, even though we were still inside the circuit of the walls. Twenty years ago much of Iznik was given over to orchards and vegetable gardens, but only in this south-west quarter had it retained the peculiar atmosphere of a city invaded by the country. Houses were grouped in villagelike clusters. Boys divided their time between playing football and tending flocks of sheep and goats. And here (as advertised) was the Roman theater, underpinned by gigantic vaults that looked like so many entrances to the underworld. Built by Pliny the Younger in the second century, abandoned in the seventh and thereafter much plundered for building materials, by the time of the Lascarids it was a grassy knoll surmounted by a church and a cemetery. On the last day of May 1991 the local people sat or strolled among the ruins, enjoying the early evening air, and a sleek young chestnut stallion pranced nervously in a meadow.

A curving track led from the theater to the Saray Kapi, the least visited and least pretentious of Nicaea's gates. A simple brick arch springing from massive stone piers, it was blocked as we approached by the lumbering passage of an oxcart laden with kindling and driven by an irascible old woman who emphatically did not want to be photo-graphed. Beyond the gate a clear, shallow stream flowed across the track and not many yards away lay the motionless pool that was its source, fringed with reeds and over-arched by a lattice of willow boughs. Nothing could have been more peaceful, more apt for the weekend watercol-orist's brush, yet, in the fields beyond, the army of Raymond IV, count of Toulouse, had encamped during the siege of 1097. I heard no spectral fanfares or reveilles, but felt the pressure of many presences. The past was very close, and the walls, unencumbered by any new construc-tion, stretched away to the east punctuated by great round bastions of pale stone and warmly colored brick, closely invested by tall poplars. From these same towers the name of Alexius Comnenus had been proclaimed while purple standards were unfurled.

Between the outer and inner walls (an interval of a few yards and a thousand years) lines of young olive trees leaned all one way and goats grazed, casually attended by a few children or women in bright head scarves. Poppies grew on eroded parapets, and as the sun dropped toward the lake the walls began to glow as if the light had taken on solid form. Hoopoes, those most elegantly costumed of birds, flew in and out of cracks in the masonry where they had made their nests, and a pulse seemed to beat in the stones.

THE DYING MOTHER

Some fifty years after his death, John Vatatzes was canonized by the Orthodox Church, but there is nothing very saintly about the controlled fury of the letter he wrote to Pope Gregory IX in 1237. The pope had rebuked the emperor for his attacks on the Latins occupying Constantinople, and Vatatzes countered by declaring that the papal missive would appear to be the work of "a man experiencing the final stages of madness. . . . For we would do an injustice to the laws of nature, to the principles of our people, to the graves of our fathers, and to the holy and sacred places if we did not with all our strength seek to recover Constantinople." For all the care they devoted to their Asian territories, the overriding aim of the Lascarids had always been the recovery of Constantinople, and by the time of Vatatzes' death in 1254 the city was completely surrounded by Byzantine territory. By a cruel irony of fate the honor of its recapture fell not to any member of their family but to the usurper, Michael VIII Palaeologus, who celebrated his triumph by blinding the last of their line, John Lascaris, the eleven-year-old son of Theodore II. Nor did the removal of the capital to Constantinople bring any benefit to Nicaea or the other cities of Byzantine Asia. The brilliant interlude was over, and it was time for the curtain to be raised on the disappointing final act of the tragedy.

After nearly sixty years in Latin hands, Constantinople was a depopulated slum and the contents of the Nicaean treasury were poured out in a vain attempt to restore it to something approaching its former glory. Worse, the effort of deflecting the implacable hostility of the western powers absorbed most of Emperor Michael's energies and most of the empire's military resources, with the result that the eastern defenses were fatally neglected. The *akritai*, or border guards, went unpaid, and their traditional tax exemption was rescinded. The majority of them promptly abandoned their posts and joined forces with the enemy. When Michael toured the eastern frontier toward the end of his life he was dismayed to find regions he remembered as flourishing lying desolate, but his own shortsighted policies were largely to blame.

In the last years of his reign a new Turkish power—the Osmanli or Ottomans—established itself in the region of Dorylaion (Turkish Eskişehir) within the bend of the Sangarios River, and began to drive a wedge into the heart of Bithynia. Nicaea and the other cities soon found themselves cut off from each other and the capital. Safe, for the time being, behind their great walls, the citizens of Nicaea watched and waited. As Lascarid loyalists they had no love for Michael Palaeologus or his descendants, who in any case were too busy fighting among themselves to offer much succor to their oppressed subjects in Asia. Emir Orhan—leader of the Osmanlis—offered generous terms, and in 1331 the Nicaeans concluded that surrender was in their own best interests. Those who wanted to leave were allowed to do so unmolested, taking their holy relics with them. According to one account the majority chose to stay and soon came to terms with the conqueror. But there are other versions.

Writing at about the time these events occurred, Demetrius Cydones claimed that the Turks had "completely destroyed cities, despoiled churches, looted graves and filled everything with blood and corpses," while Ostrogorsky remarks in passing that Nicaea fell only "after a heroic struggle." Furthermore, when the Arab traveler Ibn Battuta passed through the city in 1333 he found it derelict and uninhabited. Still more confusingly, 1333 is the date of the founding of the oldest Ottoman mosque in Nicaea (or Iznik as we should now call it). What are we to make of these apparent contradictions? How can they be converted into a coherent narrative? Since there is no reason to doubt Ibn Battuta's description of what he saw with his own eyes, we have to assume that most of the population left in 1331. It is also likely that even before the final surrender many had fled to the safety of Constantinople: fourteenth-century Byzantine sources speak of great influxes of refugees from Asia. Then, in a matter of months after Ibn Battuta's visit, Orhan began the process of restoring and repopulating the city. Since the Turkish conquest was so recent most of the "new" inhabitants would have been Greek Christians, and it is quite possible that some of the "old" inhabitants returned, attracted by Orhan's good government and religious tolerance. Who would not prefer to live in a dynamic and expanding emirate rather than in a dying empire?

The process of peaceful assimilation went ahead rapidly, and in 1339 and again in 1340 the patriarch of Constantinople, horrified to learn that Nicaean Christians were converting to Islam in large numbers, wrote futile encyclicals urging them to save their souls. Instead many preferred to save themselves the obligation of paying the *haradj*, a capitation tax to which all Christians within Ottoman territory were subject, and it is from these Byzantine converts that the majority of Bithynia's present population is descended. Byzantine Nicaea ends with a prolonged diminuendo in which one can detect the faint, choral sound of a people's desire to endure.

Theodore Metochites, who died in 1332, lived just long enough to hear of Nicaea's fall. He tried to account for the loss of Anatolia in a series of laments, but failed to think of a good enough reason for it. Why had God abandoned the empire? It was true that the Greeks had sinned, but he could not believe that they had sinned so grievously that they deserved this terrible chastisement. If the reason was not the sins of the Greeks, perhaps it was the virtues of the Turks? Surprisingly, Metochites gave considerable credence to this idea, but in order to do so he had to depict the Turks (whom he persisted in calling Scythians) as a free and simple people, uncontaminated by civilization. One would not know from reading Metochites that under the Seljuk sultans the Turks had developed an advanced, urban civilization that was quite as prone to complexity and corruption as its Byzantine counterpart. Metochites' Turks are an antiquarian fiction pieced together from references to Scythians in the pages of Homer, Herodotus and other ancient authors. In fact his enumeration of aboriginal Turkish virtues is remarkably close to Plato's praise of Sparta and just as unconvincing.

Metochites was a devout Christian, yet in the end he was forced to resort to the Hellenistic and pagan concept of tyche. It was this blind and arbitrary fortune, not the Christian God, who governed the affairs of men. Empires rose and fell, the Assyrians giving way to the Persians, and the Persians to the Macedonians, and the Macedonians to the Romans: "And these events occur in an alternating fashion according to chance of both time and tyche. Nor is there anything constant in human affairs nor unchangingly eternal." If there was any consolation in this bleak realization it was of a purely intellectual kind, and what emerges from Metochites' laments is an overwhelming sense of personal loss. Anatolia was his "nourishing mother," and now as she lies dying there is nothing he can do to help her:

> O most beautiful Ionia, most beautiful Lydia, Aeolia, Phrygia and Hellespont, lands . . . where I dwelt so pleasantly and . . . from a tender age! Now I am left a mournful exile, pouring out tears and lamentations in the manner of sepulchral sacrifices. O my dearly beloved cities, plains, mountains, valleys, rivers, groves and meadows, origins of every joy . . . now I am greatly pained in my recollections of you; my heart melts instantly as do my thoughts, and I am unable even to breathe. . . . Anatolia has departed from the Roman state! O this destitution! O this loss! We live in a few remnants of a body, that formerly was so great and beautiful, as though the majority of the most vital members had been severed. And we continue to live in shame and derision, wholly incapable in the means of existence and life.

THE DISAPPEARANCE OF THE RED

East of Hagia Sophia, Iznik's main street is shaded by plane trees and bordered by fountains, barbershops, cafés and pharmacies. (Even in quite modest Turkish towns there are astonishing numbers of pharmacies.) As you emerge from this tunnel of shade and activity a park opens to your left and it is here that you will find the Nilüfer Hatun Imaret. The word *imaret* is usually translated as *soup kitchen* or *hospice*, but in fact it can be applied to any charitable foundation attached to a mosque, and this handsome edifice was intended to provide lodgings and a place of study for itinerant scholars and holy men. With its cluster of softly rounded red-tiled domes (the highest occupied by the inevitable stork) and its alternating courses of masonry and brick, the imaret could easily by mistaken for a late-Byzantine building. It is more than likely that Greek artisans had a hand in its construction, which would be singularly appropriate since it was built in 1388 by Sultan Murad I, in memory of his mother. Her Turkish name, Nilüfer Hatun (meaning *Water-Lily Lady*), conceals the fact that she was the daughter of a Greek nobleman, perhaps one of the *akritai* whose alienation from the Byzantine government led them to join forces with the Ottomans.

Nilüfer was not the only Greek lady in the harem of Murad's father, Orhan. In 1346 Orhan had married Theodora Cantacuzena, daughter of the Emperor John VI Cantacuzenus. The marriage has occasioned much comment from moralizing historians, who entertain themselves with lurid vignettes of a weeping princess dragged off to spend the rest of her days languishing in a Turkish harem. This is taken to be a powerful symbol of the abject condition to which the empire had been reduced, but John Cantacuzenus and his spirited daughter must have seen things very differently. John VI was one of the most intelligent of the late Byzantine emperors, and he consistently preferred his Turkish neighbors to the unreliable and self-seeking westerners. Orhan was John's trusted ally. He did not persecute his Christian subjects and even spoke some Greek: he was a barbarian but a gentleman. Nor should we assume that this was a purely political match: both Byzantine and Turkish sources insist that Orhan had fallen passionately in love with Theodora. The Turkish poet Enveri asserts that John Cantacuzenus had three daughters who were "lovely as houris," and the loveliest of them all was Theodora.

It was no doubt a matter of regret to John that his otherwise excellent son-in-law was a Muslim and a polygamist, but he was determined to put the best face on things. The marriage was celebrated on the outskirts of Selymbria to the sound of choirs, trumpets, flutes and viols, and Greeks and Turks feasted together for several days. Only then did Theodora embark with her husband and set sail for Asia, where she took up residence in Bursa. Whether or not

Orhan was in love with his young bride, he treated her with marked respect. She was not obliged to convert to Islam, and rather than waste time lamenting her fate, devoted herself to improving the conditions of Christians and the poor.

The imaret now serves as Iznik's museum. It stands in the midst of a mason's yard of sarcophagi, tombstones, columns and capitals, and it is only from these fragments, set out in rows on carefully cropped lawns, that we can gain some idea of the richness and variety of Nicaea's vanished Byzantine architecture. We can see this most vividly in the way the capitals change. In the time of Constantine, the Corinthian order still lent a standardized magnificence to the empire's public buildings. At first the formula was simply varied: the Corinthian acanthus leaves were shown as if petrified in the moment of being ruffled by a breeze, or they were so deeply incised and undercut that they appeared as lacelike, nearly abstract patterns. But by the sixth century, craftsmen were emboldened to abandon the acanthus altogether: there are basketweave designs with vestigial Ionic volutes, designs of inter-weaving vines and bold rosettes in high relief. And there is a motif of foliate tendrils spilling out of a central vase that is nearly identical to a motif on capitals unearthed at the Church of Saint Polyeuctus. It gives an impression of invention barely contained, as if the sculptor could have gone on elaborating these tendrils forever: a wind from Asia has lifted the dead weight of late classicism.

The ceramics in the Iznik museum are not as impressive as might be expected. Much finer examples of Iznik ware can be found in London and New York, but in default of the anticipated glories, it is interesting to learn that Seljuk, Byzantine and early Ottoman pottery is frequently indis-tinguishable. Glazes are brown or green and motifs are often figurative. Animals, birds and horsemen are especially common, and some Byzantine fragments show curious cartoonlike images of birds catching worms, but these are all very dim precursors of Iznik ware, which did not assume its classic form until some time shortly after 1514. In that year the aptly named Sultan Selim the Grim invaded Persia, captured Tabriz and, as part of his war booty, brought back a number of ceramicists whom he settled in Iznik. It would be wrong to think of Iznik ware as a purely imported art, however: its famous red did not exist in Tabriz—perhaps it was a response to the Turkish love of brilliantly contrasted color or the chance discovery of a master craftsman with experimental inclinations. However that may be, its period of refulgence was surprisingly brief.

The power of the Ottoman state and the beauty of Iznik ware reached their apogees during the reign of Suleiman the Magnificent (1520–66) but, for reasons that are hard to understand, Suleiman ordered the murder of his two most gifted sons, thus irreparably damaging the Ottoman bloodline. He was succeeded in the last years of the sixteenth century and the early years of the seventeenth by an extraordinary parade of drunkards, weaklings, sadists and imbeciles. The decline was not immediately apparent. Suleiman's surviving son, Selim II (sometimes known as "the Sot") devoted his time exclusively to drinking and poetry, leaving the business of government in the hands of the great Bosnian vizier Sokollu Mehmed Pasha. The mosque that Sokollu built in Istanbul contains some of the most exquisite of all Iznik tiles, but in 1578 he was murdered, and the sultanate rapidly descended into anarchy. Anatolia was in a continual state of revolt. In a mass movement known as "The Great Flight" thousands of peasants, driven off their land by roving bands of Turkmen and Kurdish irregulars, attempted to make their way to Europe. At the same time the economy was undermined by massive inflation, resulting from the influx of bullion from the Spanish American colonies. These were not the kind of circumstances in which a delicate and costly art like the making of Iznik ware could be expected to flourish, and deterioration becomes apparent in the early seventeenth century, when impurities entered the red. Disturbances continued until the middle of the century. Part of Iznik was destroyed by fire, and its ceramicists were dispersed to Istanbul, Kütahya and Rhodes. The red grew duller and duller and at the same time the life went out of the greens and blues. The weakened colors overran, as if too much water had been added to the glaze, and by the end of the century what had once been compared to the reddest tulips and tomatoes was reduced to a muddy brown. The secret was lost, never to be recovered, and with the disappearance of the red, Iznik ceases to be of any significance in the affairs of the world.

IZNIK TO BURSA

The road to Bursa passes along the southern shore of Lake Ascania. Here the mountains swept down steeply to the water, and the villages were clustered on spurs of the hills, while below the road numbers of people, taking advantage of the first good drying weather after a month of nearly continual rain, were washing their carpets and kilims in the lake. Once the lake was past, the road began to descend toward the port of Gemlik, on the gulf of the same name. Gemlik is ugly, and its once beautiful gulf is lined with ranks of apartment buildings resembling unfinished fortifications, yet it is the ancient Cius. It was from here that Alexius Comnenus had his boats hauled overland to the lake.

From Gemlik we crossed a low pass to the west and came down into the fertile plain that lies before Bursa, capital of the early Ottoman sultans. Billboards lined the road and we might have been approaching any small American city were it not for a radiant white object looming ahead of us that at first I took to be a particularly stupendous cloud formation. On a second look this turned out to be the sunlit snowfields of the Bithynian Olympus, which the Turks, with typical directness, simply call Uludağ, The Great Mountain, and such, at well over eight thousand feet, it certainly is. This is the mountain that provided snow to cool the drinks of emperors, and it was once a great center of monasticism, preceding Mount Athos by at least two centuries: here Romanus Lecapenus had sent the book of his sins, and other pious emperors came on pilgrimage. Now its snows were dazzling: what had fallen as rain in Istanbul delighted us in Bursa, even as we climbed out of our bus into the filthiest bus station I had ever seen.

Bursa, alas, is not as gracious as I remembered it being twenty years ago. The center of the old city is cut in half by a four-lane highway that roars straight past Beyazid I's Great Mosque and can only be crossed by underpasses. Worse still, the nobility of the Yeşil Türbe (Green Mausoleum), last resting place of the benevolent Sultan Mehmed I, is now quite literally undermined by a road tunnel that has been gouged out of the mountainside immediately behind and below it. It would have been naïve to have expected that the center of an expanding city could have remained preserved in amber for twenty years, but I was appalled nonetheless: if any city deserved to be spared the depredations of the automobile it was surely Bursa, which I recalled as a place of florid wooden houses, plane trees, roses and rushing streams. I probably made some intemperate pronouncements on the subject of Turkish vandalism, but after an afternoon's exploration I began to wonder about the accuracy of my memories— so much seemed to have shifted, become more distant, smaller, less vividly colored, and surely not all of this could be blamed on modernization.

Of Byzantine Prusa little remained twenty years ago and as little remains today. There are some reused columns in the vestibule of the Green Mosque, and more in the tomb of Murad II; the tomb of Osman, the founder of Ottoman fortunes, has a beautiful patterned marble floor that has survived from a church that stood on the same site, and the ruined walls of the citadel are also Byzantine work. It is not much to show for nearly a thousand years of history, yet Prusa must have been a place of some consequence, since, on occasion, it had come to accommodate the entire imperial court. Its mountain air, lush wooded setting and thermal springs made it an ideal place of retreat from the rigors of administration and campaigning.

THE FOUNTAINS

Although there must always have been suburbs to the west, where the thermal springs are located, Byzantine Prusa was largely confined within the walls of the present citadel district or Hisar. It was only after Orhan had captured the city in 1326, at the end of a ten-year siege, and made it his capital, that mosques, hans and a bazaar district were built immediately to the east of the Hisar.

The capital was soon moved to Adrianople (modern Edirne) in Thrace, but all the early sultans had a special affection for Bursa; it was here that they preferred to be buried, and magnificent mosques and tombs were spread over a wide area along the precipitous foothills of Mount Olympus. By the time that the Koza Han was built in 1451, Bursa was the loveliest city in western Asia. The Han itself is quite as harmonious and graceful as anything produced in Renaissance Italy. Its broad, tree-shaded courtyard is bordered by spacious, two-story arcades and has an octagonal pavilion at its center; the upper story of the pavilion contains a miniature mosque (or *mescit*) approached by an elegant staircase, while the lower story shelters a fountain with a large pool, also octagonal, that seems to radiate calm throughout the building.

Bursa has always been a city of fountains, and recently there have been attempts to keep the tradition alive. The most ambitious of these is the huge fountain in the Koza Park, just to the south of the Han. Multiple water jets spurt, twist and flail in apparent homage to an inscrutable, concrete monolith at the center of a foaming pool. As a piece of hydraulic engineering it is impressive, but it is not beautiful and the Koza Park is a treeless square that seems designed to drive you to seek refuge under the twenty domes of the Great Mosque that borders it to the west.

According to tradition the mosque's twenty domes are the result of a pledge made by the formidable Sultan Beyazid Yildirim, known as Beyazid the Thunderbolt (so named for the speed and decisiveness with which he smote his enemies). In 1396 Beyazid was faced by an army of a reputed 100,000 crusaders. They had invaded his Balkan territories, and he promised his God that he would build twenty mosques if he were granted victory, but having disposed of the crusaders with contemptuous ease at the battle of Nicopolis, he began to have second thoughts; twenty mosques seemed a tall order even for a man who styled himself "Lord of the Universe and Sultan of Rum." His architect came up with a satisfactory solution. The Great Mosque of Bursa was one of the largest structures the Turks had ever built; it had more domes than any other mosque in the sultan's territories and their number was at least an allusion to the terms of the pledge. Allah had been honored, but architectural historians have generally been unkind about the results, finding the mosque clumsy, complaining that the twelve piers that support the domes make it impossible to perceive the interior as a single unified space. This may be true, but it will not concern an unprejudiced person who has spent some time in Beyazid's mosque.

On entering one of its three splendid doorways adorned with designs of honeycombs and stalactites, you are at once struck by the massiveness of the piers, painted with bold flourishes of calligraphy and strange designs of trophies and looped-back portieres that seem to have been copied from the stage set of some dimly remembered baroque opera. The second thing that strikes you is the honeyed quality of the light that falls through a central glass dome onto a three-tiered fountain resembling a monumental cake stand. The glass dome was originally open to the sky so that rain or snow could fall into the fountain, and the whole space glows softly with this light that comes from its center. The third thing you notice is the sound of the place, which is the sound of prayers and falling water, of subdued conversation and shuffling bare feet.

I have never entered a religious space that was more populous or less forbidding. Old men washed their feet in the fountain or sat on the floor chatting with their friends. Our presence disturbed no one—although we were the only westerners in evidence—and flocks of people moved constantly across the carpeted floor. Many of them appeared to be merely taking a short cut, shoes in hand, across the mosque, but this did not seem in any way disrespectful: in Bursa, the Great Mosque is truly the heart and soul of its city.

Then, without warning, a woman began to scream and jabber in a high-pitched, furious voice. We, of course, had no idea what the reason for her complaint might be, but the other people in the mosque reacted phlegmatically; some even tried to reason with her, but she continued to scream with the force of an enraged prophetess until gently conducted out, still pouring forth imprecations. As soon as she was gone, the mosque's calm, murmurous activity resumed as if nothing at all had happened, as the waters of a fountain might close over a shard of glass.

THE FALL OF THE THUNDERBOLT

Beyazid the Thunderbolt burst onto the historical stage in the most spectacular fashion at Kosovo, the fateful "field of blackbirds," where, on the morning of 15 June 1389, his father, Murad I, was preparing to do battle with a Serbian army under the leadership of Prince Lazar. Before battle could begin, however, a Serbian nobleman claiming to be a deserter with information that would be useful to the Turks was admitted to Murad's tent, and at once plunged a knife into the sultan's heart. Such, at least, is one of the many versions of the incident that have come down to us. What is certain is that Murad was killed and it did the Serbs no good at all. Enraged and vengeful, Beyazid took command without delay, scattering their army, executing Prince Lazar and slaughtering the Serbian nobility. According to tradition, the field of blackbirds was drenched with the blood of 77,000 Serbian dead. At the end of what he must have thought a very good day's work Beyazid had his younger brother strangled to avoid any possibility of a dispute over the succession.

Beyazid may have been a conquering hero to the Turks (and there can be no doubt of his energy and courage), but he was also impulsive, choleric, ungenerous and stupendously arrogant. He was something of a paradox, for although he might appear to be the archetype of "the terrible Turk," both his mother and his paternal grandmother were Greek. This did not make him well-disposed to the Byzantines.

In the festivities and ceremonies of his court Beyazid may have sought to rival the splendors of Byzantium's heyday, but he appears to have taken a sadistic pleasure in tormenting the emperors in Constantinople.

At this time there were no fewer than three Byzantine emperors—John V, his son Manuel II, and his grandson (and Manuel's nephew) John VII—ruling over a pathetic remnant of empire that consisted of little more than their capital and a small province in the Peloponnese. Of the three, Manuel had by far the most distinguished personality. Beyazid is said to have remarked of him, "If anyone did not know that he was emperor, they would certainly

have deduced it from his appearance," and it may have
been for this very reason that the Sultan took every opportunity to remind Manuel of his subservient status. While a
vassal and virtual hostage at the Turkish court, he was
often poorly lodged and kept short of food, and in 1390 he
had to accompany Beyazid on a campaign against the
beleaguered city of Philadelphia (Turkish Aleşehir), the
last remaining Byzantine possession in western Asia.

For more than half a century, cut off from all outside help
but ably led by the heroic bishops Theoleptos and Makarios
Chryskephalos, the Philadelphians had resisted the Turks.
How they managed this is something of a mystery, but now
Beyazid had decided to pluck this irritating thorn from his
flesh, and Manuel was forced to participate. Historians have
criticized him for his compliance, but in truth Manuel had
no choice, whereas Beyazid could have chosen to spare the
emperor this quite unnecessary humiliation.

When, in the following year, news came that his father,
John V, had died, Manuel was still a hostage in Bursa.
Somehow he managed to evade the sultan's vigilance and
hurried back to Constantinople to be proclaimed Senior
Emperor. The depleted populace welcomed him and
intellectuals hailed the long-awaited arrival of the philosopher king, but the Thunderbolt flew into a rage and very
soon wrote to Manuel saying: "If you do not accept my
orders and do as I command then shut the gates of your
city and govern what lies behind them, for everything
beyond the gates belongs to me." Three months later the
orders came: Manuel was to accompany the sultan on an
extended campaign against Kastamonu in northern
Anatolia. He wrote miserable letters to his friends in the
capital describing the desolation of the land. Ancient and
once famous Greek cities were depopulated and nameless,
and often the emperor could not tell where he was.

Worse was to follow. In the winter of 1394 Beyazid ordered all his Christian vassals, including Manuel and the surviving Serbian princes, to attend him at Serres in Macedonia. As Manuel later wrote:

> The tyrant thought the moment favorable to accomplish the massacre which he had for so long contemplated, so that in his own words, having cleared the ground of thorns (meaning us) his own people would be able to dance on Christian soil without scratching their feet. . . . He therefore ordered his general, a eunuch, to kill us all in the night, threatening him with death if he disobeyed. But God stayed the hand of the assassin, and the sultan, far from punishing his disobedience, thanked his servant for delaying the execution of his command. But this dark soul could not entirely wash away the blackness of his character. He vented his rage on some of our officers, putting out their eyes and cutting off their hands.

On the following day Beyazid was apparently remorseful, showering Manuel with gifts and protestations of affection, but the emperor felt that he had been reduced to the status of a beaten child and concluded that the sultan was now beyond reason. He shut himself within the walls of his city, and refused Beyazid's further summonses. Beyazid promptly blockaded Constantinople. After his victory at Nicopolis the blockade became full-scale siege, and Manuel left to seek aid from the western nations, leaving his nephew John VII in charge of defence. The arrival of a suppliant Roman emperor in England was cause for amazement, and Adam of Usk was moved to exclaim: "My God! What dost thou, ancient glory of Rome? Shorn is the greatness of thine empire this day; and truly may the words of Jeremiah be spoken unto thee:

'Princess among the provinces, how is she become tribu-
tary?' "

Such effusions were all very well, and everyone seems to
have been impressed by Manuel, but meanwhile the citizens of Constantinople were starving and no practical help
was forthcoming. In these circumstances John VII behaved
with dignity and courage. In 1402, when Beyazid demanded
that he surrender the city, John replied: "Tell your master
that we are weak, but that we trust in God, Who can make
us strong and can put down the mightiest from their seats.
Let your master do as he pleases." John surely trusted in
his God but he had also received encouraging news from
the east, where a new Mongol-Turkic power had appeared
in the person of Timur, the Tamburlaine of Christopher
Marlowe's play. He was probably more Turkish than
Beyazid and claimed to be related to Genghis Khan. His
empire now encompassed much of Asia, and he had left
pyramids of skulls outside the cities he had conquered. In
1400 he had entered Anatolia, captured the important city
of Sivas and killed its inhabitants, including one of
Beyazid's sons.

Furious insults were exchanged between the two Lords
of the Universe. Timur even had the temerity to demand
that Beyazid return to the Christian emperor of Constantinople all the lands he had stolen from him, and dismissed
his rival as an "ant" who should not provoke elephants.
Battle was joined on 28 July 1402, near Ankara. Beyazid
had enjoyed an unbroken series of military successes and
had grown overconfident, but Timur was an infinitely
more formidable foe than quarreling crusader princes or
emperors without empires. The Thunderbolt's army was
smashed to pieces, and although he fought with desperate
courage, he ended the day as Timur's captive.

Legend maintains that Timur made Beyazid his slave

and had him carried about in a cage, but this "cage" is now thought more likely to have been a litter; it is easy to see how, in the retelling, an enclosed litter might acquire bars. Beyazid may have been treated with courtesy, but even if this were so the fallen sultan was still forced to watch impotently as Timur methodically sacked and plundered the cities of his empire. Bursa, on which he had lavished so much care, was pillaged and burnt, and the horses of Timur's cavalry were stabled in its mosques. On 8 March 1403, Beyazid could stand it no longer and killed himself. We do not know what method of self-extinction he chose, but if the cage is legendary, we may be fairly sure that he did not beat his brains out against its bars, as Marlowe has him do in *Tamburlaine*. It was surely sufficient that the master of humiliation should, in effect, have died of shame. In Constantinople hymns of thanksgiving were sung and scholars pondered sententiously on the calamitous downfall of this new pharaoh and second Sennacherib. On returning from his long western tour Manuel found rival Ottoman princes vying for his favor, and willing to recognize him as suzerain and "father" in order to win it. The empire could draw breath again.

THE IMITATION OF PARADISE

However he may have been treated while a captive, Beyazid's corpse was accorded every honor, and was returned to Bursa to be interred in the tomb he had built there. The tomb is part of a vast *kulliye* complex that Beyazid was building on the extreme eastern edge of the city at the time of his defeat. In direct line of descent from the great charitable foundations of the Byzantine emperors and the Seljuk sultans, the early Ottoman kulliye invariably included a mosque, a medrese (Koran school) and the tomb of its founder. As one might expect, Beyazid's kulliye was particularly ambitious, and was to have included two medreses, an imaret, a tekke (or dervish monastery), a bathhouse and a palace. Perhaps he intended to retire here after he had conquered the world. Today only a mosque, the tomb and one medrese remain, but that is enough. The tomb is surprisingly modest and the mosque lacks the exquisite Tabriz tiles that make the Green Mosque such a magnet for tourists, but its majestic, five-arched portico is a masterpiece that seems to anticipate the freshest inventions of Moghul India. Strong and graceful, chaste but not severe in its ornamentation, it is built of pale marble and commands a wide prospect that takes in the city, the plain and blue, distant hills. Whatever faults the Thunderbolt may have had, indifference to beauty was not one of them.

Bursa contains three other royal kulliyes built by Beyazid's father (Murad I), his son (Mehmed I) and his grandson (Murad II), and of these the Muradiye kulliye of his grandson is by far the loveliest. It is here that you will find Bursa as it was twenty, fifty or a hundred years ago. To get to Muradiye, which is located at some distance to the west of the city center, you must start from the Great Mosque, climbing the steep steps that lead up the side of the citadel hill to the tombs of Osman and Orhan, where sincere pilgrims still outnumber the tourists. Beyond them the walk takes you through parks and tea gardens perched on the edge of a sheer cliff (to walk from one end of Bursa to the other is to have the sensation of stepping from balcony to balcony) until at the western edge of the hill you see, far below and some way off, a cluster of domes and red-tiled roofs rising out of cypresses and plane trees. This is your first glimpse of Muradiye, where Murad II lies buried, surrounded by murdered princes.

It is unwise to get there too late in the afternoon, although the light is most brilliant at that time. When we arrived at five o'clock we found the gates to the cemetery locked. We could see the roses and the tombs and the inviting shade of the plane trees, but we were shut out. Luckily the custodian had not yet left for the day and our exclamations of dismay and pleading looks softened his heart. We were admitted, and he began to open tomb after tomb, each one seemingly more beautiful than the one before.

A broad cobbled path bordered by neatly trimmed shrubs led up to the sultan's tomb, its doorway canopied by sweeping eaves edged with gold calligraphy. Apart from this solitary touch of extravagance the tomb is severely unadorned, in keeping with Murad's ascetic temperament, but the princes' tombs that lie beyond are another matter altogether. All are domed octagons, constructed in the Byzantine fashion with alternating bands of brick and masonry, and they are lavishly decorated. The tomb of Prince Mustafa, for example, has Iznik tiles of the very best period: there are red carnations and red tulips and wild hyacinths, all woven together by sinuous green stems sprouting small graceful leaves. In the tomb of Prince Cem, the upper walls and the fretted arches are adorned with calligraphy, arabesques and floral fantasies in vivid shades of vermillion, blue, green and gold. It is almost too much for the eye to take in, and has nothing whatsoever to do with western concepts of what is appropriate in sepulchral monuments, yet it seems an eminently suitable last resting place for the gallant Cem, poet and exile, who was murdered in 1495 on the orders of his brother, Sultan Beyazid II.

The Thunderbolt had set the precedent when he disposed of his brother on the field of Kosovo, and the prolonged civil war that broke out among his sons, after his capture and death, confirmed the wisdom of his action. It became customary for a new sultan to slaughter his brothers, and sometimes his male cousins for good measure. Usually they were strangled by mutes. Cem fought hard against his fate. When his brother claimed the throne in 1481 he raised the banner of revolt, captured Bursa, made it his capital and proclaimed himself sultan. He ruled for eighteen days before being forced to flee abroad, finally seeking refuge with the Knights of Saint

John in Rhodes. Embarrassed by the arrival of so distinguished a fugitive, the knights shipped him on to France,
where he spent several miserable years penning bitterly
nostalgic verses before moving to Italy. There, for a handsome price, his erstwhile protector Pope Alexander Borgia
had him poisoned at the behest of the sultan who, having
sought Cem's death for nearly fifteen years, now accorded
him a magnificent burial.

Even fratricide cannot cast a pall over the Muradiye. It
is the least gloomy of cemeteries, and its spirit is best
appreciated by simply sitting for a time on one of the stone
benches by the fountain that stands in front of Murad's
tomb. The fountain consists of a deep octagonal marble
pool, from the center of which rises a simple bowl of the
same marble. Clear water wells up slowly in the bowl and
overflows imperceptibly into the pool, hardly disturbing
its surface. Shadows of plane trees fall across it, and
beyond it there are burgeoning rosebushes (and all their
blooms are either deep pink or white), and beyond the
rosebushes the domes of the sultan's mosque are softly
outlined against a brilliant ceramic sky. The princes' tombs
could be mistaken for pleasure pavilions, and you begin to
feel that you are turning into a figure in a Persian or a
Turkish miniature, yet something of the spirit of medieval
Hellenism still lingers here in the restraint, modesty of
scale and harmonious proportions of the buildings; it is
impossible not to be touched by the obvious care and
devotion that is daily expended on the place.

THE BURNT HOUSES

When we visited the Bursa tourist information office to ask how we might get to the village of Gölyazi, the response was bewilderment and confusion. Evidently no one had asked this question before. There was much earnest peering at maps, and we were solemnly ushered into the office of the smartly suited director. No, he insisted, there was no *dolmuş* service to Gölyazi, and why did we want to go there in any case? "Well," I responded mildly, "I thought it might be interesting." A glance at a map suggests as much: Apollyont-Gölyazi is situated on an island just off the tip of a long promontory that projects into the waters of Lake Ulubat; it is also the site of the Roman and Byzantine city of Apollonias.

As it turned out, the information officers had vastly exaggerated the difficulties of our modest expedition. On the following morning we walked into the bus station, told the first person to approach us where we wanted to go and within minutes were sitting on a bus bound for Bandirma that would drop us off at the turning for

Gölyazi. At the worst we would face a six-kilometer walk, but as kindness to strangers is a matter of honor in rural Turkey, I was confident that someone would come to our aid. And so it turned out. After perhaps thirty uneventful kilometers the pale turquoise waters of the lake came into view to the left of the road, and before very long we were hurtling down the Gölyazi peninsula in the open back of a pickup truck.

Like so many Turkish place-names, Gölyazi has a specific meaning, in this case "summer lake." Filling a shallow bowl in front of a range of mountains, the lake stretched out to east and west, oneirically calm, scattered with wooded islands that had once sheltered communities of monks. As the land narrowed almost to a point I noticed sarcophagi thrown about in the undergrowth to either side of the road—a sure sign anywhere in Anatolia that an ancient city is nearby. Beyond a stretch of marshy land occupied by a closed restaurant and an unoccupied campground (apparently sited with the idea of keeping local mosquitoes well fed) stood the scant remains of a city gate. It was clear that the marshy isthmus we had just crossed had once been a part of the lake, that Apollonias had been linked to the mainland and its necropolis by a short causeway, and that the high, conical hill ahead of us had been the first of two islands on which the city stood.

Parting company with the kindly farmworkers and fishermen who had picked us up on the road, we began to walk along the straggling street that rounded the western side of the hill. A small boy politely approached us and insisted that we pause to admire his dog. More children gathered when we turned aside to examine a ruined nineteenth-century church. It was surprisingly large, with a triple-arched, rudimentarily baroque façade showing no trace of Byzantine influence. Until their expulsion in 1922–23, in the course of the so-called exchange of populations, the church must have been the focal point of a prosperous community of Greeks.

The Treaty of Lausanne, which was supposed to regularize the exchange of Greeks for Turks and Christians for Muslims, in fact did little more than acknowledge a fait accompli. In many regions of Anatolia the flight of the Christian population had begun at least a year before the treaty was signed in 1923. Immediately after the defeat at Dumlupinar, for example, the Third Corps of the Greek army had retreated north through Bithynia to Mundanya on the southern shore of the Sea of Marmara, very close to Apollonias. It seems likely that many, if not all, the Greeks of Apollonias, fearing Turkish reprisals, followed in the wake of the army. Their numbers were swelled by refugees from the large Greek community in Bursa. We can gain some idea of the situation in Bithynia from firsthand accounts of events in nearby Thrace, written for the *Toronto Star* by a young reporter named Ernest Hemingway. In a dispatch dated 20 October 1922 Hemingway wrote:

> In a never-ending, staggering march the Christian population of Eastern Thrace is jamming the roads to Macedonia. The main column crossing the Maritza river at Adrianople is twenty miles long. Twenty miles of carts drawn by cows, bullocks and muddy-flanked water buffalo, with exhausted, staggering men, women and children, blankets over their heads, walking blindly along in the rain beside their worldly goods. . . . A husband spreads a blanket over a woman in labor in one of the carts to keep off the driving rain. She is the only person making a sound. Her little daughter looks at her in horror and begins to cry. And the procession keeps moving . . .

In all, the enforced migrations of 1922–23 involved nearly two million people, including 390,000 Muslims expelled from Greece and 1,250,000 Greeks and 100,000 Armenians expelled from Anatolia and Thrace. Within the course of a year the population of Greece was increased by one third. It is not known how many died along the way or succumbed to malnourishment and disease after they had reached "safe" territory. The Anatolian Greeks had never regarded Greece as their homeland: they had lived among Turks for so long that many of them did not even speak Greek; their ancestors had been in Anatolia for two thousand years and more; they had built cities and temples, churches and monasteries beyond number; even after conquest, under the generally tolerant rule of the Seljuk and Ottoman sultans, many of them had continued to prosper, but now all of that was ending amid scenes that seem horribly familiar seventy years later, when newspapers and TV channels are loud with stories of "ethnic cleansing."

The doorway of the church at Apollonias was blocked with piles of stones and brushwood, and it was home to a flock of newly shorn sheep. It resembled a gutted barn, the little that remained of its roof being supported on crude wooden posts. It was a ruin without beauty or dignity, imbued with all the bitterness of places where an ancient way of life has been abruptly terminated in living memory. As we were about to leave, a stork swept over our heads, alighted on the point of the church's pediment and folded its great wings, becoming motionless like a finial.

Beyond the church, the street turned a corner and for the first time I was able to appreciate the full beauty of Apollonias. Across a placid expanse of water scattered with blue and red fishing boats lay an island crowded with red-roofed houses, spiked by cypresses and encircled by ruined towers.

We hear little of Apollonias until the late eleventh century, when it fell victim to the disasters that followed in the wake of the Byzantine defeat at Manzikert. It must

have been captured by the Turks at about the same time as
Nicaea (circa 1080), and fell under the jurisdiction of a
vigorous emir who was known to the Byzantines as
Elchanes. For a time Elchanes seems to have operated free
of the control of either the Seljuk sultan or the Byzantine
emperor, however he was very soon confronted by a determined adversary in the person of Alexius Comnenus.
Since we are dependent on Anna Comnena for our dates
(and Anna is notoriously vague in this respect) it is hard to
say exactly when Alexius turned against Elchanes, but
1092 or 1093 seems plausible. At first Elchanes succeeded
in outwitting his Byzantine opponents, but when Alexius
advanced on Apollonias with his main army, the emir
apparently lost heart, and since Alexius offered generous
terms (as was his civilized custom) he surrendered. Anna
tells us: "Together with his closest relatives he deserted to
the emperor and was rewarded with countless gifts,
including the greatest of all—the holy rite of baptism."
When they heard the news of Alexius' generosity, other
local Turkish chiefs followed Elchanes' example and
returned with the emperor to Constantinople, where they
became Christians. Some of them were also rewarded
with the impressive, but perhaps rather meaningless title
of *hyperperilampros*. Anna follows this information with a
daughterly encomium on the theme of her father's saintli-
ness, but Alexius, as we know, was a practical politician
and statesman: his aim was the reconquest of Anatolia, not
sainthood. At Apollonias he initiated his enlightened
policy of co-option and assimilation of the Turkish leadership.

The fate of Apollonias thereafter is typical of all the
Bithynian cities. In the early twelfth century Turkmen
nomads raided as far as the Marmaran shore and the walls
of Apollonias were massively strengthened as a consequence. During the reign of John II Comnenus and his son

Manuel it was spared any serious alarms, and prosperity returned, but from the death of Manuel in 1180 until 1205 the city suffered miserably from the combined effects of continual revolts and raids. The Lascarids of Nicaea restored good government but the reprieve was short-lived, and by the early fourteenth century Apollonias was in Turkish hands. From this point on it ceases to be a place of any consequence. It is a cheerless tale, but it should be remembered that for much of this period the citizens of Apollonias must have contrived to go quietly about their usual business, drawing rich catches of perch and pike, sturgeon and crayfish from their beautiful lake.

In recent years pesticides and fertilizers have greatly reduced the catch, and from what I could observe the fishermen seem to be able to find nothing but large and ferocious-looking pike that were slopped, still twitching, into baskets in the main square. Shaded by planes and willows, the square is the main focus for the essential masculine activities of tea drinking, cigarette smoking and conversation. At the western end of the square we came upon the massive remains of a Byzantine gate—one of its towers still standing to a height of perhaps forty feet. The arch of the gate had fallen, but it was possible to make out that it had once been surmounted by a high, vaulted chamber. Not far from the gate, up a rutted, gently winding street, was the solid stump of a great tower that had perhaps formed part of the acropolis or citadel mentioned by Anna Comnena. Beyond the tower I was startled to come upon an entire block of timber-framed houses that had burned to the ground very recently. Amidst a chaos of charred beams and collapsed walls the former occupants rummaged about despondently. In general the people of Gölyazi seemed cheerful enough, yet there was a pervading sadness about the place: clearly poverty was a constant threat, and the squalid, unkempt appearance of some houses and streets suggested that there were families that had come close to giving up. It was as if a bright, painted scene of village life had been left out in the rain.

Soon the street began to descend toward the southern shore of the island, and I started to notice a surprising regularity to the plan of the town. Streets were roughly straight and met at right angles, which would be very unusual in a modern village that had developed on the basis of a haphazard, medieval street plan. Late Byzantine and early Turkish towns were entirely unplanned, so it seemed possible that Gölyazi had retained something of the original, Hellenistic grid-plan of ancient Apollonias. The remarkable thing about Byzantine cities in Anatolia is not their near collapse in the seventh century so much as the tenacity with which they clung to existence, even when much reduced in circumstances and surrounded by the ruins of their lost grandeur.

The towers of the southern shore were built of handsome ashlar masonry; trees and a profusion of white and yellow flowers grew from them. Flocks of jackdaws flew up from the ancient stones or peered down quizzically from rooftops; a stepped street led off to the left, shaded by vines, the walls of its houses painted white but for a band of deep oxblood red at the base; to our right, boats lay motionless on waters that had risen so high during the rains of May that tree roots were flooded, and trees appeared to spring straight from the lake surface. On our way back to the Bursa road we followed a winding path that led up the hill. On its summit we found ridges and depressions suggestive of many buried structures and detected a large concavity scattered with pieces of white Proconesian marble that must once have been a theater. To the west, islands and headlands stretched to the horizon, and beyond a dark stand of cypresses the island of Apollonias appeared like a brooch pinned to a silk robe.

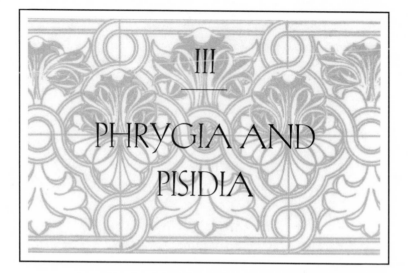

III

PHRYGIA AND PISIDIA

THE IMPERIAL ROAD

In Anatolia, during the course of a journey of only three or four hours, it often seems that one passes through half a dozen different climates and landscapes, each of which appears capable of supporting its own distinct people and culture. Between Bursa and Afyon we first traveled east across a broad plain, then turned south and began to climb a pass; as we did so the snow-capped peaks of Mount Olympus came into view across fields of red earth bordered with poplars. Next came the fertile valley of Inegöl, after which the mountains closed in again and the road began to wind its way through alpine ravines cloaked with dense pine forests; we might have been in Bavaria or Austria. But beyond the little town of Bozüyük, the landscape opened out and the trees and villages grew more isolated. By imperceptible degrees we had climbed to the Anatolian plateau. Covered with grass and flowers, the land rolled on with magnificent simplicity to a remote horizon, and the long, straight road we were traveling toward the city of Eskişehir was the old Byzantine military road, along which numberless armies had marched back and forth from Constantinople to the eastern borders, carrying the imperial standards aloft and invoking the names of Christ and the Virgin Mary.

The first sight of Central Anatolia often seems to inspire western writers to an ecstacy of generalization. The great English traveler Gertrude Bell says of it: "It is Asia with all its vastness, with all its brutal disregard for life and comfort and the amenities of existence; it is the ancient East, after so many millenniums of human endeavor, returning to its natural desolation." At first glance this might appear an unexceptional piece of rhetoric, but was it not precisely in the East that many civilized amenities were invented? We now know—as Bell did not—that some of the world's first recognizably urban communities grew up in the plain of Konya, along the southern rim of the Anatolian plateau. And how "natural" is the desolation she observes? It seems certain that many areas of the plateau that are now close to being steppe or semidesert were once forested: desolation may be the result of human endeavor, not a sign of its failure in the declining years of the Ottoman Empire (when Bell was writing).

Cement factories heralded the approach to Eskişehir, their dust bleaching the surrounding hills and fields. Eskişehir stands on the site of the Byzantine city of Dorylaion, and it was somewhere near here on 1 July 1097 that the First Crusade inflicted its second great defeat on the Turks. In her brief description of the battle, Anna Comnena makes no mention of a city of Dorylaion, only of a plain, for by 1097 the city had lain ruined and deserted for nearly twenty years. For more than three centuries prior to that, however, it had been one of the most important cities in Anatolia. It guarded the gateway to the central plateau, and it was here that the troops of the Opsikion and Thrakesion *themes* would muster when the emperor went on campaign in the east. It was for the benefit of these troops that the city contained seven bathing arcades, each of which could accommodate one thousand men.

By the time Manuel I Comnenus decided to refortify Dorylaion in 1175, in preparation for his ill-fated campaign against the Seljuks of Konya, it had all but disappeared, and the once fertile and populous valley of the River Tembris, in which it lay, was inhabited by only a few thousand Turkmen nomads who fled before the emperor, burning their tents as they did so. John Cinnamus, historian and secretary to Manuel, gives this melancholy account of Dorylaion's dereliction and former glory:

> There was a time when this Dorylaion was one of the great cities of Asia and very noteworthy. A gentle breeze blows upon the land, and it has about it very extensive level plains of extraordinary beauty which are so rich and fertile that they give forth rich grass and supply ripe ears of grain. A river sends its streams through it and it is beautiful to see and sweet to taste. There is such a quantity of fish swimming in this river that no matter how much those fishing take, fish are never lacking. Here, formerly, splendid mansions were built by the Caesar Melissenos, the villages were populous and there were natural hot springs, stoas and baths, and all such things as bring pleasure to men. These things did the land provide in abundance. But the Turks, when the invasion of the Roman lands was at its height, had razed the city to the ground and made it completely destitute of people, and they obliterated everything in it, even the thin trace of its former dignity. It was such a city.

Revisionist historians have sometimes attempted to play down the destructiveness of the initial Turkish invasions of the eleventh century and the Turkmen raids that plagued the Anatolian Christian communities from that time until the conquest, but in order to do so they have to ignore the ample and unambiguous testimony of Byzantine writers: cities were destroyed, agriculture was disrupted, famine was a constant threat, and even though certain Turkish leaders tried to protect them, entire populations were forced to flee from their ancestral homes to escape massacre or enslavement. To admit as much does not imply any denigration of the remarkable cultural attainments of Seljuks or Ottomans. The fate of the people of Phrygia was particularly miserable. Despite the best efforts of the Comneni and the Lascarids, the empire was never able to reestablish effective control over Dorylaion and its surrounding districts for very long. Like the rest of Phrygia, it became a no-man's-land in which both emperors and sultans pursued a scorched-earth policy. Repeated attempts were made to drive the nomads back beyond the bend of the Sangarius River, but the border was highly permeable and the Tembris valley provided excellent pasturage for their flocks. It was also a strategic base for profitable raiding into Bithynia, and it was here, in about 1288, that Osman began to transform these raids into a campaign of conquest. By this time even the name of Dorylaion had been forgotten, but the name of the Turkish town that began to grow up in its place preserves at least a dim memory of the vanished city: Eskişehir means "old town."

Modern Eskişehir is not a worthy successor to the charmingly pastoral, late-antique city described by Cinnamus. The gentle slopes of the Tembris valley are now bare of trees, and although it may have its secrets, the town presents a very grim aspect to the passing traveler. It has expanded very rapidly in recent years and the new construction is uniformly shoddy: apartment buildings appear half-finished or already half-ruined; streets and sidewalks are potholed or still under construction; dust and dirt are all-pervasive; the Tembris (now known as the

Porsuk) is reduced to a muddy trickle more like an open sewer than a river, and the mansions, baths and stoas of Dorylaion are buried very deep indeed.

As the bus left Eskişehir I was delighted to discover that we were taking a minor road that led directly south over the Phrygian uplands. In high summer or early autumn these uplands would have resembled a gigantic piece of scorched canvas, but now, at the end of a sodden spring, this canvas had been attacked by a delirious fauvist who had smeared and spattered it with eye-popping colors. The brilliant land rose and fell in great waves that broke against heaps of reddish rock formations. There was so much to see and the distances were so great that I began to worry about eyestrain, so when I first glimpsed a cluster of domes, turrets and minarets floating on the horizon, looking exactly like an Edmund Dulac illustration for *The Arabian Nights*, I did not quite believe what I saw. I closed my eyes, opened them and consulted my map, which told me that I was not hallucinating: I was looking at Seyitgazi, the former Byzantine city of Nakoleia.

Emperor Valens (364?–378) defeated the usurper Procopius at Nakoleia in 366 and forced him to hide in the forests that then surrounded the place. The forests have vanished and in later years Nakoleia does not seem to have been a city of much significance, but to the Turks it became a holy place: here, on a high hill above the town, it was believed that the semilegendary warrior of the faith Seyit Battal Ghazi was buried. His career gave rise to many legends, among which was the tale of a Byzantine princess who so loved Seyit that she joined him in death. The Byzantine sources make no mention of this improbable romance, but it so moved the mother of the great Seljuk Sultan Alaeddin Kaykobad I (1219–36) that she erected a splendid mausoleum on the reputed site of his grave. A little later the dervish leader Haci Bektaş established a monastery on the same site, and it became a center for Muslim proselytization of the Christian communities to the north and west. The process of conversion was greatly assisted by the extremely liberal (and indeed protofeminist) views of the Bektaşi, who, like the Mevlevi dervishes, did all they could to minimize the differences between Muslim, Christian and Jewish beliefs. It is strange and touching that the border ballads, epics and romances of Arabs, Turks and Byzantines should so frequently involve tales of love that transcend the barriers of race and religion. To fight against the infidel was the apogee of heroism, yet at the same time the ordinary people of Anatolia seem to have dreamt of an age when they could live in peace, love one another and marry. It is therefore appropriate that the highest cluster of domes at Seyitgazi should be the domes of a Byzantine church—perhaps the cathedral of Nakoleia—and that the architecture of Byzantines, Seljuks and Ottomans should combine here so harmoniously.

The little river Parthenios flows through Seyitgazi, and we now began to follow its narrow valley to the southwest. The floor of the valley was intensely cultivated but the steep hills on either side were devoid of trees. This changed as we climbed out of the valley into the highlands of Phrygia. We entered a region of mesas and outlandish tufa formations, cloaked with magnificent forests of umbrella pines—trees so widely spaced over a cloth of bright green grass that the whole landscape resembled a very peculiar park, designed according to the preferences of some eccentric English or Italian nobleman. Having crossed the pass, we descended very gradually toward Afyon, and I looked for the opium poppies after which the town is named (Afyon means opium in Turkish) but, being ignorant, I did not see them. I was expecting a blaze of red, but opium poppies are either ivory white or dark purple. The plain before Afyon—the Byzantine Akroinon— is desiccated and salt-sewn. It was here, in 740, that Emperor Leo III inflicted a decisive defeat on the Arabs after a long, bitter and bloodily fought battle, and it was here that Seyit Battal Ghazi was killed. Beyond this scrubbed and desolate plain I saw the enormous black volcanic cone that rises out of the center of Afyon. Turkish friends in Istanbul had asked me why I was going to Afyon, since there was nothing to see there, but now I knew how wrong they had been: Afyon looked as if it might be almost as splendid and mysterious as its full name, Afyon Kara Hisar—Opium Black Citadel.

A SHORT HISTORY OF SUNROOMS

Although most guidebooks pay it only cursory attention, Afyon is one of the pleasantest towns on the Anatolian plateau. The architecture of the modern town is predictably undistinguished, but compared to Eskişehir (which I had feared it might resemble) Afyon positively glows with civic pride. The streets are clean and well cared for; there is a park with fountains and outdoor cafés; there are hotels with terraces and roof gardens from which one can watch the sun sink behind the "black citadel"; there are excellent restaurants, one of which has florid baroque mirrors and uniformed waiters. But Afyon's principle charm (apart from the friendliness of its people) lies in its unusually well-preserved old quarter, which a traveler in a hurry might miss altogether, since most of it is hidden in a long narrow valley to the south of the citadel rock, and the streets that link it to the modern town are inconspicuous. These streets begin by twisting through a lively bazaar district where virtually anything can be purchased, including fine carpets, but definitely not the opium for which the town is famous. In the butchers' quarter there were impressive piles of bloody bones haunted by gaunt dogs, and just beyond the bazaar was a remarkably stylish new civic building with an elegant four-story atrium centered on a broad sweeping staircase. This suggested that Turkish architectural genius may not be completely dead, and the dull pink and blue of its external walls, which would have been a postmodernist affectation in New York, seemed extremely appropriate in Afyon's old quarter, where most of the houses are painted in more vivid shades of the same colors. We pressed on, but began to worry that we had somehow missed the Great Mosque, which was our immediate goal. We seemed to be getting very close to the edge of town.

We had not missed the Great Mosque, but we might have done so, since from the outside it is an inconspicuous, virtually undecorated rectangular structure surmounted by a low pitched roof. It is not small, but "great" seemed an exaggeration. The mosque's interior is quite another matter, giving a sense of space out of all proportion to its actual size. Completed in 1272, the structure is a rare example of a wooden Seljuk "hall mosque." The carved beams of its flat ceiling rest on a formal grove of reddish wooden columns topped by exquisitely fanciful stalactite capitals. The plan is of the utmost simplicity and must be very ancient—predating the birth of Islam itself. I was reminded of the columned halls or *apadanas* of the Achaemenid Persian kings at Persepolis. Being happily engaged in examining the details of the roofbeams and the capitals, I did not at first notice the floor. Photographs had shown it scattered with richly colored carpets and kilims; now there was only a level desert of the dreariest industrial-gray carpeting. I asked the obliging gentleman who had opened the mosque for us what had happened to the kilims. He replied without a moment's hesitation and with unconcealed bitterness that they had all been "stolen by Germans." When I expressed horror, and asked how such a thing could have happened, he simply shrugged and turned his palms toward the heavens. Subsequent enquiries revealed that the kilims had all vanished overnight, presumably at the behest of western European or American carpet dealers, but no one knew their nationality, let alone their identity, and there was little chance that the kilims would ever be recovered. This news was imparted with unanswerable fatalism. What could one do? The West was rich, Turkey was poor. It was easy to bribe people.

The path to the citadel starts just across the street from the Great Mosque. At first it loops back and forth across grassy slopes, but as the rock becomes sheer you must embark on a punishing ascent of some seven hundred steps. The rock is certainly dark, if not exactly black, but it is splashed with bright orange lichen and misted with delicate mauve and yellow flowers that grow wherever a crevice will give them footing. History is inscribed in the rock of Afyon. Its crenellated Seljuk and Ottoman battlements rest on Byzantine foundations. The view from the summit also provides a vivid glimpse into geological time. To the west the citadel is embraced by a broad semicircle of hills like an immense grass-grown theater, while the eastern limits of the town are marked by jagged black rock outcrops: it becomes clear that you are standing at the center of an eroded volcanic cone. All around you a mountain has vanished, carried away by wind and water.

We were not alone on the citadel of Afyon. A family was picnicking by the gate, and as we scrambled about the rocks, two young men seemed to be always a few steps ahead of us or behind us. It was clear they wanted to talk, but were restrained by politeness or shyness. After a while we struck up a conversation, though how we did so is something of a puzzle, since we spoke little Turkish and they less English. Although they looked hardly more than eighteen it turned out that they were traveling salesmen from Uşak, whose bizarre and, I thought, rather hopeless mission was to sell Crock-Pots to the housewives of Afyon. They proudly showed us their brochures, and then, as we were about to leave, they stood together on the highest rock and began to sing. Their harmonies were nicely practiced and the melody they were singing was long and sweet and infinitely wistful. In Turkey, men like to sing, and they often have fine voices. Drinking sessions, which usually involve staggering amounts of potent raki, are more likely to end in tearful song than fistfight. This fatalistic melancholy and love of long, melismatic melodies is surely drawn from the land of Anatolia, from its vast distances littered with ruins, its vague and shimmering horizon stabbed by inhospitable peaks.

The view from the citadel revealed the full extent of the old town, and we decided to explore its blue and rose-colored streets further. No two houses were precisely the same, but many, perhaps a majority, had projecting upper stories. This is a feature that we tend to think of as typically Ottoman, but it was also a common feature of Byzantine houses, and, since the Turks had no tradition of domestic architecture when they first entered Anatolia, must represent the continuation of this Byzantine tradition. Although no examples have survived from the Byzantine period, the written evidence is conclusive. A projecting upper story was known as a solarium or a *heliakon*, and the emperors issued voluminous legislation in an attempt to control this and other aspects of urban construction. They seem to have been particularly concerned that the mansions of the wealthy should not overshadow the houses of their humbler neighbors. When, for example, an old woman complained to the Emperor Theophilus that a new palace built by his brother-in-law Petronas had completely deprived her of sunlight, Theophilus investigated the affair and finding the old woman's complaint to be justified ordered that Petronas' palace be torn down. In these circumstances *heliaka* became prestige items: by claiming more sunlight than your neighbor you demonstrated, in the most graphic fashion, your superior wealth and influence. The *heliaka* were also much appreciated by the highborn ladies of Byzantium who until the eleventh century were generally expected to lead very secluded existences: from the latticed windows of their sunrooms they could observe the activities of the street without themselves being observed. By the early tenth century, *heliaka* had become so numerous and so large that some streets in Constantinople received no sunlight at all and the Emperor Leo VI decided something had to be done. He therefore issued an edict whose text has come down to us. The emperor praises the building regulations of "the ancients," but goes on to observe that "the constructions that are called balcony-belvederes (which take their name from the sun, being called *solaria*)" had "received at law neither mention nor regulation. This is now in need of decision, that is, we need to define and resolve the difficulties that, as might be expected, can arise." Leo's attempts at definition are frustrated (at least for the modern reader) by the labyrinthine syntax of Byzantine legalese, but the resolution of the problem is clear enough: ". . . we have decreed that no one can construct a building of this kind unless at least ten feet separate him from his neighbor."

How effectively this measure was enforced is impossible to say, but the structures that rise on either side of Afyon's cobbled streets must closely resemble the solaria of Leo's edict. The women of Afyon, however, show no inclination to stay hidden away in their upper stories. On the evening of 4 June 1991 the streets were lively with women and children. Entire families had come out to take the air and enjoy the glamour of the declining light; they sat on doorsteps, talked animatedly and served each other glasses of strong tea. In one street two women were busily applying a coat of brilliant aquamarine paint to the front of their house; in another, a plump but graceful woman of mature years insisted that we photograph her while she posed coquettishly in front of a turquoise doorway. We also photographed her sitting on a step surrounded by a group of her relations and friends; behind this group a young woman of exceptional beauty peered out shyly from an upper window that was framed in peacock blue and set in a wall washed with deep rust-red. Children followed us everywhere, but were so good-natured they never became a nuisance. The streets led directly out onto green hillsides to the south of the town and here people were strolling arm in arm and boys were flying kites.

BEFORE EXILE

There were no cars for hire in Afyon, but luckily the town possessed one of Turkey's very few useful tourist information offices, where we were advised to hire the services of a taxi driver named Vedat. Vedat was short and wiry and had bright, intelligent eyes. I liked him at once and within minutes we had arranged an expedition to the rock-cut church of Ayazin and the nearby Phrygian site of Aslantaş. Vedat also urged on us the attractions of the Phrygian royal city of Midas Şehri, but since this was some fifty to sixty kilometers away in the heart of the uplands, and had no Byzantine remains that I knew of, it seemed an extravagance and I declined the offer. Vedat accepted the decision gracefully but with some evident disappointment.

We began by traveling north, back along the Seyitgazi road, but before long Vedat turned off to the east along an unsurfaced track that wound dustily across a plain patched with fields of opium poppies. Purple and white; white, purple and green—the landscape grew increasingly dream-like, and we passed parties of women riding their donkeys out to work in the fields. Although they carried primitive hoes, and in all likelihood faced a day of backbreaking labor, they were as brilliantly dressed as if setting out for a wedding, and sat proudly in their saddles. They did not resemble in any way the submissive black-clad Muslim peasant woman of western legend. To our left rose a fantastically eroded escarpment out of which suddenly emerged the dome and central apse of a church in the classic Byzantine style. I wanted to stop and get out immediately, but Vedat gestured that I should calm myself ("all in good time" might have been the best translation) and drove on confidently to the outskirts of the village. Here he consented to stop, smiled and pointed to the cliff face above us. It was completely inscribed with the architectural record of nearly two thousand years of human endeavor: there were pediments and pilasters, architraves and arched porticoes with primitive Ionic capitals. These, I assumed, were the façades of Phrygian and Roman tombs, but interpretation was impeded by the fact that the Byzantines had reused and extended these tomb spaces when they came to hollow out their dwellings and churches. Unmistakably of the Byzantine period were barrel-vaulted churches with carefully sculpted blind arcading and small chapels with apses that were hardly more than niches, and from all of these one looked out onto swaying fields of purple poppies. In one chapel was a reminder that Greek Christians had still lived here in the early years of our century. Someone had carved a message in the wall and, not for the last time, I cursed my lack of Greek: all I could make out was the Roman numeral XIII, the name KONSTANTINOS, and the date 1914.

But it is the large church that we had passed earlier which constitutes the main reason for visiting Ayazin. The church seems to be in the process of forcing its way out of the rock. The central apse with its three small windows has emerged fully, but the dome remains half-encased in the escarpment. It is as if one were privileged to watch a moment of an infinitely slow process, to be measured in thousands of years, by which architectural form grows out of natural form. The lofty interior has been blackened by the smoke of campfires and the four square piers that once supported the central dome have disappeared, but since the whole structure is carved out of the rock (it is, in effect, a manmade cave) such support was always unnecessary, and the dome still floats serenely above its pendentives.

The plan of the church is of the classic, cross-in-square type that dominated the Byzantine middle period and remained popular until the fall of the empire. The cross-in-square has a nave and transepts of equal length, a crossing covered by a dome carried on four columns or piers, and in the more ambitious examples four subsidiary domes that cover the corner compartments which fill out the square. It is a design that stresses unity, symmetry and harmony, and at Ayazin it is executed with a care and precision that is surprising in so remotely located an example: there are no irregularities, everything is perfectly aligned.

While we were at Ayazin an emerald green lizard skittered about in the dimness of the apse, looking more like an animated piece of costume jewelry than any reptile, and outside women still passed in the dust of the road, dressed in purple and turquoise like figures from miniatures. Then, in the arcaded chamber to the south of the church, I discovered a second graffiti, and this one I was able to translate.

Someone had scratched the crude outline of a Greek cross into the rock wall and beside the cross they had carved three times the date 1922, the year of Dumlupinar.

The site of the battle was hardly more than thirty miles from Ayazin. The cross and the reiterated date took on the properties of a wordless protest and prayer for deliverance. Shortly after this graffiti was carved, all the Christians of the Afyon district followed the defeated Greek army in headlong flight, west toward Smyrna. There, on the waterfront, they were soon joined by the Greek and Armenian inhabitants of the city, all of them desperate to escape the advancing Turks. Thus perhaps as many as half a million people were gathered on a narrow quay only half a mile long when the city was set alight behind them. They were trapped between a wall of flame and the sea. It would have been an easy matter to rescue them: out in the bay the ships of the British, American, Italian and French navies floated at anchor, but they made no move to help the tormented people on the quays. Instead the Western Allies, who had done so much to bring this nightmare into being by encouraging the Greek government to embark on a course of action that was sure to enflame Turkish nationalist passions beyond reason, now assured the Turkish authorities of their neutrality, and in strict accordance with this policy any refugees who managed to swim out to the ships were turned back: many drowned as a consequence.

As the fires died down, the Turkish soldiery moved in, with results that could have been foreseen. Women were raped and unknown numbers of men were rounded up and marched forcibly back toward the Anatolian interior. In effect, a modern city was being subjected to the horrors of a medieval sack. Out on the waters of the harbor, meanwhile, the civilization of the West maintained its rituals. Naval officers invited each other to dinner parties. It was unfortunate that guests were sometimes delayed by corpses caught in the propellers of their boats. The sounds coming from the quays were distressing to be sure, so the officers turned up their phonographs and the strains of Dvořák's *Humoresque* and Gigli singing selections from *I Pagliacci* floated out over the harbor and the smoking ruins of what had been the most beautiful city of the Eastern Mediterranean. Concerning the fate of the Greek who carved that date in the church of Ayazin it is perhaps better not to speculate.

THE DOMAIN OF THE MOTHER

As we were about to leave Ayazin, Vedat once again brought up the subject of Midas Şehri. Money was not the issue. He was so determined that we should see the place that he lowered his price. Clearly, in Vedat's eyes, Midas Şehri was something we must not miss: it had become a matter of honor, which made further refusal impossible. We accepted the offer and set out with Vedat now in good humor.

Returning to the Seyitgazi road, we traveled north for a few miles, then turned off onto a deeply rutted path we would undoubtedly have missed if we had tried to find it on our own. The path led across marshy fields and along the side of a low but steep-sided plateau, which I learned later was known as Kohnus Kale (*kale* meaning "castle"). Vedat stopped abruptly in a field of flowers and announced "Aslantaş," but there did not appear to be anything much to see, apart from a few small openings in the sheer side of the plateau. Dutifully, we got out of the car and followed Vedat across the field to the rock face, where he stopped beneath a square, carefully carved opening that I took to be the entrance to a tomb. But still I could see nothing remarkable. Then my eyes adjusted to the light and the shadow and the patterns of lichen on the rock, and I saw the lions—two of them on either side of the tomb entrance, powerfully muscled and much larger than life-size, caught in midleap with fangs bared. I was reminded of the lions on the gate of Mycenae, but these were much finer. Now that I saw them, it was difficult to imagine how I could have not seen them. Moving farther around the edge of the plateau, we came upon the shattered remains of a sanctuary that had fallen from the cliff. The massive, snarling head of a lion lay upended on the grass, and beyond that was a half-buried pedimented façade covered with elaborate geometric designs: in the buried half of the façade there would have been a niche containing a statue of the goddess Kubile, for it was in such wild and lonely places, the Phrygians believed, that the Great Mother preferred to dwell.

Considering the significance of their contribution to the early development of the civilization we like to think of as "western" and "European," we know astonishingly little about the Phrygians. They came from the Danube and Thrace, and invaded Anatolia at the end of the Bronze Age. They spoke an Indo-European language, and by the middle of the eighth century B.C. had developed a rich and original civilization. For a time their kings held sway over the whole of central Anatolia. Their wealth is remembered in the legend of King Midas. They were skilled metal workers, mosaicists, architects, sculptors, carpet-weavers and musicians. Their magnificent bronze vessels have been found at many sites on the Greek mainland, where Phrygian luxury goods were highly prized. The so-called kilim designs of the Phrygian shrine-façades appear on Greek pottery, and on Turkish kilims still being produced today. The Phrygians built mostly in wood, but when the façades of their great megaron halls are translated into stone in the rock faces of the highlands, the resemblance to the typical Greek temple façade is striking, yet in the eighth century B.C. Greek architecture was still in its archaic phase.

Phrygian greatness was short-lived. In or around 676 B.C. they were overwhelmed by a new wave of barbarian peoples, known to the Greeks as Cimmerians. Their cities were burned, yet their influence persisted and their religion spread throughout Anatolia and into the Greek lands: Kubile-Kybile-Cybele is close cousin to Artemis, "Lady of the wilds and Mistress of beasts," and it may be no coincidence that the Virgin Mary is said to have died at Ephesus, where Artemis had her principal shrine. Perhaps the early-Christian propagandists realized that the people of Anatolia would not have been much impressed by a religion that deprived them entirely of their Divine Mother.

The road to the great city of Midas Şehri passes through wild forested country that contains only a few isolated villages. The design of the houses in these villages does not seem to have changed much since the beginning of the Iron Age. They have flat, densely thatched roofs and simple porches supported by wooden posts, flanked at the top by small brackets with rounded ends, suggesting a primitive prototype of the Ionic order. In most of these villages you will find fragments of ancient masonry built into the walls, and some of the finest of these fragments were obviously taken from Byzantine churches. Over the years the villagers have quarried them so thoroughly that no freestanding masonry structures of the Byzantine period or earlier have survived. It is lucky for us that the Phrygians and the Byzantines took to carving directly into the rock.

We came down at last into a green valley, flanked to the south by a long mesa, the land at its foot scattered with gigantic, detached boulders. It was very easy to understand why the Turks called such formations "castles": the steep sides of this mesa so closely resembled shattered ramparts that we could not at first distinguish nature's imitation of architecture from the genuine article. It was only when we passed through the village at the foot of the rock that we realized we had arrived at the City of Midas. Rising above the village was one of the most extraordinary monuments in all of Anatolia—the great shrine of Kubile that is known erroneously as the Midas Tomb. The shrine (it was never a tomb) consists of a façade, fifty-six feet high, completely covered with geometric designs and surmounted by a massive pediment, which is, in turn, crowned by a form like a broken clasp. Patterns of diamonds adorn pediment and frame, while the design that fills the central panel of the façade resembles the plan for a labyrinth, made up of interlocking squares and Greek crosses. At the foot of the façade is a large square niche which once held a statue of the goddess.

A few yards to the right of the shrine was something that, in its way, was almost as remarkable—a rock outcrop so hollowed out with Byzantine tombs that it resembled an enormous petrified sponge. The number of the tombs and their size suggested that a substantial Byzantine population had dwelt nearby. In the village of Kümbet, less than five miles to the west, the dedicatory inscription of a certain Epinikos has been found. He has been identified with a man who rose to high office in Constantinople in 475, only to be disgraced and executed three years later, having fallen foul of the Emperor Zeno. It is from such scraps and thin whispers of ancient voices that we have to piece together the life of the people of Byzantine Anatolia.

The sky to the north had darkened and there were rumbles of thunder, but the storm was still some way off and did not appear to be heading in our direction. Nevertheless we thought it best to waste no time, and, accompanied by Vedat and the custodian, set out along the northern slopes of the acropolis rock. Here there is a broad natural terrace that must have been the site of the lower city, and before we had gone very far we came upon something that made me wonder again at the skills of the Phrygians. A long staircase emerged from a steeply angled tunnel in the rock face and curved gracefully across the slope of the hill before plunging back into the rock. Since the tunnel was blocked, we climbed down the steps and found ourselves in a large artificial cavern that must have served as a cistern. At this point there was a deafening clap of thunder and the rain began. It was rain such as I have rarely seen, and within half a minute the steps we had just descended had turned into a torrential cascade. The cistern seemed about to revert to its original function. It was obviously not a place where we could shelter for long, but the steps were now impassable. Luckily a section of the cavern's ceiling had fallen in, and we were able to scramble up a mound of loose earth and climb through the gap. This achieved, there was nothing to do but run as fast as possible for the shelter of the Byzantine necropolis, where we found a tomb comfortably equipped with stone benches and prepared to wait out the storm.

Lightning danced between the summits of the hills, which periodically vanished entirely behind thick curtains of rain, while hammer blows of thunder fell on the rock above our heads. Such a storm would have been impressive in any location, but a few yards from a shrine to the Great Mother it was doubly so. Since the Phrygians believed she had fallen from the sky in the form of a black meteorite, they would surely have regarded storms as manifestations of Kubile, and Kubile was not always benevolent. Her attitude toward males seems to have been particularly severe: she could only be served by eunuchs, and during the ecstatic ceremonies with which she was honored, young men would spontaneously castrate themselves.

In time Kubile relented and made her exit with a cacophonous swishing of her skirts. She had delayed us by more than half an hour, so we were obliged to make our circuit of Midas Şehri with indecent haste. We saw another great pedimented façade, facing westward and only half finished, the rock protruding above it like a canopy; we saw a curving ramp scored with deep parallel ruts worn down by chariot wheels, and many flights of stairs ascending to the acropolis or descending into the rock. There were vaulted cisterns so grandly conceived that I began to wonder if, in addition to their practical function, they had served some religious purpose. On the level summit of the rock, where palaces and temples had once stood, we found a stepped altar bearing a lengthy inscription, and from here there was a wide view of the territory that had been controlled by the lord of Midas Şehri. The fact that this northwestern corner of their kingdom had been so heavily fortified suggests that the Phrygians were expecting an invasion. An invasion did come, but it came from the east and they were taken completely by surprise. The Cimmerians poured over the Caucasus into the region of Lake Van and swept westward into Anatolia, destroying everything in their path. We know little about them, but the destruction of the Phrygian kingdom made such an impression on the Greeks that the Cimmerians are remembered in their mythology as a people who dwelt in a land of perpetual darkness.

As we descended the ramp on the south side of the rock, past shrines and Hittite bas-reliefs, the custodian—who had faithfully accompanied us on our hectic tour—pointed to the fields below us and told us that a Byzantine city lay beneath them. I was doubtful but curious. There was, after all, the evidence of the necropolis, and the city of Santabaris was somewhere nearby. It lay on the military road from Dorylaion to Akroinon and produced at least one notable public figure—a certain Theodore Santabarenos, a devious and ambitious cleric who played a leading role in the sinister events that clouded the last years of Basil I.

THE CRIMES OF
THEODORE SANTABARENOS

The Emperor Basil I, the Macedonian, had a firstborn son named Constantine, whom he loved above anyone else in the world. His other sons—Leo, Stephen and Alexander—counted for nothing, and Leo, the second-born, he had always disliked. On Constantine he doted, and Constantine was quick-witted, brave and handsome beyond any man or boy of that time. Before he was ten years old, he received the imperial crown and was enthroned beside his father. At the age of twenty he campaigned victoriously against the Saracens of the east, clad in golden armor, riding into battle beside his father, mounted on a magnificent white charger, but on the third of September of the same year (it was 879) Photius, the patriarch, stood before the bronze gates and cried out:

Come forth O King! Thou art summoned to appear before the King of Kings.

In an instant Constantine had died of a fever. Grief and terror descended on his father (for he remembered the blood through which he had waded to reach the throne), and never for a moment during the seven years that remained to him did he enjoy tranquility. Another man might have found consolation in the knowledge that he had three sons still living, but the tormented emperor seemed close to madness. By all rights Leo should now have assumed the privileges that had been Constantine's, but Basil could not bear the thought of it. He wandered in an interior wilderness, and so dark was his glance that few dared approach him. He longed only to see Constantine once more.

In his despondency Basil fell into the power of the patriarch and his creature, Theodore of Santabaris, and this Theodore undertook to raise the spirit of the dead prince. Basil and Theodore therefore repaired to an unfrequented wood outside the capital and Basil was instructed to conceal himself in thickets while, at some distance, Theodore performed the summoning. After a time the emperor heard the sound of hooves and saw, or thought he saw, a familiar figure riding toward him, mounted on a white charger, clad from head to foot in gold and carrying a great lance. Unable to contain his joy and longing, Basil broke from his hiding place and ran toward his son, but the vision melted away at his approach.

Come forth O King! Thou art summoned . . .

Whether Theodore resorted to necromancy or merely contrived some ingenious illusion cannot be known, but the emperor was convinced and ordered a church to be constructed in the place where he had seen the apparition. Now Theodore had his ear, and for reasons no one has fathomed, began to poison it with slanders against Leo. The prince, he whispered, was plotting against his father, and Basil readily believed him: he had lost one son, now he imprisoned a second, and came close to putting out his eyes. But in the streets of the city the people denounced Leo's slanderers (for they knew him to be a worthy young man) and in a private dining chamber of the palace a caged bird called out continually "Poor Leo, poor Leo," and Basil relented.

Basil met a strange death, and if it were not reliably attested by Simeon the Logothete it would be hard to believe. In the summer of 886 he was out hunting near the palace of Apamea when he became separated from his companions. He rode on, and before long came upon a gigantic stag drinking from a stream. Emperor and stag looked at each other, then the stag charged and, hooking its antlers under the emperor's belt, dragged him off helplessly into the depths of the forest. The sight of his riderless horse alerted his attendants and they set out to find him. The stag was encircled and killed with lances, but it was too late. All who were present swore they had never seen a stag of such size. The emperor was carried back to the Great Palace in agony, dying nine days later from a hemorrhage of the stomach. His corpse was displayed in the Hall of the Nineteen Couches, and the patriarch stood before the bronze gates and summoned Basil forth to meet his king:

The Lord of Lords awaits thee. Put off thy crown.

On the day of Leo's coronation there was general rejoicing, but amid the acclamations Theodore of Santabaris was silent, and with good reason, for Leo had not forgotten the prison in which he languished or the terror of the heated irons that had been held before his face. As soon as he had the time for such matters he had Theodore arrested and charged with treason. There could be no doubt as to his guilt. Leo prescribed the usual punishment, and the man who had caused an emperor to see visions was deprived of his sight, spending the last thirty years of his life in exile, in darkness.

AMORION 1:
EMPERORS AND IMAGES

As full of interest as they turned out to be, I had not come to Afyon to see Afyon or Ayazin or Midas Şehri. I had come to find the ruins of Amorion, a city whose name echoes persistently through the history of Byzantium during the eighth and ninth centuries. Unfortunately I had no clear idea where it was. The *Phaidon Cultural Guide*—the only guidebook to mention it—placed it forty kilometers southwest of Sivrihisar (a town 121 kilometers to the northeast of Afyon), but failed to give further directions or even the name of the nearest village; a footnote in John Julius Norwich's *Byzantium: The Early Centuries* placed it fifty kilometers southwest of Sivrihisar, near a village called Asarköy, but my map revealed no place of that name. And even if I should succeed in finding Amorion, I did not know whether there would be anything to see. As far as I could tell, Amorion was one of the very few major Byzantine cities in Anatolia that had not disappeared beneath a later Turkish town, but the Phaidon *Guide* restricted itself to the remark: "Ruins of several buildings survive." Norwich was a little more forthcoming: "Amorion is now reduced to a few ruined buildings and the remains of a defensive wall. It is as yet unexcavated." Cyril Mango, in *Byzantium: The Empire of New Rome*, allowed that it had been considered "a center of major importance" in its day, but added "its ruins are still visible and show that it was quite a small place." This did not sound very promising, but I kept an open mind and repaired once more to the tourist information office, where the same young woman who had recommended Vedat produced a map showing, in crude pictographic form, all the main historical sites in the Afyon region. For a time I confused matters by referring to the map in the Phaidon guide, which placed Amorion to the north and west of the Afyon-Sivrihisar road, but once I had made myself clear the question was immediately resolved, and the road lay open. Everything I had read was wrong: Amorion was to be found just outside Hisarköy, a village no more than ten kilometers from the easily accessible town of Emirdağ. All we had to do was take a bus.

Amorion rose to prominence as the capital of the Anatolikon *theme*, and by the early years of the eighth century it was the greatest city in Anatolia. It had close associations with the Emperors Leo III, Constantine V and Theophilus. Its associations with the last-named were especially close: Theophilus had been born in the city, and his line—the Amorian dynasty—was named after it. All three emperors were committed iconoclasts.

The origins of iconoclasm are notoriously obscure, and later Byzantine writers (who were all iconophiles) mutter darkly about the influence of Jewish magicians, but from its early days the Church had been troubled by the idea that the veneration of sacred images might lead to outright idolatry, which would open the way to a lapse into paganism. This unease seems to have been strongly felt in Anatolia and especially in Phrygia. A bishop of Nakoleia was one of the first people to condemn the icons, and not long after, in 726, Leo III issued an edict banning all representation of Christ, His Mother or the saints in human form. The famous mosaic of Christ above the palace gate was destroyed, and the people of Constantinople rioted, but in Anatolia the measure met with widespread approval. To its supporters iconoclasm was a necessary purification of doctrine, and its efficacy seemed to be proved by a series of splendid military victories over Arabs and Bulgars—sure signs of divine favor. Leo had been *strategos* (i.e., governor and commander-in-chief) of the Anatolikon before he made his bid for the throne, and Amorion, his former headquarters, became one of the chief strongholds of the new doctrine, offering loyal support for his reforms and those of his son, Constantine V.

Although it may seem more than a coincidence that the Caliph Yazid II (720–724) should have issued an edict banning all human representation in art only five years before Leo issued his iconoclast edict, modern scholars see no pressing reason to look beyond the borders of the empire for the origins of iconoclasm; nor do they set much store by the outrageous slanders of iconophile, Byzantine writers, who gave Constantine V the unflattering soubriquet "Copronymos" (literally, "dung-named"), but misconceptions persist. It is often assumed that the iconoclasts were puritanically hostile to all images, and therefore to art itself. Norwich even proposes that the restoration of the icons in 843 was the reaction of "a naturally artistic people . . . so long starved of visual beauty," but his own evidence disproves this sentimental notion. The iconoclast emperors were opposed to sacred images as a matter of theological principle, but secular imagery presented no such problem. Constantine V destroyed many religious mosaics, but immediately replaced them with new mosaics on secular themes: churches were decorated with opulent compositions of foliage, fruit, flowers and birds; palaces and other public places with scenes of hunting, chariot races, military victories and genre scenes based on ancient Hellenistic models. Sadly, none of these mosaics have survived, but their existence is well attested, even in sources virulently hostile to Constantine. As for Theophilus, the last of the iconoclasts, he was so addicted to beauty that he deserves to be called an aesthete.

He cannot have been more than seventeen when he came to the throne, but from the first this highly cultivated young man seems to have had an ambitious building program in mind, and the great artistic revival that is usually credited to the Macedonian dynasty (866 onward) actually begins in his reign with the construction of the Pearl—an exquisite suite of rooms decorated with mosaics of animals, within the precincts of the Great Palace. The Pearl was followed by the Camilas, a three-story complex with mosaics of figures picking fruit and a children's room painted with frescoes. Since he also ordered the construction of a fountain in the form of a golden pinecone and an artificial garden in which the trees were made of precious metals, and filled his throne room with gilded bronze automata in the form of songbirds and lions, Theophilus would have been astonished to learn that iconoclasm involved hostility to art. No emperor before him had possessed such refined taste or such a lively sense of fantasy. There had been great builders among his predecessors, but Theophilus expressed himself through building to an unusual degree. On the one occasion on which he lapsed from his avowed moral principles and betrayed his wife in the arms of a beautiful palace attendant, he was overcome with remorse and in order to prove his love for his family constructed a pavilion called the Carianos for the exclusive use of his daughters.

The palace of Bryas on the Asiatic shore of the sea of Marmara (near modern Maltepe), reveals another and equally attractive aspect of his personality. It was designed in close imitation of the palaces of the caliphs in Baghdad. The Arabs might be the sworn enemies of the empire, but, for Theophilus, this was no bar to enthusiastic appreciation of their art and culture. He is even said to have imitated Hārūn ar-Rashīd's reputed habit of going about his capital in disguise to seek out injustices. Theophilus would undoubtedly have preferred relations between the two empires to have been conducted on the basis of détente and cultural exchange, but the caliphs who were his contemporaries, al-Ma'mūn and al-Mu'tasim, pursued an extremely aggressive policy toward Byzantium, raiding Anatolia on a yearly basis. Since the concept of a holy war was completely alien to Byzantine thought, Theophilus seems to have been genuinely puzzled by the caliphs' enthusiasm for slaughtering harmless Cappadocian peasants and plundering already much-plundered towns along

the eastern borders, but his offers of peace were interpreted as signs of weakness, and the young emperor—who
did not lack courage—was periodically obliged to respond
in kind. In 837 he led an army into Arab territory and
sacked the important border stronghold of Sozopetra. He
then returned to Constantinople to celebrate his triumph:
the streets of the city were strewn with flowers and its
buildings hung with carpets and silks, but the festivities
were barely concluded when the enraged al-Mu'tasim,
swearing vengeance for the sack of Sozopetra, set out from
Samarra (the vast new city he had constructed on the
banks of the Tigris) at the head of an army 80,000 strong,
and above this mass of humanity waved banners embla-
zoned with a single word: AMORION.

AMORION 2:
THE FIELDS OF SORROW

Emirdağ is an agreeable, bustling market town with a wide
main square. It is also copiously supplied with taxis.
Within minutes we had found a driver who was familiar
with Amorion and were driving east across the plateau
with the car radio ululating at high volume. To the south

was the blue outline of Mount Emirdede, and ahead of us a low line of hills broken by a narrow pass, beyond which the houses of Hisarköy came into view, huddled against a hill and shielded by a few poplars and willows. Even in early June the place looked desolate, and in winter life must have been very hard. It seemed impossible that it could ever have been the site of a great city, defended by emperors and besieged by caliphs, but that long, low, flat-topped hill behind the houses was Amorion.

There was no path up to the ruins, so we simply scrambled over a wall and waded through long grass to the summit, where we were lustily welcomed by three grizzled herdsmen. Two young heifers frisked about like schoolgirls, and sheep grazed amid the poppies and thistles that grew from the foundations of Amorion's walls. These foundations could be followed all the way around the edge of the hill, and they revealed the walls to have been of rubble construction, faced with finely cut ashlar masonry. Halfway down the hill at the northeastern edge of the site was the stump of a tower. On the plain below a solitary woman was working in a field, in the company of a black dog, their presence serving to emphasize the vastness of the level distances that stretched beyond them. The streams that rose here wandered away disconsolately toward the north and east, where they eventually emptied themselves into the Sangarius as it moved in a series of great loops toward the Black Sea. Within the circuit of the walls only one stone, isolated like a monolith, remained standing; there was also a tombstone, thrown down and defaced with graffiti, but still showing a cross set in a recessed panel at its center. For a time I thought this was all there was to see, but on the south side of the hill I stumbled upon a deep excavation, which, according to Norwich, Mango, et al., should not have been there. The archaeologists had uncovered one of the city gates and a stretch of paved street flanked by a series of rectangular chambers, perhaps guardhouses. Some of these structures had been built with carefully laid courses of ashlar masonry; others seemed to have been thrown together in haste, using any materials that came to hand, including at least six tombstones, one of which had recessed panels framing delicately executed sprigs of flowers.

It was when I looked out from the ruins of the gate that I realized the full extent of Amorion. It had not been confined to the hilltop, as I had first assumed: on the plain below us the line of a defensive wall, enclosing a broad stretch of ground, was clearly visible. There must have been a lower city, covering several times the area of the upper city or acropolis on which I stood. Carved fragments of a very beautiful purple-veined marble lay about in the grass alongside trenches the archaeologists had dug. Professor Mango had been misinformed: this had been a very large city by the standards of the early Middle Ages. When it fell to al-Mu'tasim, Amorion is said to have contained 70,000 people, and even if we take into account the reinforcements that Theophilus had sent to defend the city and the inhabitants of outlying villages who had taken refuge within its walls, this would still leave a permanent population of at least 35,000. Very few of these people survived the events of August 838.

Once he was apprised of the caliph's invasion and its destination Theophilus made a brave attempt to halt the Arab advance at Dazimon, near modern Tokat, in northeastern Anatolia, but his army panicked under a hail of arrows unleashed by the caliph's mounted Turkish auxiliaries, and it was only with difficulty that the emperor himself escaped. His troops dispersed in all directions, taking with them the rumor that Theophilus was dead. In consequence he was forced to return at once to the capital to show himself and quiet the growing disorder. Amorion was left to its own devices, and al-Mu'tasim arrived there on the first of August. He at once put his siege engines to work, but the fortifications of Amorion were strong and for nearly two weeks the caliph made little headway until a traitor revealed to him a weak point in the walls where they had been undermined by a spring. Soon a breach was opened and on 15 August the Arab army poured into the city. Part of the garrison made a final stand in a monastery, but it was set alight and they, and the monks inside, were burned alive. In all, 30,000 people were slaughtered and over 1,000 women were raped. The spoils were then methodically divided and the entire city was burnt to the ground. The surviving inhabitants were forced to accompany the Arab army on its sudden retreat across the Anatolian desert: news of a rebellion had reached the caliph and time could not be wasted. Many of the prisoners escaped, others were left to die of thirst in the broiling heat of an Anatolian August, and another 6,000 were beheaded for no very good reason. Legend has it that when the caliph arrived back in Samarra only forty of his prisoners remained, and seven years later even they were executed for refusing to forswear their religion.

News of Amorion's destruction was greeted with dismay in Constantinople, but in truth it had very little effect on the empire as a whole; it might even be said to have brought some benefit, since it spurred Theophilus to introduce much-needed military reforms. Nor did it bring any benefit to the caliphate, which soon entered a period of irreversible decline. In sum, the sack of Amorion was a singularly futile act of inhumanity. Its effect on Theophilus was devastating nonetheless. He at once took to his bed with a high fever, and his heart and digestion were perma-

nently weakened. He took the destruction of his birth-
place as a calculated personal insult—which was indeed
what al-Mu'tasim had intended—and he also realized that
it was now impossible to claim that iconoclasm brought
victory, an idea that was very dear to him. He must have
known that the doctrine in which he believed so passionately was dying. His own wife, the Empress Theodora,
venerated images in the privacy of her apartments and he
did not love her any the less for it. In the end he seems to
have accepted the inevitable. On his deathbed in 842 he
said nothing for or against sacred images, but was
concerned only to secure the future safety of his family.
On 20 January of that year he died of dysentery, sincerely
mourned by his subjects. He was not yet thirty. Al-
Mu'tasim had died a few weeks earlier. It was the end of
an era: Theodora soon restored the icons, and never again
were the armies of the caliphate to pose a serious threat to
the existence of the empire.

It is good to know that archaeologists are now paying
Amorion the attention it deserves, but the place still has a
lonely and forgotten air. It should not be thought that the
history of the city stopped dead in 838, however. Al-
Mu'tasim had not had time to demolish its great walls and
eventually it was reoccupied and partially rebuilt. It never
regained its former prominence, yet it prospered enough
to be considered worth sacking once again by the Turks
some two centuries later. Even after this it remained the
seat of a bishop, and only disappears entirely from the
historical record in the early fourteenth century. Today
one stands in fields of tall thistles imagining the streets and
houses, the barracks, baths and churches beneath one's
feet. To the east the dust storms stirred up by hostile
approaching armies seem to revolve uselessly in the air.

THE GARDENS OF NIS

About halfway between Afyon and Eğridir poppies give way to roses, and the production of opium to the production of soaps, perfumes and bath oils. At the same point you pass from Phrygia to Pisidia. The landscape is spacious and grand, and it is in these hills on the edge of the plateau that the rivers Maeander and Kayster have their origin, flowing westward to the Aegean and the cities of the coast. The rich Maeander valley with its many towns and monasteries was particularly important to the Byzantines during the twelfth and thirteenth centuries, and both the Comneni and the Lascarids of Nicaea made strenuous attempts to defend it against Turkish raids, but the river valleys gave easy passage through the mountains, and they were not always successful. Fortresses were built, destroyed and rebuilt. Greek villagers and townspeople fled westward, but were sometimes abducted en masse and forced to settle in Turkish territory. When imperial authority weakened, as it did at the end of the twelfth century, the local Greek magnates rose in revolt and called in Turkish tribesmen to aid them. The misery of the common people of western Anatolia was complete. Even the great shrine to the Archangel Michael at Chonai, in the upper Maeander valley, was sacked and stripped of its famous mosaics. Today almost no one recalls these bitter events. The land appears peaceful and prosperous, and the scent of the roses is overwhelming.

You come upon Lake Eğridir without warning: from a narrow valley full of rose fields, the road emerges suddenly onto a high ledge, and there below you is the lake, colored an extraordinary shade somewhere between turquoise and peacock blue. As lovely as any of the Italian lakes, and possessed of a perfect climate throughout spring, summer and autumn, Lake Eğridir is nearly fifty kilometers long, lies at an elevation of 3,000 feet and is ringed by mountains that rise to 9,000 feet. The town of Eğridir, with its ruined ramparts and red-roofed houses, stretches lazily out along a promontory. Beyond the promontory, and connected to it by a causeway, is an island with many old Greek houses and almost as many restaurants and family pensions. The Turks call the island Yeşil Ada (Green Island), but it was known to its former Greek inhabitants as Nis. It was here that we decided to stay, in the Sunset Pension belonging to the delightful Uzun family—Mehmet and Fatma, their daughter-in-law Zehra and her two small sons. The latter were identical twins with gleaming blond hair and the charming habit of presenting their grandparents' guests with flowers. Close by the pension was a small harbor for fishing boats, and immediately behind it was a simple, barnlike church that had been falling slowly into ruin, through sun and snow, since the early 1920s. The shoreline was fringed with masses of red and orange poppies.

An uncrowded island at the center of a lake is a perfect

place to do nothing, but I grew to love the walk to and from the town. The causeway had been planted with trees, and the water on either side of it was never the same color: to the north it tended toward deep turquoise, while to the south it was usually a paler blue in which the mountain that rose behind the town was exactly inverted.

The main reason to go into town is the medrese, which has a magnificent doorway in the Seljuk style, framed in carved bands of abstract ornamentation as delicate as lace and canopied by stalactite formations. The capitals of the columns surrounding the inner courtyard appear to be Byzantine work—part of a long Anatolian tradition of architectural recycling. They are massive, out of all proportion to the columns that support them, and a number are of very unusual design, being composed of four spread-winged birds so comically plump that it is impossible to imagine them ever lifting off the ground. Both the medrese and the neighboring mosque are mementos of Eğridir's brief fourteenth-century heyday, when it was the capital of the independent Hamid emirate, and a thriving center of commerce in which the products of the plateau and the southern coastal plain were exchanged. It impressed Ibn Battuta as a rich and powerful city, but once incorporated into the expanding Ottoman state in 1391 it sank back into a comfortable provincial obscurity on which tourism—so far—has intruded very gently.

The happiest populations are those that escape history, and the only thing that disturbs Eğridir's tranquility today is a splendidly incompetent brass band from the nearby army camp that periodically marches into town playing Sousa in the style of Charles Ives at his most experimental. Indeed, Eğridir was too tranquil for its hoteliers. Alarm over the Gulf War had reduced the flow of visitors to a parched trickle, and I often found myself apologizing for the unfortunate misconceptions of my fellow westerners, who imagined that events in the remote southeast could affect Eğridir. A brand-new and (by Anatolian standards) startlingly elegant hotel was without a single guest, and the smartly dressed staff had nothing to do but stare wistfully out at the lake and the majestic outline of Mount Barla.

On the island I became agreeably lost among lanes winding between decaying wooden mansions. There was something very deceptive about these lanes: every time I aimed for the north shore I found myself emerging on the south shore, and vice versa. Many of the houses appeared to be abandoned, and through shattered windows I could see faded murals in the upper rooms, but sometimes a line of washing strung out between the trees of an overgrown garden would reveal that at least part of the house was still inhabited. In one garden a weathered boat, unused for generations, lay on its side in the shade of a vine. The old gray house beyond it was shuttered and locked. The church behind the pension was also locked, but it was easy enough to peer through the empty windows at collapsing rafters and a floor piled with brushwood and broken furniture. Once when I emerged from my wanderings onto the north shore (having aimed for the south) a young man called out to me from a garden—switching rapidly from German to French to English. His name was Mustafa. He offered me a glass of raki and we fell into discussion of the vanished Greeks of Yeşil Ada.

It seems likely that they were a Byzantine remnant population who had taken refuge on the island during the anarchic years that followed the battle of Manzikert. At any rate the island had been purely Greek for centuries after the Turkish conquest, and according to Mustafa this had become a cause of resentment. When the Greeks went into town in their boats (there was no causeway) they were pelted with trash and insults, but on one occasion the imam of Eğridir had cause to go out to the island, and the Greeks noticed that they were not abused, so they invited some of their Turkish friends to join them on the Green Island. Thereafter, Mustafa claimed, the Turks had lived on the northern shore and the Greeks on the southern shore, and relations between the two communities were untroubled until the terrible years after World War I in which the Turkish nation struggled for survival, years that left no space for civility or tolerance.

Mustafa's grandparents had told him about these events, and I assumed that they had occurred at the end of the last century, by which time the Greeks of Eğridir had lost their language. Even the liturgy had been translated into Turkish, and when they wrote, they wrote Turkish in the Greek alphabet. Mustafa insisted that Greeks, who spoke excellent Turkish, still came back to the island to find the houses where they were born. How must they have felt confronted by the dereliction into which their childhoods had fallen?

Even at noon the gardens of Nis seemed twilit, but the sun shone brightly on the patio-restaurant of the Uzuns, on the games of the twins and on the infrequent fishing boats passing on the unruffled lake.

HIDDEN CITIES

Mustafa was not just a source of local lore, he was a bright intelligence and a crafty facilitator. As soon as he discovered that I wanted to visit the Pisidian cities to the south of the lake, he offered to be my guide and arranged to borrow his father's car for two days.

In antique texts the Pisidians are routinely referred to as "wild," "turbulent" and "warlike." Even after they became subjects of the Roman empire they continued to value their independence highly, and liked to stay out of the way of emperors or their agents. The results can be disconcerting for the traveler, and the road to Adada seemed long. It first climbed away from the lake toward a high pass, then swept down into a lush plain encircled by mountains. Poppies brightened the roadside and birds flew off. The plain was followed by a ravine cloaked with romantically dark pines. I realized that the stream hurrying along by the side of the road was not draining north to the lake, as I had assumed at first, but south toward the Mediterranean; the road had imperatives of its own, however, and began to climb away from the stream in wide loops. The mountainsides were scattered with dwarf pines like stubble; some bluish, distant peaks showed stripes of snow, then a new vista opened out, and we saw a red-roofed village far below, spiked by a solitary minaret, and began to descend toward it. The entire process was repeated. And repeated. Finally we came to a halt on the flower-strewn summit of a pass, miles from anywhere, convinced that we had missed the turning. It seemed scarcely credible that anyone—even the notoriously ungovernable Pisidians—could have built a city in such a place.

We were about to turn back when something entirely unexpected occurred. Gluck's "Dance of the Blessed Spirits" came over the car radio, and the sound of this supremely western and "classical" music in such an unlikely setting somehow encouraged me. We drove on, and within two hundred yards had found the turning. When Adada came into view, Gluck's serene flute melody was still playing, and for a moment I could have imagined that the city's temples and tombs had been summoned into being by the music. The spell was abruptly broken when we got out of the car, to be greeted by the earsplitting braying of a donkey penned in the sanctuary of a temple.

Turkey is so overprovided with well-preserved classical cities that it is easy to become blasé, but in Pisidia the wild grandeur of the settings and the lack of visitors restores one's sense of wonder. At Adada the walls and doorways of the temples still stand to their original height, but the porticoes that stood in front of them have fallen in a jumble of finely carved entablatures and column shafts. From the temple area a straight street leads across a grassy plateau to the tree-shaded agora, surrounded by the

Lefke Gate, Nicaea/Iznik.

Tomb of Şehzade Mustafa,
Muradiye Cemetery, Bursa.

View of Apollonias/Gölyazi.

View of the citadel
from the streets of
Afyon.

Sculpture at
Sagalassos.

Interior of Karatay Medrese, Konya.

The "exedra" at Binbir Kilise, lower town.

Church number thirty-one at Binbir Kilise, upper town.

Interior of the east church at Alahan.

The ravine at Aloda with the author at far right.

General view of
landscape near
Ürgüp, Cappadocia.

Keşlik Monastery/
Monastery of the
Archangel, chapel of
Saint Stephen,
Damsa Valley,
Cappadocia.

The Red Church,
Cappadocia.

Doorway of a *han*, with
muqarnas decoration,
on the road to Aksaray,
Cappadocia.

Rock-cut façade,
Yaprakhisar, Ilhara Valley.

Direkli Kilise (The Church with the Columns),
Ilhara Valley.

Church of Saint George. Fresco showing Basil Giagoupes
and the Lady Tamar standing on either side of
Saint George. Ilhara Valley.

The Pantokrator Monastery seen from the west. Istanbul.

Interior of the Pantokrator looking from the funerary
chapel toward the north church, Istanbul.

remains of stoas and broad flights of steps that climb to a craggy acropolis, defended by tall, Hellenistic towers. Much of Adada would appear to date from the Hellenistic period (that is to say, between Alexander's conquest of Asia and Rome's) and the absence of churches implies that it was already deserted by the beginning of the Byzantine period. It was perhaps too remote or its land too poor to sustain urban life for very long. It seems to have played no part in history, and herein lies its great charm. It is impressive and touching to see how finely things were made, and how lavish were the amenities provided for the citizens in this modest town lost in the folds of the Taurus.

There is something Arcadian about Adada, but Sagalassos is dramatic and severe. It is also much easier to find, being close to the road that goes down from Eğridir and Isparta to Antalya and the Mediterranean coast. At the little town of Ağlasun a road leads off to the right and begins to twist violently up a precipitous mountainside to a height of 5,500 feet. The city conceals itself until the last minute, then appears as a chaos of gray masonry hurled down across a series of bleakly treeless natural terraces, backed by cliffs honeycombed with tombs. After a time the heaps of stones resolve themselves into temples, forums and basilicas. On all sides are carvings of lions' heads, vines, acanthus leaves and elegantly incised Greek inscriptions. Toward the western edge of the site we came upon the bust of a man, his head wreathed in curls, glancing suspiciously to one side. The approach to the theater was guarded by a handsome, diamond-patterned snake. It lay still as a heraldic device and at first I assumed it to be dead, but when (over my protests) Mustafa threw stones in its direction, it took off, slithering through the long grass at tremendous speed. I stepped very carefully after that.

By all accounts the Sagalassans were the most belligerent

of the Pisidians, and they had the temerity to resist Alexander after his triumphal entry into Asia in 334 B.C. According to Arrian, his biographer, Alexander began his attack on the city by advancing directly up the mountainside. If this is true—and anyone who has been to Sagalassos must find it hard to believe—it is an impressive tribute to his genius as a commander, and to the courage and discipline of his troops, for the slope is so steep that even an unopposed ascent would have been difficult. The unarmored Sagalassans threw themselves heroically and uselessly against the shields and spears of the Macedonian phalanx. Five hundred were killed and the rest put to flight. Alexander made his way north into Phrygia to meet up with his main army and began the long march into Asia that would bring Hellenism to Bactria and the banks of the Indus. The capture of Sagalassos may be no more than a minor skirmish in this far-flung triumph, but the city's magnificent theater is a token of how completely its citizens, for all their initial resistance, came to accept the culture of the Greeks.

The *cavea* of the theater nestles into the grassy slope of a hill. It looks large enough to contain at least 10,000 spectators, and stands to its full height, but in places where an earthquake has undermined them the regular semicircles of its seats break into convulsive waves. From the highest seats one looks down on an orchestra overgrown with grass, and on the rubble of the stage building, amid which a solitary lintel, tilted at a crazy angle, still rests precariously atop its doorway. And beyond that the land descends in blue, undulating stages for over a hundred kilometers toward the sea. It is strange to think of the words of Aeschylus, Sophocles and Euripides ringing out in these hills where, today, not a word of Greek is spoken.

In the early Byzantine period, theaters became symbols

of paganism and immorality, yet they continued in use. The great dramas were no longer performed, but there was music and dancing, mime, acrobatics, farce and political satire, and the fulminations of ecclesiastics could not keep people away. It was only in the second half of the seventh century that the theaters were finally abandoned. This has been described as a triumph for the Church, but it probably had as much to do with plague and invasions: by the end of the century it is unlikely that a city such as Sagalassos could have mustered enough citizens to fill even half its theater. Yet the texts of the classical dramas were preserved and studied in the libraries of Byzantium, and for a further four centuries Anatolia maintained its position as a stronghold of Hellenism—a last remnant of the world Alexander had created. The history of Sagalassos during this period is obscure, but by the twelfth century the city lay empty in an uncertain border zone between Greeks and Turks. At the time of our visit its sole occupant was a bored custodian who complained bitterly about the lack of visitors. He also assured us that we must have imagined the snake. He had never seen one.

In the hills south of Sagalassos, the cities of Kremna, Milyas and Ariassos lie hidden. I would have liked to have seen them all, but at the first of them I noticed that Mustafa was showing signs of fatigue or outright boredom, which he politely attempted to conceal. It was possible to sympathize: at Kremna the fragments of sculpture thrown down in abundance on the steps of the forum began to look too florid and the whole urban scheme seemed monotonous and decadent, as if the life had gone out of the city long before its people abandoned it. Mustafa confessed that he preferred the lake at Eğridir to any ruin. And yet the place is unforgettable. Its great colonnaded street is now a deep trench choked with toppled pedestals and columns, like a preparatory sketch for some romantic vision of urban apocalypse, and the whole city looks down from a high precipice toward the valley of the river Kestros and the cities of the Pamphylian plain with the air of a man who knows he has been forgotten but will not show that he is conscious of the insult.

NEVER THEREAFTER

At Eğridir in the evening, clouds sometimes gathered around the brow of Mount Barla and broad shafts of light, piercing the clouds, struck the steel blue of the water, and a cold breeze blew down from the hills to the north of the lake. It was somewhere in these hills in 1176 that the Sultan Kilic Arslan II decisively defeated the Emperor Manuel I Comnenus at the battle of Myriocephalon. It is impossible to be more precise about the location of the battle: the fort of Myriocephalon was already ruined in Manuel's day, and today it has vanished entirely. All we know for certain is that Manuel set out from Chonai, where he had paid his respects to the Archangel Michael, and marched slowly east toward Konya, and that just beyond Myriocephalon the sultan trapped his army in a narrow pass known as Tzivritze.

There is also some uncertainty as to why the battle took place at all. In the aftermath of the recapture of Nicaea and the passage of the First Crusade, the Byzantine position in Asia had greatly improved. The three Comneni— Alexius, John and Manuel—had reestablished control over the whole of western Anatolia as well as the Mediterranean and Black Sea coasts, and the Seljuk state was now effectively confined to the central plateau. By 1176 Byzantines and Turks had been in close and continuous contact for a century, and an uneasy but workable balance of power had developed.

Byzantine writers are consistently hostile to the Turkmen nomads who raided Phrygia and the other border zones, but their attitude to the Seljuks of Konya was much more complex. By the second half of the twelfth century the Seljuk sultanate was a well-organized, civilized state and its ruler, the wily and determined Kilic Arslan II, was noted for his benevolence toward the many Christians who lived within his borders. There was considerable diplomatic and cultural exchange, and Muslim merchants were allowed to trade within the empire. There were Turks in influential positions at the Byzantine court (notably members of the Axoukh family), and Greeks in similar positions at the Seljuk court. Manuel demonstrated his admiration for Seljuk culture in the most concrete fashion by building a hall in the Seljuk style (complete with stalactite ceiling) within the precincts of the Great Palace, and for eighty days in 1161–62 he played host to the sultan himself.

Manuel was famous for his magnificence and liberality, and Kilic Arslan was duly dazzled by the splendors of the imperial capital and the gorgeous festivities that were staged for his benefit, including a mock naval battle. It was, no doubt, a wonderful and very expensive show, but its purpose was strictly political: it was intended to convince Kilic Arslan of the futility of any attack on the God-guarded City and its Empire, and although he was far from unsophisticated, the sultan seems to have been convinced. That, at least, is the impression he wished to give. Sultan and emperor pledged friendship during the course of a series of intimate suppers, and Kilic Arslan swore to return certain cities to the empire. He would also supply troops at Manuel's request. In effect he had accepted client status.

From the Byzantine point of view the situation was the best that could be hoped for: a friendly Turkish state was permitted to exist, but Byzantine prestige and influence remained paramount throughout Anatolia. Why then did Manuel turn against Kilic Arslan in 1176? It was true that the sultan had gained most from the peace, but even Byzantine writers imply that there was insufficient provocation. There had been Turkmen raids, but this was partly the result of Manuel's own negligence, and it was recognized in Constantinople that the nomads were acting independently of the Seljuk government, which had its own problems with them. Kilic Arslan had failed to hand over the city of Sivas, as he had promised, but this hardly justified an all-out attack on his capital when a mere show of force would probably have been sufficient to restore the favorable situation that had existed fourteen years earlier. The capture of Konya might have eliminated the Seljuks, but it would have done nothing to solve the problem of the nomads. The empire did not have the resources to hold down such a large, hostile and mobile population, and it is arguable that the absence of a central Turkish authority, to whom the Turkmens owed at least nominal allegiance, would have made matters worse.

Manuel's foreign policy had always been bold and imaginative. With time it had perhaps become overambitious, involving Byzantium too deeply in the internal politics of Italy, Hungary and the crusading states, to the detriment of the vital Anatolian provinces. Manuel loved glory, had his victories depicted in mosaic on the walls of his palaces, and adopted high-sounding, Justinianic titles. Had he now succumbed to delusions of grandeur? It seems unlikely: he was much too intelligent. The truth of the matter was probably that Manuel needed a spectacular victory to overawe his many enemies. The empire had never been more isolated. His interventions in Italy had succeeded only in uniting the Venetians, the papacy, and the German emperor, Frederick I Barbarossa, against him, and he must have known that Kilic Arslan was in communication with Barbarossa. This opened up the remote but alarming prospect of a concerted attack on the empire from east and west, something all his predecessors had striven to prevent.

These considerations must have revolved in the emperor's mind as he led his army east from the fortress of Choma-Soublaion into Turkish territory. The army was enormous—the entire column stretching for several miles—and at its center was an elaborate and cumbersome siege train. It also included many foreigners: Englishmen made up the majority of the imperial guard; the troops guarding the right wing of the siege and baggage train were under the command of the crusading knight Baldwin of Antioch, and there were significant numbers of Christian Turks. They advanced into desolation. The sultan had burnt the villages and fields; Turkmens "numerous as locusts" made constant attacks, and corpses of dogs and pack animals had been thrown into wells and cisterns. Forced to drink contaminated water, much of the army succumbed to dysentery. When Kilic Arslan sent offers of peace, Manuel's most experienced commanders urged him to accept, but he would not hear of it, and continued his slow advance. When the main Turkish army attacked in the pass of Tzivritze, the vanguard of the imperial army had little difficulty in fighting its way through to open ground, where it halted, but the huge siege train had stalled and the Turks fell on Baldwin's troops. A sandstorm completed the confusion: no one could tell friend from foe and the killing became indiscriminate.

For the first time in his life Manuel lost his nerve. He was on the verge of abandoning his army when the commander of the rearguard came to his rescue. Together they managed to link up with the vanguard, and some semblance of order was restored. The siege train had been lost, Baldwin had been killed and most of his troops with him, but the rest of the army was largely intact. As dawn broke on the day after the battle, emperor and sultan called a halt, and opened negotiations. Historians have expressed amazement at the mildness of Kilic Arslan's terms (Manuel was merely obliged to dismantle his new fortifications at Choma and Dorylaion), and have given much of the credit for this civilized behavior to the sultan's grand vizier, who was a member of the distinguished Byzantine family of Gabras. They perhaps underestimate the seriousness with which Turks (then and now) regard the laws of hospitality. Kilic Arslan had been Manuel's guest for three months, had shared his table and accepted valuable gifts; the sultan himself would have been dishonored if the emperor had been stripped of all dignity. The retreat was orderly, but the imperial troops were horrified to see that the Turks had severed the genitals of the slain.

The immediate aftereffects of Myriocephalon were negligible, yet at the time the battle was considered a catastrophe for the empire, and modern historians have concurred. Manuel himself compared it to the defeat of Romanus Diogenes at Manzikert. Manuel had not been taken captive, the army had not been annihilated, but Myriocephalon dealt a staggering blow to his personal prestige. Nor could he ever forget the terror that had taken hold of him in the pass of Tzivritze. William of Tyre, who visited Constantinople in 1179, the year before Manuel's death, has left us a vivid account of the emperor's state of mind:

> From that day the emperor is said to have borne, ever deeply impressed upon his heart, the memory of that fatal disaster. Never thereafter did he exhibit the gaiety of spirit which had been so characteristic of him or show himself joyful before his people, no matter how much they entreated him. Never, as long as he lived, did he enjoy the good health which before that time he had possessed in so remarkable a degree. In short, the ever present memory of that defeat so oppressed him that never again did he enjoy peace of mind or his usual tranquility of spirit.

Manuel's western enemies made no attempt to conceal their pleasure at the news of his defeat, and the German emperor wrote to him in the most insulting terms, addressing him as "King of the Greeks," claiming that he, Frederick, was the true Roman emperor: Manuel should pay him homage and submit to the authority of the pope. The fragility of the Comnenian revival was apparent to all. While a victory at Myriocephalon would not in itself have ensured a Byzantine reconquest of Anatolia, it would have made it a very real possibility: defeat and its consequences placed that possibility forever out of reach, and the stage was set for the final defeat of Hellenism in Asia.

Manuel was the last emperor who seemed to embody in

his own person the full splendor of the imperial myth. Now his magnificence was revealed to be hollow, and his claim to the inheritance of Constantine and Justinian was treated with contempt. With his death in 1180, Byzantium ceased forever to be a great power. For a time Constantinople maintained its position as the greatest city in Christendom, but less than a quarter of a century later even this was lost.

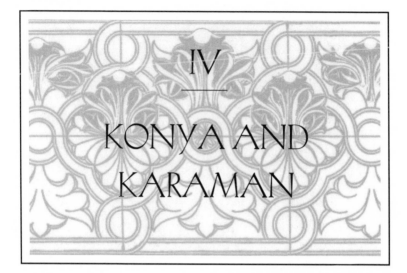

IV

KONYA AND KARAMAN

THE ROAD TO KONYA

Parties of businessmen would sometimes come to the Sunrise Pension in the evening to eat Mrs. Uzun's fried bass and drink raki. As yet another bottle was opened, Mr. Uzun would look in our direction and raise his eyebrows expressively. An unfailingly polite man of distinguished bearing, Mr. Uzun clearly didn't want us to think that all Turkish men were drunks. He need not have worried: we were the last people who would have disapproved of them on this account, and he had reckoned without the two Australian couples who arrived on the day before our departure for Konya. They were people who loved to talk and drink: conversation was interspersed with frequent cries of, "That was good. I could drink another bottle of *that!*" It occurred to me that Konya's most distinguished citizen, the great poet and Sufi mystic Celalledin Rumi, would have thoroughly approved of their behavior. It was Rumi who proclaimed that "being sober is not living," and wrote ecstatically of "the simple wine that makes me loose and free."

The road to Konya makes a long loop to the north of the Dedegöl mountains before turning south to Lake Beyşehir. Broad and shallow and scattered with more than twenty islands, Lake Beyşehir is the largest of the Pisidian lakes but its shores are thinly peopled. In the twelfth century, and in all probability for long after that, the islands were still inhabited by Greek Christians, but when John II Comnenus campaigned in the area in the 1120s he found that these Greeks—whom he must have regarded as his natural subjects—were less than delighted by the arrival of the imperial army. They had no desire to be liberated from the Muslim yoke, and obstinately refused to acknowledge the emperor's authority, with the result that he was obliged to reduce the islands by force.

John was renowned for the justice and benevolence of his rule, and might reasonably have expected a better welcome, but it was half a century since an emperor had exercised effective authority in the region and the original Byzantine population had been forced to come to terms with the Turks. More than that, they had learned to appreciate the easygoing overlordship of the Seljuks and were happy to be spared the exactions of imperial tax collectors. Although sincerely concerned for the welfare of his subjects, John Comnenus still had to find the means to support a large army of mercenaries and a splendid court. The man who claimed to be Emperor of the Romans, God's Viceroy on Earth and the Equal of the Apostles might (and did) attempt to curb the excesses of his nobles, but he could not afford exaggerated economies. Furthermore, the sultans' exemplary religious tolerance meant that there was no particular advantage to the rule of a Christian monarch. "Thus," as Nicetas Choniates sententiously remarked, "custom strengthened by time is stronger than race or religion," and it was this, as much as any military defeat, that doomed the Comnenian reconquest.

The eastern shore of the lake was marshy and fringed with reeds. The mountains that rose from the farther shore were smudged with snow and I remembered how, in the autumn of the previous year, I had flown over the lake on my way from Adana to Istanbul. It had looked like a pool of turquoise paint into which someone had poured milk, and the islands were a dark reddish purple. I thought then and I thought now of the lonely ruins of Kubadabad, the summer palace of the Seljuk sultans, which lay on the western shore of the lake. The road to the site is bad by all accounts, and I did not know of anyone who had succeeded in getting there, yet I regretted that I had not chosen to make the attempt. Of the great medieval palaces—the palaces of the Abbasid caliphs in Baghdad or those of the Fatimid caliphs in Cairo, or the Sacred Palace and the Blachernae in Constantinople—little or nothing remains except the awestruck descriptions of contemporary writers, so it would have been worth putting up with a good deal of discomfort in order to stand amid the rubble of Kubadabad's halls and look out at the same vista of lake and islands that had greeted the eyes of Alaeddin Kaykobad I, most magnificent of all the Seljuks.

From Beyşehir, with its wooden mosque and elegant mausoleum, the road turned sharply northeast, almost doubling back on itself, into a valley patched with green and flowering fields. In the thirteenth century this had been the main caravan route from Konya to Beyşehir and thence down across the Taurus to Alanya on the Mediterranean coast, where the Seljuks had established their winter capital. As the road began to climb out of the valley into a range of dry and stony hills, a large caravansaray came into view. With its broad gateway and polygonal towers it resembled a fortified palace, yet like the hundred or so other examples of the Seljuk caravansaray, it was built at state expense to provide free accommodation for all travelers, regardless of race, religion or social status. The larger caravansarays had their own medical staff and provided new shoes for the poorest travelers, and it is the systematic provision of such welfare services—which also included hospitals, libraries, soup kitchens and insane asylums—that made the Seljuk sultanate perhaps the most advanced state of the entire medieval period (and considerably more advanced in this respect than the majority of modern states). It is especially pleasing to note that Seljuk insane asylums maintained resident orchestras, whose music was employed to soothe the melancholia and depression of inmates. It is perhaps no wonder that the majority of the Seljuks' Christian subjects saw no reason to pine unduly for the return of Byzantine rule.

Any traveler who came by foot over the hills from Konya would have needed new shoes by the time they reached the caravansaray. The land is desolate and inhospitable—the color of parchment and bone—and coming from the direction of Beyşehir you might think you were entering a desert rather than approaching a city and a fertile plain.

A SUNBURST

It was Konya (the former Byzantine city of Ikonion) that the Seljuks chose as their capital after they had been driven out of Nicaea in 1097, and by the early years of the thirteenth century it had grown into one of the greatest cities of the Islamic and Mediterranean world—a magnet for scholars, poets and artists, and home to a syncretic civilization of exceptional brilliance and sophistication. The modern traveler should not expect a vision of medieval ramparts, minarets and domes, however: the sight that greets you when the road breaks from the hills is a vast, dusty sprawl of apartment buildings.

Despite its glorious tradition, Konya today is a dull and conservative town. The one restaurant that serves wine caters only to heavy drinkers, misdirected tourists and would-be gigolos. The place has a guilty air, the food varies from poor to inedible, the wine is sour and overpriced. Even connoisseurs of Seljuk architecture may experience some disappointment: of the city's five undisputed architectural masterpieces, two are in a semiruinous condition, and the greatest of them all, the Alaeddin Mosque, has been closed for restoration for as long as anyone can remember. Of the palace of the sultans only a moldering brick stump remains, protected by a grotesque, parabolic concrete canopy.

Substantial sections of the palace were still intact in the nineteenth century, and travelers have left descriptions of carved and painted ceilings. At that time the city also retained most of its double circuit of defensive walls. The towers were a hundred and forty in number and rose to fifty feet; the gateways were adorned with relief sculpture, including images of lions, elephants, eagles and angels, but in a horrifying act of vandalism, all this splendor was razed to the ground so that Konya could be equipped with a banal system of European boulevards. What the Mongols had refrained from doing, the Turks have inflicted on themselves. The loss is appalling and incomprehensible. It is equally hard to understand why the Alaeddin Mosque cannot be opened to the public. The whole complex took a century to complete and contains the tombs of eight sultans, among them the massive octagonal mausoleum of Kilic Arslan II. By all rights it should be one of Turkey's greatest national shrines. As it is, the visitor can only admire its broad, asymmetric façade and read accounts of its tombs and courtyards, its prayer hall supported by a forest of forty-seven Roman and Byzantine columns.

The Alaeddin Mosque stands on the edge of an oval hill (the original citadel hill of Konya and a settlement mound of great antiquity) and just below it, across a busy road, is the Karatay Medrese. Here disappointment gives way to delight. The medrese's marble portal shows the Seljuk hybrid at its richest and most refined. The central doorway is flanked by attached, spiral columns with stylized Corinthian capitals that represent a clear allusion to late

Roman and Byzantine models. These columns are flanked in turn by panels filled with geometric designs that would not look out of place on the façade of a Phrygian shrine, and above the doorway is a niche filled with a restrained *muqarnas* design—a piling up of many miniature niches with foliate motifs in seven registers—framed by a softly pointed arch. The upper panel of the portal is studded with three intricately carved bosses and otherwise filled with a magnificent interlace design, executed in white and bluish-gray marble. But the mere listing of details cannot begin to convey the perfection of the Karatay portal and may, indeed, give an impression of ornamental excess. Nothing could be further from the truth, for the relationship of the various elements is exquisitely judged. Here the irreconcilable is reconciled—aboriginal Central Asiatic and Anatolian motifs with the most sophisticated devices of Persian, Arab, Armenian and Byzantine design.

Since it gives access to a medrese, the portal is also a doorway to enlightenment in a quite literal sense. "Medrese" is usually translated as "Koran school," but this gives a very limited idea of the functions of these remarkable institutions, where, in addition to the Koran, philosophy, medicine, mathematics and astronomy were studied. If they did not actually invent the medrese, it was the Seljuks of Konya who perfected it both as an institution and an architectural form.

The interior of the Karatay Medrese is one of the loveliest surviving monuments of Islamic art. It demonstrates that the Seljuks considered poetry to be an essential adjunct to learning. You enter obliquely through a domed antechamber in one corner of the building that does little to prepare you for the glorious central space, which consists of a great square hall with a fountain, covered by a dome nearly forty feet in diameter. On the far side of this hall, beyond the fountain, is an *iwan*—a vaulted, open-ended hall of a type that can be traced back two thousand years to the palaces of the Parthian kings. But the miracle of the place is the faience tile mosaic that covers the dome, *iwan* and the upper part of the walls. The pendentives that support the dome are opened fans, colored jade green, white and black; and on the surface of the dome a pale turquoise interlace design is interspersed with forms resembling sunbursts or chrysanthemums. It is an interior that seems to mirror, with absolute calm, all conceivable intricacies of thought.

A MURDER AND
ITS CONSEQUENCES

The Karatay Medrese now serves as Konya's ceramic museum, and although it is the museum itself that is the main item on display, no one should leave without looking at the archaeological finds from the palace of Kubadabad that are exhibited in a side chamber. On a wall of this chamber is a drawing of a reconstruction of the palace, which reveals its design to have been purely Persian. Throughout the history of the Seljuk sultanate, Persian culture continued to have great prestige value: Persian was the language of literature and polite society. What is more surprising is the palace's small scale. Here the emphasis was on comfort and delight rather than oppressive demonstrations of the ruler's power. At the center of Kubadabad was a small courtyard off which an *iwan* opened; beyond the *iwan* (which was doubtless the main reception hall) were the intimate apartments of the sultan and his household and a broad terrace with a pavilion overlooking the lake. It must have been the perfect place to escape from the burning heat of the Anatolian plain, but its real splendor was its tile decoration.

The star-shaped tiles from Kubadabad are outstanding examples of Seljuk figurative art. Animals (especially a prancing, braying donkey) are portrayed with a delightfully naturalistic vigor, but it is the human figures that are most fascinating. By the time Kubadabad was built (circa 1220), the Turks had been in Anatolia for almost a century and a half, and there had been widespread intermarriage with the Byzantine population. The sultans themselves took Christian wives, and yet the artists who painted the tiles adhered to purely Central Asian ideals of beauty, and the men and women of Kubadabad have broad faces with high cheekbones and narrow eyes. This lingering fidelity to the pre-Islamic traditions of their distant homeland may account for the Seljuks' ready acceptance of figurative art, an acceptance that was not limited to ceramics. The Arab traveler al-Harawi attests to the existence of marble statues of men and women in the gardens of Konya in the twelfth century. None of this statuary has survived, but it is possible to get some idea of how it may have looked from the relief sculpture stored in the Ince Minare Medrese, particularly the great winged figure that once stood above one of the city gates: it wears a crown, its wings are outspread (each plume carefully delineated), its knees are bent as if it were running through the air and its robes are rippling.

All of this was, of course, contrary to the strict dictates of Islam, but Alaeddin Kaykobad I, the builder of Kubad-abad, seems to have been incapable of narrow-minded-ness. He took an intense personal interest in the arts and the sciences, and was one of the greatest builders of the medieval period: sometimes it seems that there is no place of any significance in Central Anatolia that does not claim to have been a mosque, a medrese or a caravansaray that was built by Alaeddin Kaykobad. His kingdom extended from the Black Sea to the Mediterranean and as far east as Lake Van. The building of roads, bridges and caravansarays permitted the growth of trade and communications and the sultan's benevolence reached into every corner of the realm, but with hindsight we can see that this brilliance and security could not have lasted.

By 1230 the Mongols had been on the move for more than a decade. They had devastated southern Russia and shattered the kingdom of Georgia and the vast empire of the Khwarizm Shah (the eastern neighbors of the Seljuks). In a sense the Mongol invasions followed the pattern of the Turkish invasions: once again a nomadic Central Asian people had been mobilized into an invincible military machine and had set out on the path of conquest, but, compared to the Mongols, the Turks had been models of restraint and good manners. In 1222, for example, a Mongol army had spent a week systematically extermi-nating the entire population of Herat, which numbered in the hundreds of thousands. In the previous year the great cities of Merv and Nishapur had suffered similar fates. At Merv only four hundred craftsmen were left alive.

Alaeddin Kaykobad's response to the approaching cataclysm was finely judged. He avoided provocation and responded to the Great Khan's violent demands for total submission with courtesy, as if they were couched in the normal language of diplomatic exchange. At the same time he worked to establish a grand alliance of Christians and Muslims to counter the threat, but in 1237 he was poisoned. Rarely has there been less justification for an assassination, and there can be little doubt that the poison was administered with the knowledge and connivance of his son, who now became sultan as Kaikhosru II. At a stroke Seljuk greatness was ended.

Kaikhosru proved to be as inept as he was unfilial. He fell into the power of an evil chief minister who embarked on the murder of his opponents, including most of the best commanders in the army. The Turkmens rose in a revolt that was only suppressed at the cost of thousands of lives and in 1243 the Seljuk army was annihilated by the Mongols at the battle of Köse Dağ. Kaikhosru II survived, which was perhaps rather more than he deserved, but he was forced to accept vassal status, and the eight sultans who ruled between 1243 and the extinction of the dynasty in 1308 exercised little real authority. Popular uprisings against Mongol rule were followed by savage reprisals. There were further Turkmen rebellions and rival sultans divided the realm amongst themselves. Caravansarays were besieged and roads between major cities were closed for months at a time. Trade and agriculture became so disrupted that the economy came near to collapse and there was widespread famine.

It would be wrong, however, to think of this as a period of unrelieved misery and misrule. The reign of Alaeddin Kaykobad had given such a strong impetus to the development of Turkish culture that even the Mongols could not prevent its further efflorescence. The cities of Anatolia had been spared the wholesale destruction that had been visited upon the cities of Khorāsān and Persia, and not all the Mongol governors were either unreasonable or uncultivated. The Seljuk administration continued to attract men of remarkable abilities, who did what they could to alleviate the sufferings of the populace, and maintained traditions of charitable and artistic patronage. The decades that followed Köse Dağ saw the construction of some of the greatest masterpieces of Seljuk architecture, including the Karatay Medrese (1252), the Ince Minare Medrese (1264) and the Blue Medrese in Sivas (1271). The Seljuks' decline, like that of their Byzantine neighbors, was not lacking in either dignity or beauty.

THE PATH TO RUMI'S TOMB

Celaleddin Karatay, distinguished founder of the medrese that bears his name, was a Greek. He was also a high court official, a devout Muslim and an intimate friend of Rumi. It was not uncommon for Greeks to exercise power and influence at the Seljuk court, but whereas Celaleddin had begun his career as a page and had risen through the slave system, others were aristocratic Byzantine exiles. The Gabrades, for example, who provided the sultans with three grand viziers, were former governors of Trebizond who could trace their ancestry back to the tenth century. There was even a branch of the Comnenus family in Konya, founded by a nephew of the Emperor John II, who escaped to the Seljuk court after quarreling with his uncle over a horse. In Konya he became a Muslim and married a daughter of the sultan. His descendants were still living in Konya at the end of the thirteenth century.

There were parallel developments at the Byzantine court. Take the case of John Axoukh, a young Turkish slave whom Alexius I chose as a companion for his son John. If Alexius wished to demonstrate that Turks and Greeks could become one people, he had chosen well: the imperial heir and the Turkish slave soon became devoted friends, and when John succeeded his father he made Axoukh his chief minister. A Turk had thus risen to the highest position the empire could offer, short of the imperial throne. Axoukh's son, Alexius, was for a time an important figure, bearing the title *protostrator*. He was married to a granddaughter of John II, and like his father, claimed to be related to the Seljuk royal house.

The Axoukhs were not alone: we know of at least five other Byzantine noble families of Turkish origin. Nor was Kilic Arslan II the only sultan to spend time in Constantinople. In 1196 his son Kaikhosru I was forced to flee Konya as the result of a dynastic dispute and sought refuge at the Byzantine court, where he remained for nearly eight years and married into the highest levels of the aristocracy. His ready acceptance into Byzantine society was no doubt facilitated by the fact that he was half-Greek, as was the Sultan Kaikaus II (1246–57), who was twice obliged to take refuge with his Byzantine neighbors. The mother of

Kaikaus was the daughter of a priest, and his administration was dominated by his Christian Greek relatives. During his reign, Byzantine influence at the Seljuk court reached its apogee—a circumstance aptly symbolized by the fact that Kaikaus took to wearing the purple boots that for centuries had been the sartorial prerogative of the emperors.

Kaikaus became suspect in the eyes of his Turkish Muslim subjects. He had taken things too far, but he had not really departed from tradition. The sultans had always shown a marked respect for Byzantium, even as they made war against it. They never forgot that they ruled over former Byzantine territory and called themselves sultans of Rum, which is to say, sultans of Rome, since to them the Byzantines were always Romans. Rumi himself acquired his name because he had come to dwell in "the land of the Romans." It was only the western Christians who questioned the Byzantines' right to that proud title, and it was the westerners, not the Seljuks, who reduced Constantinople to ruins and desecrated its churches in 1204.

In the matter of relations between Christians and Muslims, Greeks and Turks in thirteenth-century Anatolia, the example of Rumi is at once exceptional and representative. In him the tolerant and eclectic nature of Seljuk society found its most complete expression, and it is fitting that the high turquoise cupola of his tomb should still dominate the skyline of old Konya. It is the point to which all eyes are drawn. In photographs its turquoise can look garish, but in the sharp air and clear light of Anatolia it is like a shout of joy. Even to an irreligious visitor it remains a touching symbol of amity between faiths and races.

I approached Rumi's tomb with some nervousness. I knew it was still an important place of pilgrimage and wondered how the pilgrims might react to the presence of infidels. Konya, as I have said, is a conservative town. I arrived well before the place opened, defensively clutching a volume of Rumi's verse, to find a small crowd already gathered at the gates. Entire families had chosen this day to pay their respect to the master. Everyone seemed perfectly relaxed and no one looked at me askance. I reflected that Rumi, for all his greatness as a poet and mystic, was not a forbidding figure, so there was no reason to expect a visit to his tomb to be a grim religious duty, and before long we were all shuffling respectfully through the gate. We crossed a courtyard and a series of airy, vaulted bays opened before us. The Turkish visitors immediately produced cameras, and flashbulbs were soon detonating in all directions. I relaxed at once.

There were displays of costumes, carpets and musical instruments, with particular prominence given to the *ney*, a flute whose wild and melancholy tones accompany the dervish dances. There were also objects like huge glass vases, which turned out to be antique lamps. And there were tombs. The tomb of Rumi's father stood bolt upright, supposedly a sign of his posthumous astonishment at his son's achievements. Rumi's own tomb was a kind of sarcophagus, richly clad in red, blue, green and gold, and capped by a great turban. Above it was a honeycombed and painted vault. People crowded at the rail to get a closer look, but good manners prevailed and, as Rumi would have desired, foreigners and infidels were most definitely welcome. I too was a pilgrim in my way. I felt no sense of religious awe, but I was very happy to pay homage to the poet who had written

Long nights I have passed with the priests,
And I have slept with pagans in the market places.
I am the green eyes of jealousy, the fever of sickness.
I am cloud and rain, I have swept down over the meadows,

Yet the dust of mortality never touched the hem of my garment.
I have gathered a treasure of roses in the Field of Eternity . . .

Rumi believed that God had taken him from his native
Khorāsān and brought him to "the land of the Romans" so
that he "might mingle with them and lead them to the
good doctrine." His interpretation of that doctrine was
extremely liberal however, and the only methods of
conversion he ever employed were kindness, friendship
and good example. Conservative Muslims who congratu-
lated themselves on their innate superiority to the infidel
were the targets of his withering scorn. He would remind
them that "Though the ways are various, the goal is one.
Do you not see that there are many roads to the Kaaba?"
He further believed that "Love for the Creator is latent in
all the world and in all men," and in a quatrain of the great
Divan-i Shams i Tabriz he goes so far as to dismiss the
terms Jew, Christian and Moslem as "false distinctions."
His relations with Konya's Christian community were very
close. His disciples included Greek painters, architects and
artisans, and he assiduously cultivated the acquaintance of
priests and monks, whom he always treated with the
greatest respect. (On one occasion he is said to have
greeted a monk from Constantinople by bowing no fewer
than thirty-seven times.) Even Christians who remained
steadfast in their faith were fascinated by his teachings and
attracted by the peculiar radiance of his personality. His
favorite retreat was the Monastery of Saint Chariton on
the edge of the hills outside Konya. The learned abbot was
a particular friend, and the two men would spend days
together, meditating and conversing. As a result, the
Christians of Konya came not only to respect Rumi, but to
love him. The depth of that love is demonstrated by the
extraordinary scenes that took place at his funeral.

THE BREAD
AND THE FLUTE

After the body of the Master had been brought forth on a litter,
the nobles and all the people bared their heads. Men, women
and children gathered in the streets of the city and such a
tumult arose that it seemed the resurrection was at hand. And
all wept, and the men marched behind the litter, crying out
and tearing at their clothes so that they walked almost naked,
such was their grief.

Everyone came—the Christians and the Jews, the Greeks,
the Arabs and the Turks—and all of them marched beside the
body of the Master, the Christians holding aloft their sacred
books, which were very precious and beautifully illuminated.
They recited verses from the Psalms, the Pentateuch and the
Gospels, and uttered lamentations according to their customs.
And the Muslims could not drive them back, try as they might
with blows of the cudgel or the flat of the sword.

The noise became so great that it reached the ears of the
sultan in the seclusion of his palace and he summoned the

chiefs of the monks and priests and demanded to know what this event had to do with them—for did they not know that the Master was a Muslim and a revered imam? And they answered:

"In him we have comprehended the true nature of Jesus Our Savior and of Moses. In him we have found the same guidance that is offered by the perfect prophets whose words we have read in our books. If you Muslims call our Master a new Mohammed, we Christians recognize him as the Jesus of these times. Just as you are his sincere friends, so are we a thousand times over his loving servants and disciples. It is thus that he has said: 'Seventy-two sects hear their own mysteries from us. We are like a flute which, in one mode, is the concordance of two hundred religions.' Our Master is the sun of truth who has shone upon mortals and accorded them his favors. Does not the whole world love the sun, which illumines alike the abodes of the poor and the powerful, the Christians and the Muslims? Our Master is both the sun and the window that admits the light of the sun. He is like bread, which is indispensable to all who live. Has it ever been known for a hungry man to run from bread? Just so is our Master essential to us."

At this the sultan fell silent, and all his ministers with him. Then a flute was heard and twenty groups of excellent chanters recited words the Master himself had written:

"My work is to carry this love for You, as solace for those who long for You,
To walk in all the places You have walked and gaze on the trampled dirt."

A VILLAGE IN THE HILLS

At the time of Rumi's arrival in Anatolia most of the sedentary population was still Greek and Christian, but by the time of his death in 1273 the Greeks were beginning to disappear. In the last years of the thirteenth century and throughout the fourteenth the process of conversion and assimilation accelerated. It was a comparatively small step from comparing Rumi to Christ to embracing Islam, and a Greek who was a Muslim and spoke only Turkish was no longer, in any real sense, a Greek.

Today, with the exception of some Byzantine architectural elements built into the façade of the Alaeddin Mosque, you will look in vain for mementos of Seljuk Konya's Christian community. The city's principal church—the Church of Saint Amphilochios—survived until the early years of this century, when it was photographed by Gertrude Bell. It was revered by the Turks, who believed, for unfathomable reasons, that it contained the tomb of Plato, but it has vanished so completely that I was unable to locate its site. This makes a visit to the village of Sille all the more surprising. Although it is only eight kilometers from the center of Konya, Sille remained a purely Greek Christian enclave until the late nineteenth century. Up to that time its people continued to speak the Greek of their Byzantine forebears.

On the outskirts of Konya, bleak white apartment buildings were rising out of the dusty plain, and women were filling cans with water at roadside fountains. Ahead of us there appeared to be nothing but a line of forbiddingly barren hills, but after climbing a gentle rise the road descended into a fertile valley and we saw the handsome, red-roofed houses of Sille scattered among poplars and fruit trees. We might have been eighty kilometers from the city. A streambed wound through the village, crossed by many small footbridges. Sadly, the stream was dry—its waters dammed higher up in the hills and drawn off to slake Konya's insatiable thirst. On its bank was a charmingly rustic mosque with a high, wide, wooden veranda and beyond that on the hillside was a cluster of troglodytic dwellings and chapels of a kind we had seen in Ayazin and would see again, a hundred times over, in Cappadocia. These were unremarkable examples of the form, but from the natural terrace in front of them there was a fine view of Sille. It became clear that the modern village was only the residue of what had been a prosperous town. The ruins of substantial houses covered both sides of the valley, extending far above the present limits of the village like tidal wrack. When Turks settled here in the nineteenth century, Greeks must have continued to make up a large part of the population, and when they were expelled in 1923 Sille evidently did not recover from the blow.

Accounts of Sille that I read had been vague, so as we walked farther up the valley I had little idea of what to expect—certainly not a perfectly preserved eleventh-century church. This, I learned later, was the Church of the Kyriakon. It was screened by poplars, the high drum of its dome decorated with intricate brickwork patterns; the single apse was unusually deep and full. It was also surrounded by a wall and the only gate was locked, but it did not take long to find a gap and climb through. The church had been added to, altered and repaired over the centuries, and borrowed materials had been haphazardly mixed in: there were panels with spiral and rosette designs, and a row of whiskered lions' heads of mysterious provenance. But, as I had feared, the Kyriakon itself was locked. It seemed intolerable that having come so far we should be denied a glimpse of the interior.

It was at this point that we encountered, for the second time, a good-looking young man who had accosted us in Konya and offered overinsistently to be our guide. He was dressed as if for a visit to a discotheque, in an oversize, dull turquoise suit in the Italian style and was obviously chagrined that we had managed to find Sille and its church without his assistance. He was escorting two middle-aged German women and could barely conceal his contempt when I informed him that we had come by bus rather than taxi. "Rich" foreigners were not supposed to behave in this manner. Nevertheless, it was he who showed us how it was possible to scramble up the side of the apse, cling precariously to a ledge and look into the church through a tangle of barbed wire.

What I saw surprised and moved me. The interior had suffered nothing worse than the inevitable effects of abandonment and neglect. Dim figures floated on a faded blue ground on the pendentives and dome, and an ornate wooden iconostasis was still in place, surmounted by its cross. It looked as if the church had been left largely undisturbed since the last Greeks of Sille closed its doors and departed for a land they did not know, seventy years before. Perhaps the Turks of Sille had left it alone out of respect for their vanished neighbors, and for a way of life that had lasted for fifteen hundred years before a gathering of politicians in a dull resort in Switzerland decreed that it should end.

A cemetery rose up a grassy hillside to a ruined funerary chapel. To look back through the tombstones, which were streaked with ocher and orange, was to be overcome with a sense of loss. Something about that locked church—the softness of its silhouette, the way its stones absorbed the light, the way it huddled under ranks of jagged rocks—seemed to embody the Byzantine spirit at its most humane. Beyond the chapel was a limestone ravine traversed by a lofty ogival arch that had once carried water to the highest gardens of Sille—gardens that no longer existed. The diagonal stratifications of the nearby white rocks resembled heaps of torn pages and the arch was like hands joined in prayer. The afternoon was wearing on and it was time for the faithful to pray. A muezzin began his incantation, but this muezzin was a young boy with an extraordinarily high, clear voice that rose and fell like a fountain, filling the valley with liquid syllables of praise. I heard in that boy's voice something of the nearness to heaven that is a recurring theme of Rumi's poetry: "We have been to Heaven: we are the companions of angels."

TOWARD THE
BLACK MOUNTAIN

The town of Karaman lies a little more than a hundred kilometers from Konya at the southernmost point of the Anatolian plateau. The road skirts the edge of the vast Konya plain, keeping the mountains of Isauria to its right. Streams flowing down from these mountains watered the fields surrounding the neolithic settlement of Çatalhüyük, which flourished six thousand years before the birth of Christ and has some right to be called the world's oldest town. Where there is no water the prospect is desolate in the extreme, and the description Gertrude Bell gave in *The Thousand and One Churches*, circa 1909, still holds good in all essentials. The land, she says, is "barren save for a dry scrub of aromatic herbs or flecked with shining miles of saline deposit; naked ranges of mountains stand sentinel over the featureless expanse; the sparse villages, unsheltered from wind or sun, lie along the skirts of the hills, catching thirstily at the snow-fed streams that are barely enough for the patch of cultivated ground below; the weary road, deep in dust or mud according to the season, drags its intolerable length to the horizon."

The roads are less "weary" and "intolerable" these days, and we could not have gone more than halfway to Karaman before I recognized the jagged outline of Kara Dağ—the Black Mountain—rising out of the plain. This was a holy mountain: the Hittites had built a shrine on its summit and the Byzantines had covered its northern slopes with churches—so many that the area is still known as Binbir Kilise, the Thousand and One Churches.

As we drove into Karaman from the new but already ruinous bus station on its outskirts, I was shocked to discover that the old quarter which until very recently had clustered around its great citadel had been leveled to the ground. Where there had been a warren of winding lanes there was now only a mound of bare earth. But travelers should make some attempt to temper their craving for the picturesque and take into account the material needs of the people who live in the places they visit: judging by the old houses surviving in other parts of the town, the houses of the citadel quarter must have been very poorly constructed of mud brick and thatch, and their inhabitants were probably delighted to move into new apartment buildings. And, unlike Konya, Karaman had at least kept its citadel. Its massive polygonal towers stood to their original height and swallows in great numbers swooped and veered about them.

In the second half of the thirteenth century and into the early years of the fourteenth, there was intense hostility and rivalry between Konya and Karaman. The people of Konya, whether Muslim or Christian, detested the Karamanid Turkmens, whom they regarded as "wolves" and "dog-headed cannibals," and yet when they eventually succeeded in capturing Konya, the emirs of Karaman maintained the best Seljuk traditions. It was they who built Rumi's tomb and their fidelity to the Seljuk style is everywhere apparent in the architecture of Karaman, from the towers of the citadel to the exquisite portal of the Nefise Hatun Medrese.

Nefise Hatun, who founded the medrese that bears her name in 1382, was an Ottoman princess and the wife of Alaeddin Beğ, the greatest of the Karamanid emirs. Her medrese is so conservative in style that it could easily have been constructed more than a century earlier, yet if there is no advance, neither is there any sign of a decline in artistic standards. The inscription bands and *muqarnas* decorations of the medrese's portal were as fine as anything I had seen in Konya. In contrast to early Ottoman architecture, neither its style nor technique of construction show any trace of Byzantine influence, and this is only to be expected. In the fourteenth century the Ottomans were still completing their conquest of Byzantine Bithynia, whereas the heartland of the Karamanid emirate had been under Turkish rule for nearly three centuries. In the minds of architects Konya had effaced Byzantium. Nevertheless, Hoca Ahmet, the architect of the Nefise Hatun Medrese, was not above borrowing Byzantine materials when they suited his purposes. The arcades flanking the central courtyard are carried on double columns of a kind commonly found among the churches of the Black Mountain.

In Karaman it is hard to forget the presence of the Black Mountain, rising starkly out of the plain to the north of town, and it becomes easy to understand how it could have been an object of awe and veneration. According to Sir William Ramsay, "The power of the Mother Earth was displayed in making the Black Mountain the sanatorium, vineyard and orchard of the Lycaonian plain; it was clothed in vines and other fruit trees; it offered a delightful climate in the heat of summer; from its lofty summit men surveyed the whole land and communed with the gods." Its holiness must have been self-evident to the aboriginal

people of the Konya plain, the artistically inclined inhabitants of Çatalhüyük and their descendants, but looking at
the naked peaks of Kara Dağ from Karaman today it is
difficult to believe that it could ever have been a place of
vines and orchards, or that it still conceals so many
churches. A thousand and one is, of course, an exaggeration: "binbir" in this context is best translated as "a great
many," and in this sense it holds true, for this is the largest
group of masonry Byzantine churches to be found
anywhere in Anatolia.

It was obviously a place I had to visit, but it was not
clear how this could be achieved. On my map the roads
leading there were marked by disturbingly indistinct lines
of dashes, and one of my guidebooks told me to "beware of
the wild horses that live in the hills." Since Karaman has
no tourist information office I repaired to the museum,
where I found myself distracted by the leering grin of a
seventh-century mummy from the great cave-monastery
at Manazan. Tearing myself away from the gaze of this
dead Byzantine, I displayed my maps and guidebooks to
the museum employees, who looked at them all with great
sympathy and interest. Unfortunately, with the exception
of a man who spoke a bizarre idiolect he claimed was
French, no one spoke anything but Turkish. I was getting
nowhere when a resonant and authoritative voice rang out
and I turned to see a tall, stout, gray-haired gentleman
dressed in the most elaborately patched pair of trousers I
have ever seen. There appeared to be only a few square
centimeters of the original cloth left. The trousers
notwithstanding, this was clearly a person of substance.
He shook my hand firmly and announced in English, "I am
Ismail Ince, the custodian of Binbir Kilise. We will go
tomorrow. You will hire a taxi."

THE THOUSAND AND ONE
CHURCHES: ONE TO
TWENTY-FOUR

The next morning Ismail arrived at the hotel at eight o'clock sharp. He was wearing a blue suit in our honor and was impatient to set out. A few moments later our driver, Ibrahim Saygi, arrived. Although they had not met before, Ismail and Ibrahim took to each other at once. Both men were in their early fifties. Ibrahim had fine gray eyes and was mercurial and quick in his movements; Ismail's eyes were darker and sadder and he wore about him a clear consciousness of the seriousness of his position as custodian of the Thousand and One Churches; his gestures were slow and dignified but also kindly and without pomposity: he was about to show us his domain.

The suburbs of Karaman were soon left behind, and we drove north across the desolation of the plain (which was turning to dust now that the spring rains had passed) toward the treeless and eroded southern slopes of the Black Mountain. The peaks and spurs above us had once been heavily fortified by the Byzantines. This had been an important military base from which they had kept watch on the movements of their Arab enemies as they broke into the plain through the Cilician Gates.

After about twenty-five kilometers, Ibrahim turned to the left onto an unsurfaced track that began to climb steeply over the eastern shoulder of the mountain. He evidently relished the challenge and grinned happily every time a rock hit the underside of the car. After climbing for perhaps two thousand feet we crossed the pass and the landscape abruptly changed. There were pine woods and green fields and fruit trees grown wild. Among the latter William Ramsay had been able to distinguish "apple, pear, two kinds of plum, almond, peach and apricot," describing them as "the untended degenerate offspring of the formerly cultivated trees." Below us the small village of Maden Şehri lay in a broad valley. The whole of this valley had once been covered by the churches and houses of the Byzantine city of Barata. As we drew nearer to the village I recognized the ruins of a very large church lying on its eastern edge. This was Gertrude Bell's church number one.

Information about the Binbir Kilise district is hard to come by. The entry in the *Oxford Dictionary of Byzantium* is wholly inadequate; Cyril Mango's *Byzantine Architecture* manages only a few passing references and the *Phaidon Cultural Guide* gives a very inaccurate account of the churches before giving up entirely with the remark, "The Binbir Kilise district is very extensive and thus a detailed description following a plan is impossible," although it is hard to see why Binbir Kilise should be any more "impossible" than Cappadocia. The standard work on the subject remains that of Gertrude Bell and Sir William Ramsay, which I have already mentioned several times. As far as I am aware it has not been reprinted since 1909, and since it will be inaccessible to the vast majority of readers I will continue to refer to it frequently. It is a pleasure to do so, for *The Thousand and One Churches* was written at a time when scholars allowed themselves strong opinions and fine prose styles.

Church number one is presumably so numbered by Bell because it is the first church that most travelers come to, but since it is the largest church on the Kara Dağ, it is also first in another sense and may have been the seat of the bishop of Barata. Even without entering I could see that large parts of it were in good condition, but Ismail gestured for me to stay back. I soon discovered the reason. A huge shaggy hound, with a temperament as ugly as its appearance, sprang onto the wall beside the approach to the church and began to menace us with a fine display of barking, growling and slavering. We were only allowed to proceed after its truculent owner, with some evident reluctance, had chained it up. I noticed that Ismail carried a stone in his pocket at all times, and visitors without a guide would be well advised to do likewise.

At last I was permitted to enter the first of the Thousand and One Churches. In the years since I had become aware of their existence they had assumed an almost legendary status for me, but the only photographs I had seen had been old and dim, and it had been difficult to form any clear impression of the buildings. I was a little unnerved to be confronted with the real thing, sharply illumined by the harsh light of an Anatolian morning. On the double arch that led into the dark, vaulted narthex there were traces of reddish paint—paint that must have been at least nine hundred years old. The main body of the church was open to the sky, its floor carpeted with grass and flowers. The entire south side of the nave had disappeared, but the ten horseshoe arches of the northern arcade were still intact, as was the nobly proportioned apse, in front of which a small black donkey cropped the grass, paying no attention to our intrusion.

Church number one is a barrel-vaulted basilica, and this is the most common plan for the churches of the Black Mountain. It is perhaps a little heavy and lacking in refinement, yet it gives an impression of strength and power, in this resembling certain much later romanesque monuments in western Europe. What is most surprising about it, given its early date, is the complete lack of any residual classical influence. It cannot be later than the seventh century and is probably more than a century older, yet there are no acanthus capitals, no columns or vine scrolls, and the horseshoe arch is radically unclassical. Despite this, it seems unlikely that the architects and artisans of Barata would have made a conscious decision to break with the past. Style was governed by circumstance, and Barata, for all its size and prosperity, was remote from the major centers of Hellenism. Judging by surviving inscriptions, the inhabitants' Greek remained poor throughout the history of the town. The classical style may never have taken firm root here.

From the first church, Ismail led us toward the center of the valley. Here, rising from fields beyond the northern limits of the village, was a remarkable and enigmatic monument. It was massive, semicircular and capped by an impressive half-dome, measuring some twenty-five feet across. I assumed at first that it must have been the apse of a church which had otherwise vanished. But no, Ismail informed me with great firmness, it had never been part of a church. Looking again, I saw that he was right: the structure was windowless (as no apse is) and so large that any church that had been built to its scale would have been truly gigantic. What, in that case, was it? Ismail became mysterious, turning his open palms toward the heavens, and remarking that no one knew. Gertrude Bell is hardly more informative. The structure in question, which she calls an *exedra*, was attached to a walled enclosure surrounding the heavily ruined seventh church, but not to the church itself, and she thinks that it may sometimes have been used for the celebration of open-air services. This hardly seems adequate, for this is the grandest of all the monuments on the Black Mountain, and the most carefully constructed. It stands alone, keeping its secrets, like a memorial to some unaccountably forgotten world conqueror.

Beyond the exedra and the seventh church, on the extreme northwestern edge of the site, the scant remains of another enclosed group of churches were visible, but where church number eight should have been I could see nothing. This was one of the most beautiful and original of all the churches. It was an octagon from which three porches and an apse projected. In a drawing of 1826 it is still perfect and the drum of the dome is so high that it resembles a tower, or perhaps a pavilion of several stories rather than a church. The sheer delight its builders took in architectural form is evident in every detail of the design. In Bell's day, part of the apse, some of the masonry of the tower and one of the porches survived. And in the porch there were remnants of frescoes. At the time of my visit there was only a level field littered with stones and enlivened by poppies.

THE THOUSAND AND ONE CHURCHES: THIRTY-ONE TO FORTY-FIVE

When Gertrude Bell last visited Binbir Kilise in 1908, the first church still showed signs of a ninth- or tenth-century restoration and this tells as much about the history of Barata as we are ever likely to learn. The people of Barata abandoned their city as soon as the Arab raids began in the latter half of the seventh century, but, displaying the tenacity of all Byzantine Anatolians, they did not abandon the mountain. They simply moved to a location about three miles distant, fifteen hundred feet farther up the mountain and easier to defend. Here they built a new town, and, when circumstances permitted in the second half of the ninth century, they partially reoccupied the lower town and rebuilt some of its churches.

Our first sight of the upper city was a handsome church perched dramatically on the steep side of a rocky knoll. I asked Ibrahim to stop immediately but Ismail insisted that we drive on into the center of the village of Değle. Here we found ourselves surrounded by great jumbled masses of ruins into which (and out of which) the villagers had built their houses and farm buildings. Değle was once populous enough to have its own mosque, with charming murals of trees and flowers, but the mosque is now abandoned and the population is reduced to no more than two or three families. They lead a very isolated existence and were pleased to receive visitors, plying us with glass after glass of the marvelously refreshing yoghurt drink known as *ayran*.

The chaotic appearance of the upper city is not entirely a result of its ruinous condition. The place never had a regular plan, but after some exploration it became clear that there was an organizing principle of sorts. There were three or four main walled enclosures containing churches and other mostly monastic structures, and over time these enclosures had been linked by long lines of walls. It was in this haphazard fashion that a well-defended city came into being. At the center of the present village is the largest of these enclosures. It is dominated by the ruins of an elaborate cruciform tower of which a single broad arch still stands. To the west of the tower is an impressive two-story structure with parallel vaults, now collapsed. Sheep were penned in the lower story, but white goats wandered about freely, sometimes perching high in the ruins as if they knew they made a very picturesque impression against the dark, reddish stone. To the east of the tower was an ambitious church (number thirty-two) with a nave that had originally been flanked by tall galleries. Its condition has deteriorated sharply since Bell's visits, and she herself saw the beginnings of this process. In 1905 the high arcade of the north gallery was intact and the two-story narthex stood to its full height; by 1907 the arcade had succumbed to the storms of a bad winter, but most of the narthex had survived; now even this had been reduced to the level of the lintels. I looked through doors carved with crosses and over the grass-grown mounds of rubble filling the nave to the handsome apse, which alone has preserved its original shape.

On this natural terrace, suspended between the peaks of Kara Dağ and the plain, the air is sweet and the quiet all-enveloping. Yet high and lonely as it is, there is a curious sense of intimacy about the place. As you walk from church to church, much as the town's Byzantine inhabitants must have done, the life of the tenth century seems very close. I noticed, standing next to a Turkish house, what appeared to be a large earthenware jar of the Byzantine period, much repaired but still in use.

Ismail now led us away from the center of the village, across stony fields that must have concealed the traces of many streets and houses, to the northwest corner of the site, where we came upon a straggling group of buildings, many of which had succumbed to quarrying. Ismail told me that the quarrying of the ruins for building materials had continued until very recently, and Bell talks of peasants clearing the ruins merely in order to plant melons. Now, I was informed with some solemnity, these pernicious practices had been halted. Anyone who touched a stone of the Thousand and One Churches had to answer to Ismail, who was known to all the people on the mountain and was not a man to tolerate any flouting of his authority. I felt confident that the ruins were safe in his care, and at Değle his task had been made easier by the flight of the population.

Happily, Bell's building number forty-five had survived the best efforts of villagers, time and the weather, and its now rather shapeless ruins were still tall and faced in places with fine ashlar masonry. This, Ismail proclaimed, was not a church but a house, although Bell maintains that it was a monastic building. Its walls enclosed a mass of long grass and wildflowers. At the opposite end of the enclosure the remains of a domed church (number thirty-five) lay against the side of a hill. It was heavily ruined, but it was pleasant to rest on its stones for a while in a silence broken only by the intermittent murmur of a breeze in the wild fruit trees. From a nearby field Ismail uprooted a green plant that he evidently considered a delicacy. Its leaves were coated with silky white threads and its taste was fresh and pungent.

As we walked back toward the village, the peaks of the Kara Dağ rose above us, still brushed with green from the spring rains. On the summit of the highest peak Gertrude Bell visited a monastery with a fine domed church, and I regretted that I would not be able to follow in her footsteps—this would have to be the work of another year. On the lower slopes, traces of terraces, water channels, cisterns and wine presses bear testimony to the highly developed agricultural skills of the Byzantine population. These skills were the source of the remarkable prosperity and abundance that allowed them to devote so much of their time and energy to the construction and decoration of churches, yet, in a notably cantankerous passage, Ramsay asserts flatly that "there is little to be said in favour of this provincial Byzantine town," which he describes as "the home of ignorance and dulness [sic]." And this, he continues, is only the symptom of a broader "national decay," and the main agent of this decay was none other than the Orthodox Church itself. The cognitive leap is a large one, but it is instructive to follow Sir William: the nation had been delivered into the hands of the Church and "the result was that art and learning and education were dead and the monasteries were left." The triumph of the Church "meant the degradation of higher morality and intellect and Christianity."

This peculiar outburst reveals that Ramsay's view of

Byzantium was still fogged by the poisonous fumes of anti-Byzantine prejudice rising from the seductively eloquent pages of Gibbon. It shows how hard it was in the early years of this century—even for a man with firsthand knowledge of the monuments of Byzantine Anatolia—to break the habit of regarding Byzantium as a culture of superstition and decadence. In fact, despite periodic lapses into bigotry, the Orthodox Church showed no consistent hostility to art and learning, or even to the works of pagan poets and philosophers. One might point to the example of the bibliophilic Patriarch Photius in the ninth century or of Eustathius, archbishop of Thessalonika, in the twelfth, who devoted much of his time to the composition of commentaries on Homer, Pindar and Aristophanes. The point need not be labored. No doubt the majority of Barata's inhabitants were illiterate, but this had more to do with the city's remote location than ecclesiastical obscurantism. Provincial "ignorance and dulness" are not the original inventions of Orthodox Christianity, and compared to the miserable conditions that obtained in most Western European towns during the ninth and tenth centuries, Barata shines as a beacon of civilization and good living.

The period between 850 and 1050, when the upper city was at its height, was the opposite of a period of "national decay." It represents the apogee of Byzantium, when the empire, under the rule of the Macedonian dynasty, enjoyed a sustained period of security and prosperity, and learning and the arts flourished as never before. On the Black Mountain, in all likelihood, there were few elevated discussions of the respective merits of Plato and Aristotle; conversation was not peppered with allusions to Hesiod and Euripides; no exquisite ivories or enamels were produced; craftsmen did not attempt to imitate the masterpieces of Greco-Roman art, and mosaic work was too difficult and expensive, but the sustained outburst of building activity on the mountain during these two centuries is an integral part of this great efflorescence of Byzantine civilization.

As a guide Ismail was something of an artist. He had kept church number thirty-one (the one we had seen on our approach) for the last because it was the most beautiful. Its location on a steep slope offering sweeping views of the Konya plain and the distant Isaurian hills added to its charm. Its plan—a vaulted basilica—differed little from several other churches we had seen, but here everything seemed finer—the relation of the various elements, their proportions, the quality of the masonry and even the rich, tawny color of the stone. Inside, a tortoise ambled peacefully about under the graceful arches of an arcade. From the exterior the full apse banded with two broad plain moldings seemed to grow harmoniously out of the hillside. It was as perfect in its place as Greek temples are said to be. In the end even Sir William Ramsay succumbed to the allure of the Thousand and One Churches:

"The great tradition of Byzantine architecture was preserved in this remote part of the empire to the last. It did not decay and die out gradually, it merely came to an end when the Christian Empire expired and there ceased to be any theatre for its activity. It could not survive the loss of liberty. It was the latest expression of the free Hellenic spirit." When the Turks swept over the mountain soon after 1071 they did not indulge in any massacres, and for a time Greeks and Turks lived uneasily side by side. Then in the early years of the twelfth century the Greeks began to desert the mountain. The vines and orchards that they had tended with such care for so many centuries grew wild and no more churches were built.

On the way back to Karaman, Ismail insisted that we stop for lunch—a very late lunch—at his home in the bleak little village of Uçkuyu, which lies in a valley midway between Değle and Maden Şehri. Although she could not have had much warning of our arrival, Ismail's wife had somehow managed to produce a magnificent stew of eggplant and tomatoes simmered in lamb stock, accompanied by enormous, paper-thin breads that served as edible placemats and napkins. Up to this point I had only seen Ismail in his role as Master of the Mountain, but now he revealed a surprising sweetness. A neighbor's pretty little girl, wearing a red-and-white party dress with elaborate flounces, wandered in and immediately clambered onto his lap. They conversed quietly for some time; Ismail's manner was tender and respectful. The air was thick with contented bees, and a tiny white kitten picked its way unsteadily between the dishes on the stone table. Ismail's three handsome sons greeted us shyly, but their father, being a man of advanced ideas, was proudest of his clever daughter who was away in Ankara studying literature at the university. The sons were unmarried, and when I expressed surprise I was told that this was because they could not afford the price of a marriage license. Since the sum was insignificant to a foreigner with dollars, I considered offering to pay for at least one license, but Ibrahim had already made it plain that Ismail would not accept money. In return for all this help and hospitality we were merely required to deliver a cheese to Karaman—a cheese the size of a twelve-pound bag of laundry.

THE ANGELS OF THE DOOR

Traveling south by bus from Karaman, the road climbed so gradually that I was hardly aware that we were approaching the Sertavul pass, but after a time the mountains closed in, their slopes scattered with pines and dwarf oaks. In Byzantine times this had been an important route linking the towns and forts of the plateau with the great stronghold of Seleucia and the Mediterranean coast. Once the pass was crossed, the land began to fall away steeply to the right of the road, toward the vast canyon carved out by the river Calycadnos and its tributaries. It was in the swift, cold waters of the Calycadnos that the German Emperor Frederick Barbarossa had drowned in 1190 on his way to the Holy Land. My own goal, the monastery of Alahan, was much closer at hand, but I was a little doubtful of finding it since my map showed two different Alahans, nearly forty kilometers apart. Which was the right one, and would the bus driver know the difference? Ahead of us rose a massive and deeply riven rock outcrop that leant menacingly out over the road as if it might crash down at any moment. As we drew closer I noticed that the base of the rock was honeycombed with burial chambers, and more were visible in smaller rocks below the road. We were driving through the heart of an extensive necropolis, which could only mean that the site of an important civic or religious center was close by, and only a few hundred yards farther on, by a roadside café, the sign for Alahan came into view, pointing directly up the mountainside.

The amiable Turkish writer and traveler Evliya Celebi came this way in 1672. Unaware of its history or function, he referred to Alahan as "the castle of Taykenos," and said of it: "On all four sides of the castle there are hundreds of thousands of caves in the rock in each of which there is a marble working such that not even a master stone cutter of the present day would be competent to touch his pick to it. It was given to the people of that time to enchant the rocks, so that they carved every stone as if it were the work of the wood carver Fakhri, into flowers and interlaces in the Greek fashion, so fine that a man stands stupefied in amazement at the sight of them."

The ascent to Alahan is steep, and it was a relief to find a taxi lying in wait outside the café. It must also have been the only taxi for miles around. We had driven about halfway when we saw the churches of Alahan standing atop an artificial terrace that stretched for nearly three hundred yards across a precipitous mountainside. Photographs had given me some idea of what to expect, but I was nonetheless startled to encounter so much civilized splendor in this wild and isolated place. On stepping from the cab I was immediately presented with confirmation of Evliya Celebi's words. Before me stood the Door of the Evangelists, every inch of which was richly carved. On the lintel, two seraphim in full flight supported a medallion of Christ. The archangels Michael and Gabriel, who stood guard on the doorjambs, had their feet planted on symbols of defeated paganism—a bull and, more obscurely, two women in Phrygian caps. There was nothing classical about the hieratic splendor of these angels; they were posed with rigid frontality and they were dressed in the Iranian style. Above them on the underside of the lintel were the four beasts of Ezekiel's vision.

The effect of all this on pilgrims who had made their way on foot up the mountainside from the valley below must have been overwhelming, and judging by the carved fragments that still lie scattered about, the whole of the basilica beyond the door was once as richly decorated. There were partridges perched in curling vines heavy with clusters of grapes, and sporting dolphins on whose flanks the artist had not been able to resist carving scales; there were acanthus leaves, palm trees and pomegranates. And all of this work was imbued with an irresistible joie de vivre. The contrast with late Roman sculpture could not be more complete: I thought of the sarcophagus I had seen in the Konya museum on which the labors of Hercules were depicted with such vulgar realism that they were quite as tedious to look at as they must have been to perform. The difference between the posturing body-builders of the Konya sarcophagus and the vines and dolphins of Alahan is the difference between the moribund and the newly alive.

On the south side of the basilica, on the edge of the terrace, fragments of moldings and volutes lay amid the thistles and asphodel. Beyond them the land fell away for thousands of feet to the green meanders of the Caly-cadnos, coiled like a snake in its hollow. From the basilica, a colonnade of nearly fifty columns once led to the east church. A pilgrim of the late fifth century, walking east under this colonnade, would have passed a baptistery with a fine cruciform font set in its floor, and would then have paused at a small shrine, with a central niche sheltering nearly obliterated figures carved in low relief, above it a steeply angled pediment flanked by pairs of angels and partridges. As I stood in front of this shrine I wondered what religious significance its imagery might have held for a fifth-century Christian. The angels resembled Winged Victories domesticated by the endearing proximity of the partridges; the obscure figures in the niche might as well have been nymphs or Graces. The overwhelming impression was one of sheer artistic exuberance, as if the masters of Alahan could not resist giving yet another demonstration of their superb skill.

In the east church, this exuberance was reined in to accord with the conception of a great architect whose name we do not know. It seems likely that he was a native of Isauria or Cilicia (Alahan stands on the border between the two provinces) rather than an architect sent out from the capital on the orders of the emperor, since his masterpiece is more advanced in design than anything that had been built in Constantinople up to that time. Alahan was built between 474 and 491, during the reign of the Emperor Zeno, who was himself a native of Isauria. As might be expected, he favored his native province, especially after it had offered him refuge when he was briefly driven from his throne. When he returned to Constantinople in triumph in 476, it must have occurred to Zeno or his supporters to endow Isauria with a great monument. Although the Isaurians were regarded in Constantinople as little better than barbarians, their stonemasons had such a high reputation that, in the next century, Justinian employed them in the construction of Hagia Sophia. It is well to remember this when approaching the east church at Alahan, for its sophistication is astonishing. It is also virtually intact: only the narthex and the roof are missing.

On entering through one of the three west doors it is at once apparent that the world has changed since the construction of the west basilica, even though the two churches cannot be separated by much more than fifteen years. For all its extravagant decoration, the west basilica has a very simple plan of a type that can be found everywhere from Spain to Syria, but in the east church the nave is divided into four bays by majestic horseshoe arches carried on tall columns attached to masonry piers, and the third of these bays is surmounted by a tower with squinches in the form of elegant half-domed niches. It is the complexity of this plan that necessitated sobriety in the decorative scheme, but what decoration there is is exceptionally fine: corbels are carved with rams' heads; on the capitals, birds spread their wings among the acanthus leaves; door frames are embellished with vine scrolls, cavorting dolphins and fish attacked by gulls. Delightful as these details are, nothing about the east church is merely picturesque, and it was the harmonious interrelation of all these diverse elements that most impressed me—that, and the afternoon light falling through the empty roof spaces. Here was strength without heaviness, richness without excess and, to my eyes, it all seemed to anticipate the baroque. Certainly the music of the much later ages— Palestrina perhaps, or Monteverdi, even Bach—would not have sounded out of place in such a setting.

At about the same time that work began on Alahan, the Western Roman Empire finally expired after a protracted and repetitive death agony. On 4 September 476, in Ravenna, the barbarian general Odoacer forced the abdication of the boy-emperor Romulus Augustulus. The world did not tremble, and the last emperor, whose good looks and pathetic circumstances softened the heart of the new master of Italy, was merely required to retire to Campania, where he had relatives and a comfortable villa.

For decades the Western Empire had been largely a fiction—its emperors mere puppets in the hands of Germanic warlords—and in the mountains of Isauria the event must have gone largely unnoticed, yet the abdication marked an important stage in the transformation of the late Roman empire into the Byzantine empire. Odoacer dispatched the regalia of the western emperors to Constantinople, and henceforth there would only be an emperor of the east. The builders of Alahan had no prophetic agenda, yet the transformation is made manifest in the east church. Late-Roman pomposities and early-Christian simplicities are alike abandoned. The west basilica looks back to the age of Constantine, the east church looks forward to the extraordinary flowering of new forms that would lend such luster to the age of Justinian.

Scholars cannot agree whether the tower over the nave's third bay was covered by a dome (as the squinches would lead one to expect), but even if it was not, the east church is clearly the ancestor of the domed, centrally planned church that was to appear in Constantinople early in the next century, and would continue to dominate Byzantine ecclesiastical architecture until the fall of the empire some nine hundred years later. There may even be a direct link: in the troubled years that followed the death of Zeno in 491, when work on Alahan was broken off, large numbers of Isaurians were forcibly transported to Thrace, where they would have been within easy reach of the capital. Some of the stonecarvers who worked on the Church of St. Polyeuctus and Justinian's Great Church may thus have been the pupils of the men who built Alahan. Concerning the lives of artisans at the end of the fifth century we can only speculate, but of the consummate beauty of their work at Alahan there can be no doubt at all.

ANOTHER PART
OF THE MOUNTAIN

Back at the café by the road I encountered a distinguished-looking gentleman who spoke excellent French. Did he know of another monastery called Aloda? Indeed he did. Some friends of his had come all the way from Paris to see it. It was not far away, but I would not be able to find it without assistance. There was no road, not even a track, but I need not worry, his nephew Murad would lead the way. Murad was a thin child with a severely cropped head, and although he cannot have been much more than ten years old he was already an experienced guide.

We set off through the necropolis, passing arched openings in the rock where the dead of the neighborhood had been laid to rest fifteen hundred years ago, and soon began to descend the steep, crumbling side of a ravine that eventually came to an end halfway up a sheer precipice. Murad possessed the agility of a goat. I did not, and I was wearing the wrong shoes. My every step released a small avalanche and Murad had already dispatched several snakes with deftly aimed stones, following this with dramatic pantomimes illustrating the dreadful consequences of being bitten. I began to understand why Aloda was so infrequently visited.

At the end of the ravine the cliffs opened out to form a sort of natural amphitheater pierced with monastic cells. Masonry structures huddled under overhangs in a way that reminded me of cliff-dwellings in the American southwest. Aloda is so close to Alahan that it is impossible that the two were not in some way connected. There may have been cave-dwelling anchorites on the mountain before Alahan was built, and the building of that great shrine must have attracted many more, some of whom very likely settled in the Aloda ravine. But the contrast between the two monasteries could hardly be greater: Alahan displays itself grandly on its terrace—it is not for nothing that it has been called "a Christian Delphi"—whereas Aloda is hidden from view, built *into*, not on, the mountain. It has the quality of a refuge and perhaps the monks of Alahan moved to these humbler but securer accommodations during the Persian and Arab invasions of the seventh century, for it would have taken an invader possessed of truly fanatical determination and detailed local knowledge to find them in such a place. At Aloda in the seventh and eighth centuries, under the impact of intense external and internal pressures, a new world was coming into being, one that was inward-looking, mystically inclined and distinctively medieval.

I was not given much time for reflection. Murad strode on purposefully to the edge of the precipice, turned abruptly right and vanished into a hole in the rock. Scrambling after him as best I could, I emerged onto a broad manmade ramp above a dizzying drop. Not daring to look down, I walked slowly forward, focusing my gaze on the far end of the ramp where I could see the entrance to a

large cave-church; the interior of the church did little to
dispel my acrophobia, since the south wall and part of the
floor had collapsed and presumably lay smashed in pieces
at the foot of the cliff. The few houses in the valley below
looked very small and far away: mentally I reached for a
rope and a stout alpenstock. Murad was amusing himself
by throwing rocks over the edge and waiting for the sound
of them hitting bottom. The pause was alarmingly long. It
would have been nice to sit down, but this was out of the
question, since the floor (or what remained of it) was
ankle deep in what looked like several centuries worth of
goat droppings.

By scraping at the edge of this floor with my foot I was
able to uncover patches of bluish-gray mosaic. These fragments were unimpressive in themselves but they were
extremely rare: the church at Aloda, as far as I know, is the
only Byzantine cave-church to have a mosaic floor, and
since mosaic floors went out of fashion in the seventh
century, this gives some indication of a date. This was
interesting enough, but it was when I looked up at the
ceiling that I felt my efforts had been rewarded. The
roughly carved vault was covered with abstract frescoes
consisting of a design of octagonal medallions and interlocking circles painted in red, black, ocher, green and
white, adapted directly from the traditional designs of
Anatolian textiles: the church must originally have looked
as if it were tented with silks and tapestries, rather than
hewn out of the rock. The colors of the paint were still
vivid, which made it clear that the damage that had been
done to the frescoes was not just the work of time and the
weather: untold generations of small boys and bored
goatherds had amused themselves by flinging stones at the
ceiling, bringing down irreplaceable chunks of plaster
and pigment. On one wall of the church were traces of

robed and haloed figures so savagely scraped and pitted that it was impossible to tell what scene they might once have enacted.

Shadows were lengthening in the Aloda ravine, and as I had no clear idea of how to get back to Karaman before dark it was time to leave. Traffic on the Karaman road was light. At the café we were assured that a bus would be along very soon. Half an hour passed. The shadows grew longer and the rocks of the necropolis turned to gold. Murad's uncle became visibly worried and made several attempts to flag vehicles down. At last a dust-encrusted truck ground to a halt and an ill-shaven and extremely drunk man stumbled out, grinning broadly. He shook my hand, introduced himself as Suleyman, and promptly turned aside to urinate torrentially in a ditch. Luckily it was not Suleyman who was doing the driving but his mild-mannered brother-in-law, who appeared to be relatively sober. Suleyman's eyes were bloodshot and his breath stank of raki, but he was a handsome man and the most genial of drunks. As we crawled toward the summit of the Sertavul pass he entertained us with emphatic expressions of his political views: according to Suleyman, Bush, Özal and Saddam Hussein were all equally "fools" and "idiots." This was not an uncommon view in Anatolia, and it seemed only polite to agree heartily, but fatigue soon over-came me and Suleyman's expostulations began to sound strangely distant. I remember the light gilding the bank of a small river lined with restaurants in which families had gathered, the fierce red glow above the desolation of the plateau and the quiet streets of Karaman's darkening suburbs through which we made a slow and wandering progress as Suleyman distributed bear hugs and boxes of candy to the various branches of his extended family.

HERODOTUS
AND THE FIRE DANCE

If instead of returning to Karaman I had continued south from Alahan, I would soon have reached the Cilician coast, a region I had visited on two previous occasions. Here, between the cove of Narlikuyu and the river Lamas, is a fifteen-mile stretch of coast that resembles a continuous archaeological park. Valleys are crossed by the arches of an aqueduct; hills are crowned by magnificent tombs in the form of temples, and richly carved sarcophagi lie forgotten amid the orange groves. There are at least four ruined cities, none of them more than a few miles apart, and the ancient, stone-paved roads connecting them are sometimes astonishingly well-preserved. At Korykos I stumbled upon no less than five very grand fifth- or sixth-century churches, all grouped closely together and apparently unvisited by tourists. At Kanytelis another church of very sophisticated design stood on the tip of a limestone chasm several hundred feet deep. The outline of an entire urban system is so eerily complete here, like a white and gold skeleton, that the fifth century seems only a few decades distant.

On my last visit I stayed in the ramshackle little resort of Kizkalesi, hard by the ruins of Korykos. It was October and the whole town was falling asleep like a drunk at the end of a party. Vast swarms of mosquitoes descended at dusk, and most of the buildings seemed to have been improvised in the course of an afternoon. The sidewalks (when there were sidewalks) and the staircases of the hotels were so uneven that sprained ankles were difficult to avoid, yet I liked the place immediately. It had no pretensions and seemed to want you to like it. Even the short-legged dogs that haunted the doors of restaurants were unusually sympathetic and intelligent, and all the streets led out onto a broad crescent of pale sand from which I could look east across the bay to the two castles of Korykos. One rose from an island and appeared to float on the surface of the sea, while the other (the *land* castle) was a monumental palimpsest in which the heraldic devices of the last Armenian kings were juxtaposed with beautifully precise Greek inscriptions robbed from the adjacent necropolis.

It was in Kizkalesi that I experienced one of those sudden sidesteps into the past that are among the chief enchantments of travel in Turkey. I was eating a lunch of thin breads stuffed with herbs and vegetables in an open-air café. A man in his late thirties, who seemed to be the proprietor, was playing a lute, but broke off to explain with some pride that he and his family were Turkmens, that is to say, descendants of the original nomadic tribes who had invaded Anatolia in the eleventh century. I did not set much store by this until I noticed the way his mother prepared the breads. She mixed flour and water into a paste, rolled it out, then placed it on a convex iron plate heated by a low fire. This was a technique that had been observed more than five centuries earlier by the Burgundian knight Bertrandon de la Broquière as he traveled through Anatolia on his way back from Jerusalem.

On the next day I set out late in the afternoon to explore the sand-covered promontory of the double city of Elaeusa-Sebaste. The light was fading rapidly, so I was surprised to see a man sitting on a stone at the farthest point of the promontory. He seemed lost in thought, and at first I was reluctant to disturb him, but feeling that anyone loitering on the ramparts of Elaeusa at this late hour must be a kindred spirit, I wished him good evening. He was the schoolmaster of the village of Ayas, which lay nearby nestled in among the ruins, and he spoke some English. We exchanged the usual pleasantries, then, with an almost somnambulistic gesture, he produced a Turkish edition of Herodotus from a plastic bag he was carrying. I still wonder why I was so moved by this. It was, of course, pleasing and appropriate that the Greek classics were still read on the Cilician coast, but there was something more to it than that: the apparition of the book in such a place, at such an hour seemed a gesture against oblivion. Behind us a line of tombs, catching all that was left of the light, shone like a diadem on the summit of a ridge.

The schoolmaster asked me if I was interested in history. He was consulting Herodotus for references to Cilicia. He regretted that he could not read the Greek inscriptions he passed each day, and mentioned the ruins farther off in the hills. If I ever came to Cilicia again he would be happy to show them to me. As we continued to stroll together and talk of Greeks and Romans, Byzantines and Seljuks, he suddenly asserted that I must be a historian. I denied the compliment. "No," he replied emphatically, "you *are* a historian." He had the melancholy and obstinate certitude of characters in Russian short stories. I could not refuse to share a glass of tea with him, and so returned to Kizkalesi in darkness.

My final day in Kizkalesi was a Saturday, and the town had filled up with weekenders from Mersin and Adana. As night fell, the hotels grew loud with dance parties. Families crowded into restaurants decorated with murals of tropical lagoons and giant roses. On the beach a tall bonfire had been lit and bands of youths danced around it, joined occasionally by bashful girls. Immense shifting complexes of shadows flickered over the sand. The sea was very still. Then, as the flames reached their height, the young men began to leap through the fire, sometimes singly, but more often in pairs with hands clasped. There were shouts of approval from the young people. The older people sat in a circle watching the proceedings with an air of great seriousness. It was impossible to tell whether the event was a spontaneous invention or a ritual with a history. I felt as if I was witnessing victory or funeral games outside the walls of Troy.

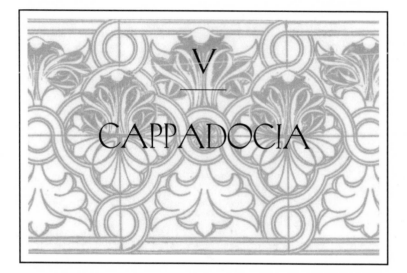

V

CAPPADOCIA

THE PLAIN OF MIRAGES

As we drove east from Karaman toward Ereğli, the Byzantine Heraclea, it occurred to me that we were once again following in the path of the First Crusade.

After their second victory over the Turks at Dorylaion, the crusaders faced a dilemma. The most direct route to Antioch and the Holy Land lay across the central Anatolian desert, but the heavy armor of the knights, the intense summer heat and the lack of water for men and horses made this impossible. On Byzantine advice they followed a much longer and more circuitous route, keeping to the western and southern edges of the plateau, but progress was not easy. Much of the Christian population had fled under pressure of constant Turkish raids, and the terrified remnant was in no position to provision a foreign army. Land had gone out of cultivation, wells were dry, cisterns and bridges had been destroyed and the old imperial roads had fallen into decay. The crusaders responded by quarreling with their Byzantine guides and advisers. The miseries of the journey were the result of more than twenty years of invasions and warfare, but the crusaders had already acquired the bad habit of holding the Byzantines responsible for all their misfortunes. The Byzantines, in turn, were deeply offended by the ingratitude and barbarous manners of the westerners.

The crusaders must at first have felt relief as they approached Heraclea, for here the plain is generously watered by snow-fed streams coming down from the Taurus, and, like its modern descendant, the Byzantine city was surrounded by lush fields and orchards, but the crusaders found their way blocked by the armies of Hasan, emir of Cappadocia, and various of his allies. Even those Byzantine authors who were most suspicious of the crusaders' intentions admired their courage: they attacked at once and the Turks abandoned the field. At the moment of victory the sky was illumined by the flight of a comet.

The plain to the north and east of Ereğli is the kind of place where one might expect to see signs, omens and visions. To the north the horizon is dominated by the outlines of the holy mountains Karaca Dağ and Hasan Dağ Gertrude Bell visited a great monastic complex on the summit of the former, while the northern slopes of Mount Hasan are littered with the ruins of churches. Its twin peaks, which rise to nearly ten thousand feet, are clearly depicted in a fresco of fantastic antiquity—it is probably the oldest landscape painting known to us—that has been recovered from the mounds of Çatalhüyük. Mount Hasan remains the presiding presence of western Cappadocia.

The road to Niğde took us very close to the foothills of Mount Hasan. Although it was by now the middle of June, the high peaks of the Taurus, which rose to the south and east, were still snow-covered. The raw hessian of the plain had been embroidered with red, yellow, purple and blue, and on every side phantom lakes shimmered into view and vanished. The air was clear and the light had the force of a proclamation: mirages in such a climate, in such a place, were only to be expected, but I was surprised to see that the surfaces of these chimerical lakes carried the inverted images of pines, where no pines were to be seen.

As we escaped from the shadow of Mount Hasan I saw another apparition rising to the north and east, some sixty miles distant. I glimpsed it only for a moment before hills obscured my view but I knew it was Mount Erciyes. Its great peak was white above blue slopes. It stood guard on the eastern limits of Cappadocia, the Land of Noble Horses, which we had now entered.

The incomparable landscape of central Cappadocia is the gift of Mounts Hasan and Erciyes. In the centuries during which they were active volcanoes, the mountains spewed out enormous amounts of ash, which solidified into the soft stone known as tufa. Wind and rain began the work of sculpture, producing in time an infinite variety of polychrome lunar forms. And it was the softness of this tufa that allowed the Byzantine inhabitants to carve out the many hundreds of churches, monasteries, homes and refuges that remain to amaze the visitor. And here, until the early years of our century, were twenty-six villages whose people still spoke a pure form of Byzantine Greek and preserved in their songs vivid memories of the exploits of emperors and *akritai*.

GABRIEL'S DIADEM

In Niğde we quickly found a cheap hotel and made a new friend—a sweet-natured young man named Orhan who was anxious to practice his English. At the center of the old town rose a high citadel rock commanding wide views of the surrounding mountains. On its summit was a handsome Seljuk mosque of the thirteenth century, with a door framed by stone lace and a sturdy minaret like a lighthouse. Fine as it was, the mosque was not my reason for stopping in the town. A few miles to the northeast, in the village of Eski Gümüş, lay one of the finest of all Cappadocia cave-monasteries. I had barely had time to mention my interest in the place before Orhan produced a friend who drove a taxi, and we set out, approaching the village along a valley full of cherry and apple orchards and shimmering stands of poplars.

Along the north side of the valley was a long and fantastically eroded rock outcrop into which Byzantine monks and villagers had carved innumerable niches and chambers. The entrance to the monastery was so unobtrusive, however, that it was easy to understand how it could have remained undiscovered by the outside world until the 1960s. Beyond a small, unadorned doorway a tunnel led through the rock into a large square courtyard with forty-five-foot high walls. Although the stone is soft, the excavation of this courtyard represents an enormous expenditure of labor.

Eski Gümüş is the only Cappadocian cave-monastery to have a fully enclosed courtyard. It is also the most southerly of them all, lying close to the Cilician Gates, the great defile that leads down through the Taurus to the Cilician plain. The two factors are related. The Cilician Gates were the preferred invasion route of Arab armies, and a monastery that was literally hidden in the rock and could only be approached through a single narrow opening had obvious defensive advantages. The average raiding party would simply have passed it by. These considerations also give some indication of the monastery's date. Until 965 part of Cilicia was in Arab hands, but in that year Emperor Nicephorus II Phocas—known as "the White Death of the Arabs," finally wrested it from their control and all raids across the Taurus ceased. It is likely that the excavation of Eski Gümüş was begun not long before that date, at a time when southern Cappadocia was still insecure but not so unsafe as to prevent the execution of an ambitious building program.

The courtyard is surrounded by chambers on several different levels, including a refectory, a kitchen (placed rather oddly above the entrance tunnel) and a series of underground chambers that were probably used for storage, but what immediately caught my attention was the high façade carved into the northern wall. Behind its blind arcade of nine narrow arches lies the church—a cross-in-square with a diminutive dome carried on disproportionately thick columns. The frescoed interior glowed with color, and even the columns were painted with simple leaf patterns. The figures in the apse were severely stylized, rigidly frontal in the Oriental manner, but those on the north wall, which were clearly the work of another hand, were imbued with a more humanist and Hellenic spirit that must have emanated from Constantinople. All the scenes on the north wall (representing, in ascending order, the Annunciation, the Nativity and the Presentation in the Temple) were remarkably well-preserved: even the faces, usually the first targets of Muslim iconophobes, remained intact. Finest of all was the figure of the Archangel Gabriel in the Annunciation.

Portrayed three-quarter view, Gabriel seems to be caught at the moment of turning away from the observer toward the Virgin Mary, who stands on the far side of a funerary niche. His right arm, clad in a full, blue-gray sleeve, is stretched out toward her in a gesture of blessing, while the folds of a long orange sash are looped over his left arm. His face is delicately drawn and bears an expression of serene tenderness; he wears a small diadem in his carefully coiffed hair. Confronted with work of such sophistication it is surprising to recall how persistently art historians have maintained that the paintings of Cappadocia are essentially crude and provincial—picturesque and touching in their way, but having little bearing on the Byzantine mainstream. The painter of the north wall at Eski Gümüş was obviously aware of the styles that were in favor in the capital, and, to my eyes, his Gabriel seems quite close to undisputed masterpieces painted more than two centuries later by the great Sienese master Duccio. No doubt some Cappadocian painters were ignorant monks whose fervent piety hardly compensated for their rudimentary skills, but the best of them do not require our condescension.

As we left Eski Gümüş, our driver insisted that there was another site nearby which we should not miss. It was a Roman bath, he insisted, known locally as Cleopatra's Bath. I knew nothing of this and nor did my guidebooks, but since my encounters with Vedat in Afyon and Ibrahim in Karaman I had learned to trust Turkish cab drivers. We drove south toward the high white peaks of the Taurus, and turning to the right, close to the charming little town of Bor, found ourselves in a shady oasis crowded with picnicking families. The scent of grilling meats and peppers filled the air and at the center of the oasis was the famous bath. This was a perfectly regular oblong pool and its framing masonry did indeed appear to be Roman work. It looked too big to have been merely a bath—even a bath built for an Egyptian queen—and there were no steps leading down to it: bathers would have been obliged to drop five feet from the brink and would then have had great difficulty getting out, which did not seem the Roman style. I thought it much more likely that it had been a sacred pool, associated in some way with the ancient city of Tyana, which once lay close by.

Whatever its function may once have been, the pool is still treated with great respect by the local people, who take care to preserve its idyllic quality: litter was noticeable only by its absence, and this despite the large numbers of people eating and drinking under the trees. But perhaps it is only in regions where they are scarce that one appreciates the blessings that the conjuncture of trees and pure water can confer. Ancient willows, filtering the intense afternoon sunlight, trailed their branches in the pool; its floor was carpeted with brilliant green moss above which a school of trout moved about in constantly shifting formations as quietly excited children fed them chunks of bread.

EVENING, BAD EVENING

In his account of the career of the Emperor Nicephorus II Phocas, the historian Leo the Deacon indulges in an unusual digression—unusual in the sense that Byzantine historians rarely lower their gaze to consider the living conditions of ordinary people. He remarks that the Cappadocians were sometimes called troglodytes because "they went underground in holes, clefts and labyrinths, as it were in dens and burrows." Apparent evidence of this strange habit is to be found under the bleak plain that lies to the north of Niğde.

Under the villages of Derinkuyu and Kaymakli are vast labyrinths of chambers linked by narrow corridors, ramps and twisting staircases that go down into the rock for as many as twenty stories. They are ventilated by air shafts over two hundred feet deep and are said to be linked by a broad subterranean road some nine kilometers long. They are popularly known as "underground cities," and it is calculated that the "city" at Derinkuyu could have held as many as twenty thousand people. They are remarkable engineering feats and have naturally attracted the curiosity of the world, but there is something appalling about them. I have only made the descent into Derinkuyu once and would not willingly do so again. By the time I reached the eighth level (the lowest level cleared so far) I had concluded that the "cities" were misnamed: villages cut into rock faces, in which all the dwellings had some access to sunlight, are one thing, but it is inconceivable that people—even people living in a violently contested border zone—could have lived in the cramped, lightless chambers of this dismal warren on a permanent basis. If they had done so they would have gone mad.

The endless sequence of rooms and passageways was so roughly carved that if you stumbled the skin was stripped from your hands and knees. There was no decoration, and, most tellingly, there were no graffiti: if, as tourist legend maintains, thousands of people huddled in these depths for years at a time while Arab armies passed overhead, they would surely have scratched their curses and prayers for deliverance into the rock. They did not do so, and the "cities" are more likely to have been temporary refuges for the people of the surrounding villages and their livestock during periods of extreme disturbance. They were the Byzantine equivalent of air-raid shelters. They bear witness to the sufferings of the Christian population of Cappadocia from the beginning of the seventh century until the mid-ninth century, when the armies of the caliphs and their agents ranged freely across Anatolia. In Byzantine chronicles we read constantly of forts and towns destroyed, of raiding parties returning to Arab territory ladened with booty, and yet the Cappadocians dug into the earth and the hills and refused to be ejected from their homeland. In their folk songs, they celebrated the warriors who defended them and lamented the fate of their women.

Some of these folk songs have survived the nine centuries that have intervened. They present a very grim picture of life during those dark times. In one of them an *akritas* builds a castle: he builds it double and triple and its doors have iron nails to keep out Death, but when he turns around he finds that Death is standing next to him within the walls. His wife tries to bargain with Death, offering him her five children in her husband's stead, but Death is a merciless angel and decides to take the husband, pausing only to inform the wife that she will be plunged into the pit of hell if she does not exercise the virtue of charity. A more complex narrative song tells of Little Constantine (the hero of many of these ballads), who marries in May and plants a vine to celebrate his marriage, but is soon called away to the wars. Once he is gone, his demonic mother and sister (who are clearly descendants of Clytemnestra and Medea) shave his wife's head and exile her to a remote place with only sheep and goats for company. When Constantine returns he asks: "Mother, O Mother, where is your daughter-in-law, where is my beloved wife?" and his mother replies: "My daughter-in-law has been dead these twelve years." There are different versions of this ballad. According to one, Constantine announces that he will bring his dead wife home and asks his mother how she should be punished, and she replies: "If you would bring her home, cut off my head." And Constantine obliges. In what may be the most chilling of these songs the young wife or beloved goes out to search for her Yannakos and finds his limbs scattered about the mountainside: "They cut his arms to their junctions. They cut him off at the knees. Evening, bad evening, and the sun sank down."

THE WHITE PATH

To the north and east of Derinkuyu the landscape grows ever more intricately pleated and folded, streaked with intense shades of pink and white and yellow. Between the folds of the rock lie narrow, fertile valleys where melons, squash, apples and vines are grown. The Cappadocian apples are firm and sweet and colored a brilliant Chinese lacquer red, the Cappadocian wines are light and fragrant and were praised by Rumi. The steep sides of these valleys are honeycombed with the small openings of pigeon houses, and the shadows of the birds flicker constantly over the fields. As they have done for centuries, farmers collect the pigeon droppings and use them to fertilize the ground: this apparently accounts for the excellence of the apples and the wine.

As you drive farther east toward Ürgüp there are valleys so tightly packed with pinnacles that agriculture is impossible. It is these pinnacles or cones that have made the Cappadocian landscape famous and driven observers into analogical frenzies: the pinnacles are said to be like obelisks or columns, like minarets or church spires, like witches' hats, chimneys, nomad tents or swords. What is not so often remarked is that a good number of them are grossly phallic, complete with realistic retracted foreskins and ponderous testicles. In this vast natural sculpture park—by turns majestic and ribald, graceful and grotesque—the traveler wanders in a state of perpetual astonishment, but the full beauty of the landscape is difficult to convey and where words fail photography rarely succeeds. Seen in isolation, the rock formations can appear merely outlandish. They must be seen in their context, surrounded on all sides by the blindingly clear distances of the Anatolian plateau. Just before the road curves south into Ürgüp, for example, there are three tall, thin pinnacles, each capped by a stone tilted at a rakish angle. The initial impression is one of gingerbread quaintness until you notice, far to the east, the great peak of Mount Erciyes hovering just above the horizon like a ghost.

Ürgüp is a town of pleasant, tree-lined streets lying at the foot of high ocher rocks that conceal monastic complexes and many-chambered refuges (smaller versions of the "underground cities"). In Byzantine times it was known as Hagios Prokopios, and was the seat of a bishop; today it is Cappadocia's main tourist center, complete with carpet stores and travel agencies offering bus tours, but this development, which has helped to give the town an agreeably prosperous air, has had absolutely no effect on the natural friendliness and good manners of its inhabitants. It was a particular pleasure to arrive in a place where, for once, I knew exactly where to go—west from the town center into the old Greek quarter, where the Hotel Elvan is to be found at the top of a steep, cobbled street. I retained fond memories of the Hotel Elvan from my travels of the previous year, and was delighted to see its vine-shaded forecourt and to hear once again the high, birdlike laughter of Fatma Bilir, who, together with her more retiring husband, Ahmet, is the proprietor of the hotel. They are charming people and although neither speaks a word of English this will not prevent the ebullient Mrs. Bilir from engaging you in animated conversation— conversation that is invariably punctuated by fluttering roulades of laughter.

The street that leads to the Hotel Elvan continues to climb along the northern slope of a ridge. It is flanked by fine nineteenth-century Greek houses, some of them so large they deserve to be called mansions. Gardens and courtyards lie hidden behind doorways surmounted by gracefully undulating moldings. The color of the stone varies from white to pale saffron. Streets pass under houses and emerge into cobbled squares with fountains. Carts of antique design are parked in alleyways. Many of the larger houses have elegant two-story loggias with arcades consisting of high rounded arches carried on very slender columns. These loggias intrigued me: they did not look very Turkish, but nor was there any sign of Western European influence—no baroque heaviness or neoclassical rigidity. In fact they looked distinctly Byzantine, resembling to a remarkable degree the so-called portico façades of certain twelfth- and thirteenth-century churches and palaces (notably those of Sancta Sophia in Ohrid and the Tekfursaray in Istanbul); and yet most of these houses must have been constructed more than seven centuries after the Turkish conquest. We know that the Greeks of Cappadocia clung tenaciously to their language and religion, but can they really have remained so faithful to the traditions of Byzantine aristocratic secular architecture over this vast period? Perhaps the loggias of Ürgüp were part of a self-conscious "Byzantine revival" inspired by the successes of Greek nationalism and made possible by the new wealth of the Cappadocian Greek communities in the nineteenth century.

On the afternoon of our arrival we followed this street of noble houses until it led us out onto the western edge of town, where there was a shattered pinnacle that had once contained a church. Most of this church had fallen away, but a niche remained containing a red line-drawing, in which an acephalous central figure extended its hands in blessing toward two smaller figures, who were, perhaps, the donors of the church. Below us to the south lay an orchard-filled valley and more mansions fronted by over-grown gardens. On its far side we could see a path climbing aslant a steep white slope, a path that took us past several troglodytic dwellings that appeared outwardly as a series of crude windows and doorways carved from the rock face, like a child's paper cutout. We met two hand-some, dark-haired young women carrying babies, who asked us if we would photograph them. They were sisters and the elder of the two was the mother of both children; she did not look much more than eighteen and was obvi-ously proud of her fertility; she lived in a landscape that suggested fertility on all sides.

The white path narrowed to a deep groove worn down by the thousands of Cappadocians who, over the centuries, had gone out to work in the fields or made their way to the neighboring village of Ortahisar. The rock resembled snowdrifts or heaps of sugar. Sometimes the white was tinged with pink so that it approximated a flesh tone; below us on either side were softly molded forms like the breasts and hips of sleeping women. Other forms resem-bled petrified waves or heaps of crumpled drapery. The path emerged eventually onto the surface of the plateau, where it seemed to lose its sense of purpose, petering out amid an upthrust of pinnacles in which determined anchorites had carved out their cells. In the mid-distance the fortress rock of Ortahisar rose above the plateau.

We returned the way we had come, but then took a different route, passing to the south of the original ridge that we had followed, and found ourselves in a grove of poplars below cave-houses painted blue and yellow. At the point where a stream bubbled up out of the earth on the southeastern edge of the town, we crossed into a large sloping field, covered with long grass and scattered with tombstones so long neglected they could have been boulders. I thought at first that this was a Muslim cemetery, until I noticed that the gravestones took the form of crosses. Until 1923 this had been Ürgüp's Christian cemetery; now it lay overgrown and abandoned, bounded by a line of poplars and the sky.

A cemetery implies a church, but I could find no trace of one in Ürgüp. This puzzled me, since substantial nineteenth-century churches had survived in neighboring towns and villages, and Ürgüp had been the center for the veneration of Saint John Roussos, whose efficacy as a healer and miracle worker was acknowledged by Christians and Muslims alike. During an outbreak of cholera in 1908, for example, the Muslims of Ürgüp begged their Christian neighbors to parade the saint's body through their quarter and women showered their best kerchiefs on the coffin as offerings. I made discreet enquiries. The people of Ürgüp showed no hostility to the memory of the Greeks, and I was led by a friendly waiter to a store selling refrigerators and microwaves. Its proprietor showed me dim framed photographs of a massive baroque church with a high dome and an ornate belfry. It had been demolished to make room for a girls' school. There was little cause for regret, since the church had been cumbersome and ugly, and after 1923 it was of no use to anyone. In that year, as a result of events in which they played no part and decisions in which they had no voice, the Greeks of Cappadocia were forced to abandon their beautiful homes, but they were not persecuted by the Turks of the district, who had never regarded them as enemies, and made their way north to the Black Sea ports, where ships were waiting to take them to Greece. They were among the last of the Anatolian Greeks to leave.

A SHORT HISTORY OF PASTRAMI
And Other Secrets of the Byzantine Table

In Cappadocia one often has the impression that there has been a fold in time—that the Byzantine Empire came to an end in 1953, not 1453, so immediate is its presence. And one need not tour a dozen painted churches in a day to succumb to this agreeable disorientation. All you have to do is visit a restaurant: much of what you will eat there would be familiar to a Byzantine of the tenth century or earlier.

The exact degree of Byzantine influence on Turkish cuisine is difficult to assess, since Islamic cuisine had already absorbed much from Byzantine Syria and Egypt when those great provinces were conquered by the Arabs in the seventh century, but directly and indirectly modern Turkey's culinary debt to Byzantium is profound. The first Turks to arrive in Anatolia were nomads, who subsisted on a severely limited diet that bears very little relation to the variety and richness of later Turkish cuisine. This is also so markedly superior to Greek cookery that it must have been in Istanbul and Anatolia, rather than Greece, that the best Byzantine traditions were preserved.

Such Turkish staples as kebabs, stuffed vine leaves and stuffed vegetables were Byzantine staples. Börek, halva and baklava are well-attested in Byzantine and classical texts. The arts of baking and viniculture were also unknown to the Turks when they arrived in Anatolia and the latter remained a Christian prerogative at least as late as the sixteenth century. The food of the ordinary people of Byzantium was very similar to that of today's Anatolian peasantry—bread, beans, lentils, olives and olive oil, vegetables, fruit and dairy products. Fish and meat were (and are) rarely eaten, but fruit and vegetables were many and varied, including apples, pears, grapes, figs, melons, cabbage, leeks, cucumbers, carrots, garlic, onions and zucchini. It would be difficult to think of a healthier diet, and while the tables of aristocrats groaned with caviar, sturgeon and wild game, their diet was also well-balanced and red meat was sparingly used. Lamb was preferred to beef, as it still is, and "beef-eating" was a term of abuse often applied to westerners.

The Byzantines did, however, have a great taste for a form of cured beef they called *paston* and the Turks called *pastirma;* it remains a Cappadocian specialty, associated particularly with the city of Kayseri. Its name will sound strangely familiar to New Yorkers, and pastirma looks and tastes very like pastrami. In fact the word *pastrami* derives from the Turkish via Romanian and Yiddish. Having inherited pastirma from the Byzantines, the Turks took it with them when they conquered Hungary and Romania, where it became a specialty of the Jewish communities; they would later bring it to America: thus the great staple of New York's Jewish delicatessens turns out to be a legacy of Byzantium.

Other elements of Byzantine cuisine reached the West more directly. From the sixth century to the eleventh, southern Italy was a Byzantine province, and from the late eleventh until the fall of the empire there was close contact between Byzantium and the Italian maritime republics. In the late fourteenth century, Byzantine scholars began to abandon the dying empire and settle in Italy, especially in Florence, where their knowledge of Plato and platonism was highly prized. It was in Florence that George Gemistus Plethon, the last significant Byzantine philosopher, enjoyed his greatest public success. There were numerous sophisticated gastronomes among these émigrés; and their arrival gave a powerful impetus to the efflorescence of Florentine cuisine that began about this time. Giuliano Bugialli in *The Fine Art of Italian Cooking* even seems to imply that the practice of dressing salads with oil and vinegar was introduced from Byzantium, and caviar is referred to in fifteenth-century Florentine texts as a food of which the Greeks were especially fond. In a sense Byzantine influence on Italian cookery was a form of restitution, for it was in Constantinople rather than strife-torn Italy that Roman traditions of high gastronomy best survived.

It is also probable that Byzantium gave the Italians lessons in table manners. The aristocrats of Constantinople were the first people of medieval Europe to use clean table linen and forks—refinements that the scandalized crusaders considered sure signs of moral degeneracy. Accounts of upper-class dinner parties of the twelfth century reveal a "polite society" far in advance of anything in the West. Dining rooms were decorated with mosaics and frescoes (often of a mildly erotic nature), with ceramic tiles, carpets and stucco sculpture. In addition, some would have contained display cases for the host's collection of objets d'art. The Roman habit of reclining on couches had been abandoned during the course of the tenth century, and the guests, who might be as many as forty in number, were seated around circular or rectangular tables that were variously inlaid with marble, gold, silver and ivory. Such parties were scenes for gossip and intrigue (against which Byzantine moralists issued stern warnings), but they were also occasions for the serious discussion of literature, philosophy and scripture, and the performance of new literary and musical works. These elegant symposia harked back consciously to Hellenistic Alexandria, yet at the same time they seem to anticipate the salons of eighteenth-century Paris. But it is the imperial banquets that took place in the Great Palace that haunt the imagination by their magnificence and strangeness.

During the reign of Constantine VII Porphyrogenitus, the western envoy Liutprand (soon to be bishop of Cremona) attended a Christmas banquet in one of the great *triklinoi* or banqueting halls of the palace. Here he found "The Emperor surrounded, in imitation of his heavenly prototype, by twelve companions, while the rest of the company, to the number of 216, was disposed in parties of twelve at the remaining eighteen tables. The plate was of gold and the weight of the three gold vases of dessert necessitated their arrival on three scarlet-upholstered chariots, whence they were hoisted to the table by ropes descending from a ceiling of gold foliage, and wound on to a revolving machine. . . . The meal was followed by a display of acrobatics, in which two boys ascended a pole twenty-four-feet high, balanced on a man's head."

At the conclusion of this performance Liutprand was so obviously bewildered that the emperor, having some mild fun at his expense, dispatched an interpreter to ask him which he thought the more wonderful, the boy acrobats or the man who had balanced the pole. Liutprand, who was not often short of an opinion, replied rather lamely that he did not know. At this the emperor "gave a loud laugh and said that he was in the same difficulty: he did not know either." The response is typical of Constantine VII. Although Gibbon finds him guilty of "intemperance and sloth," he was one of the most amiable and artistically gifted of all the emperors. He was also the author of *The Book of Ceremonies*, the definitive account of the rituals of the Byzantine court, so it is only to be expected that he would have taken pains to ensure that his Christmas dinner was as splendid and entertaining as possible. Liutprand praised some of the dishes, but, like a first-time British tourist in Greece, found others too drenched in olive oil and garlic, and he was revolted by the Byzantine retsina.

The Book of Ceremonies contains a description of a banquet which reveals that the one attended by Liutprand was a relatively unbuttoned affair. The banquet celebrating the name day of an emperor or an empress, of which Constantine tells, is more in the nature of a choral ballet than a mere dinner. The smallest gestures are choreographed and the fact that the meaning of some of the terms used (*phengia*, for example) are unknown only adds to the otherworldly aura of the passage:

> After the roasts have been served the *artoclines* go out and introduce those who should perform in the dance, namely the Domestic of the Schools and that of the Numeri, the

Demarch of the Blues and his party, the tribunes and the vicars. When these have entered within the doorway they acclaim the sovereigns, wishing them many years; and the Domestic of the Schools presents in his right hand the book of permission. The prefect of the table steps down and takes it, and gives it to the chamberlain in charge of the water. The members of the party chant an *apelatikon* in the first mode. . . . The prefect of the table then turns and stretches out his right hand, opens his fingers in the form of rays and closes them again to form a bunch; and the Domestic of the Schools begins to dance with the Domestic of the Numeri, the Demarch, the tribunes, the vicars and the demotes, turning three times around the table. You must know that the tribunes and the vicars wear a blue and white garment with short sleeves and gold bands and rings on their ankles. In their hands they hold what are called *phengia*. After having danced three times, all go down and stand at the foot of the sovereigns' table. Then the singers sing: "Lord, strengthen the Empire forever," and the people sing three times: "Lord, strengthen the Empire forever."

This entire procedure was then repeated with some changes of cast and costume, and foreign guests, unaccustomed to such things, must have despaired of ever getting to dessert. These ceremonies have often been cited as symptoms of the empire's decadence and rigidity, but Byzantium is unimaginable without them: by means of them the life of the court mimicked the imagined rituals of the heavenly kingdom. In Byzantine iconography even archangels are depicted as courtiers. In *The Book of Ceremonies* Constantine goes so far as to compare his own efforts to ensure that the ceremonies should be properly performed to the exertions of the Creator in bringing order to the world: "To neglect ceremony and to sentence it as it were to death," Constantine warned, "is to be left with a view of empire devoid of ornament and deprived of beauty."

THE DEAF-MUTE GUIDE

It was in the garden of the Hotel Asia Minor, while dining to the accompaniment of Vivaldi's *Four Seasons*, that we met the melodiously named Enrica La Viola Brunella, a strikingly good-looking Sicilian blonde who explained her very un-Mediterranean coloring by declaring: "I am a Norman! I am a Viking!" She was referring, of course, to Sicily's twelfth-century heyday, when the island was ruled by a line of Norman kings—men of exemplary tolerance and artistic tastes who imported Byzantine mosaicists to decorate their churches and palaces. Enrica had all the energy and determination one might expect to find in a Norman princess. She was also a person of genuine kindness and generosity, who loved all things Cappadocian. The phrases most often on her lips were, "I likèd it. It was very nice," and "I likèd it. It was so *beautiful*," the last word being enunciated with a florid upward swoop. She had bought an old house in Ortahisar and had ambitions for the town. Marvelous as it was, Cappadocia lacked opera, and Enrica was of the opinion that Ortahisar, with its great fortress rock, would be the perfect place to mount a production of *Aïda*. On hearing this, Haydar Hakir, the infinitely obliging Kurdish manager of the Hotel Asia Minor, hurried off to replace Vivaldi with a tape of Pavarotti. Before the evening was over Enrica had arranged for us to accompany herself and her Turkish lover Ertul (a portly but handsome man with the air of a faintly disgruntled sultan) on a walk from the village of Ibrahimpasha to Ortahisar on the following morning.

The walk began with a descent into a narrow ravine along which flowed a shallow but very clear stream. The walls of the ravine were almost white, and hollowed out with many pigeon houses. After about half a mile it became apparent that these walls were narrowing to a point; this puzzled me, since the stream was flowing in the same direction we were walking. Where would it go? The solution to this mystery was soon made dramatically clear: at the "vanishing point" of the ravine the stream made a sharp turn to the left and entered a precisely cut tunnel that was broad enough to have also accommodated a road. After perhaps a hundred yards we emerged into daylight, but soon entered another tunnel and then another. In Cappadocia one becomes almost used to the experience of walking through mountains, but this was something remarkable: a stream had been diverted through a series of narrow ridges to the fields where its waters were needed, and at the same time the villages of Ibrahimpasha and Ortahisar were provided with a secret means of communication.

In Ortahisar, on Enrica's advice, we hired the services of a child named Ercan. He was about nine years old, blond-haired and blue-eyed, thin and gawky, with protruding upper teeth and a radiant smile. He was completely deaf, but since he could produce sounds, only mute in the sense that he had never heard language and therefore did not know how to shape words. When I remarked that he was obviously intelligent and with the proper teaching could learn to speak in some fashion, the response was, "Yes, he is a clever boy, but his parents are poor and God has not been kind to him." Ercan did not seem too weighed down by God's unkindness. He was generally recognized as the best guide in the village, and he led us on a breakneck tour of painted churches hidden away in nearby valleys. In one of these was a charming Annunciation in which the angel had the air of a neighborhood gossip, leaning forward overeagerly to impart his information, but I was almost more interested in Ercan than I was in the churches he showed us. How had he come by that head of pale hair and those eyes?

The Cappadocians are the handsomest people of Anatolia. They are also among the most racially mixed and thus provide an excellent argument in favor of miscegenation. Few of them show much sign of Central Asiatic origins and this should not surprise us: when they conquered Cappadocia in the eleventh century the Turks were in the minority and remained so for many generations. The process of intermarriage with the Byzantine population began at once, at all levels of society, and this Byzantine population already had an extremely hybrid complexion.

When we talk of the Greeks of Cappadocia we are not talking about a people descended from the Greeks of the time of Sophocles. Up until the seventh century the population of Central Anatolia was made up of a mixture of Phrygian, Hittite, Gallic, Iranian and Semitic peoples, all of whom were more or less Hellenized, but the epidemics and invasions of that terrible century brought widespread depopulation. To make up for this the Emperors Justinian

II and Constantine V transported Slav settlers by the hundreds of thousands from Europe into Asia. In the mid-eleventh century, large numbers of Armenians, including members of the royal families, were resettled in eastern Cappadocia. By this time there were also significant numbers of Persians, Syrians, Kurds, Arabs, contingents of Patzinaks and Cumans (Turkic tribes from the steppes of south Russia), and the principal cities had small colonies of Jews. During the tenth century the ethnic composition of the imperial family itself was of a bewildering complexity: the Emperor Romanus II, for example, was Armenian on his mother's side and a mixture of Armenian, Slav, Greek and Scandinavian on his father's.

In sum, being Byzantine was entirely a matter of language, culture and religion. Barbarians were people who did not speak Greek and did not accept the tenets of the Orthodox Church or the emperor's claim to universal rule, and Byzantine snobbery, which could express itself in savage contempt for the manners and speech of foreigners, should not be confused with racial prejudice in the modern sense. Theirs was an ecumenical empire. Inter-marriage between the different ethnic groups was more the rule than the exception and was, on occasion, actively encouraged by the emperors: even Digenis Akritas, the hero of the great popular epic celebrating the exploits of the Byzantine border barons, was the son of a Greek noblewoman and an Arab emir. It is the persistence of this sturdy and resilient Byzantine hybrid that accounts for the startling occurrence of pale gray, blue and green eyes, of blond and red hair among the present inhabitants of Cappadocia.

THE BLUE OF HEAVEN

A short distance along the road that leads out of Ortahisar we came upon a sign pointing to the Hallaç Manastir, the Hospital Monastery. The track curved gently down into a broad valley that was already beginning to fill with shadow. On its far side rose a massive rock-formation into which a series of façades had been carved, and as we drew closer we saw that parts of these façades had been painted. The great, three-sided courtyard of the monastery was overgrown with grass and the remnants of vegetable plots. The original façades with their elaborate blind arcades had been much altered and eroded over the centuries. After the monastery was abandoned, its chambers were reused as pigeon houses, and this accounted for the strange, rectangular niches (breaking the lines of the horseshoe arches) perforated with rows of small openings and decorated with bright red and green kilim patterns designed to attract the birds.

The courtyard was completely silent, sheltered from any breeze that might have troubled the grass, and the doors leading into the chambers that surrounded it were barred with iron gates. To the west was a square chamber covered by a half-collapsed dome supported on four stout white columns. In a corner was a curious carving of a leaping human figure wearing a tunic and a pointed hat. To the north was a large barrel-vaulted hall with arcades carried on square piers. To the east lay the church, off which a funerary chapel opened to the south. The church was a cross-in-square, but an unusually lofty one, with very slender piers and exotic carvings of rams' heads on the capitals of the pilasters. There were no frescoes, apart from a brownish Virgin and Child in the apse, but arches and capitals were decorated with simple geometric designs executed in dark-red paint. It is thought the whole complex was completed during the 1060s and abandoned little more than ten years later. As we moved into the darkening center of the church through an aperture recently hacked out of its south wall, many hundreds of tiny moths fluttered up, filling the air like pale dust.

Although it lies only a few hundred yards from the main road from Ürgüp to Göreme and is one of the most architecturally interesting of all the Cappadocian monasteries, the Hallaç monastery seems to be forgotten by the world. The vast majority of visitors are so anxious to reach the overpraised and overcrowded Göreme valley that they cannot be bothered to turn aside. The approach to Göreme is dramatic enough: the road suddenly twists downward and to the left through a cluster of pinnacles, and the archaeological park opens before you—more pinnacles and cliff faces hollowed out with churches, chapels and monastic chambers—but on the three occasions on which I have visited Göreme my overmastering emotion has been frustration. In 1990 and 1991, for example, the Dark Church (Karanlik Kilise), which has some of the best paintings, was closed for restoration, and one does not have to be a snob to find the numbers of people at Göreme a real problem. Most of the churches are extremely small and if two or more coach tours have just arrived you may have to wait for upward of twenty minutes before there is room for you. The lovely Apple Church (Elmali Kilise) is particularly problematic. It can only be entered from a small, fully enclosed courtyard, which in turn can only be entered by a very narrow passageway. (It feels as if you are entering an Egyptian tomb rather than a Byzantine church.) There is no way of seeing its frescoes without being packed in with thirty or forty other people. There is also the question of what all these sweating and exhaling bodies will do to the paintings, which have been preserved because of the exceptional dryness and purity of Cappadocia's air. A Lascaux syndrome may soon occur at Göreme and more of the churches may have to be closed for "restoration" for years at a time. Small, decorated churches intended for the use of a few monks cannot withstand the twentieth-century industrialization of travel.

I have derived more pleasure from the churches concealed in the hills and valleys outside the perimeter of the park—the aptly named Hidden Church (Sakli Kilise) for example, which is unique in having frescoes that depict the Cappadocian landscape, or the Church of El Nazar, carved out of a towering white cone and painted with angular figures that exude an intensity reminiscent of Coptic art. But everything in or around Göreme pales in comparison to the Tokali Kilise (the Church of the Buckle) which lies directly by the road, very close to the entrance of the park.

Behind its unimpressive façade lies one of the greatest surviving masterpieces of Byzantine art—frescoes painted in the mid-tenth century by a certain Nicephorus. The

walls and vaults of the church's spacious transverse nave
are covered with figures that seem to float in the measures
of a courtly dance against a deep blue ground. This perva-
sive, violet-tinged blue is astonishing; made from crushed
azurite, it is so intense as to appear nearly luminous. The
figures are tall and graceful, their gestures are deeply
expressive and all are clothed in classical robes of white or
light brown. The painter Nicephorus was obviously very
proud of his skill with drapery, and he paints it like a
virtuoso, in complex pleats, folds and billows that clearly
allude to Hellenistic prototypes. The architectural backdrops and landscape elements (trees and jagged rocks) are
equally classical and there is a touching humanism about
the baptism scene: Christ stands in unembarrassed nudity
and the blue ripples of the water are depicted naturalisti-
cally.

The compositions of the provincial Cappadocian school
tend to be stiff and crowded, but the frescoes of the Tokali
Kilise leave an overwhelming impression of grace and
amplitude. Here one breathes the air of the Macedonian
Renaissance. This was not, of course, a renaissance in the
Italian sense—it did not result in a new conception of man
and his place in the universe—but, beginning in the mid-
ninth century, Byzantium was the scene of a great rebirth
of interest in the art of the classical past. The artists of
Constantinople did not have to look far for models: until
1204 the streets and squares of the city were stocked with
the greatest works of Greek and Roman sculptors, and
wealthy individuals kept private collections of antiques.
The fact that classical art was pagan in subject matter does
not seem to have been an issue of much concern to the
citizens of Byzantium: it was sufficient that the art was
beautiful. A society steeped in knowledge of Homer and
Euripides saw no reason to take exception to images of

Apollo or Helen. The results can be startling. In illuminated manuscripts biblical figures are juxtaposed with
personifications of night and dawn, rivers and seasons
copied directly from Hellenistic originals: Night has a blue
shawl billowing above her head and carries a blue torch;
King David appears in the guise of Orpheus; Saint Matthew
imitates the pose of a second-century statue of Epicurus,
and a red glass bowl, now in the treasury of San Marco, is
adorned with naked youths skillfully copied from a Greek
vase. But the peculiar flavor of this medieval neoclassicism
is best illustrated by a passage from the tenth-century text
known as the *Philopatris*. Although this passage describes a
visit to a monastery, hardly a sentence goes by without a
classical allusion:

> An old man with the grim look of a Titan plucked me by
> the sleeve and said he had been initiated . . . into all the
> mysteries, so we went through iron gates and over floors of
> bronze and climbing round and round the many steps of a
> staircase we came to a house with a roof of gold like the
> house of Menelaus that Homer described. I gazed at
> everything much as did the young man from the island
> (Telemachus from Ithaca). But I did not see Helen; I saw
> only some stooping and pallid-faced men. When they
> caught sight of us they rejoiced and came to meet us asking:
> Did we bring bad news? By their looks they seemed as if
> they hoped for the worst and took pleasure in misfortune
> like the Furies on the stage.

A PLACE IN THE COUNTRY

An inscription in the Tokali Kilise names the donors of the church as a certain Constantine and his son Leo. No family name is given, but they were evidently men of wealth and sophisticated tastes who owned estates nearby. It is likely that they were related in some way to one of the intricately intermarried families of Anatolia—the Phocades perhaps, or the Maleinoi.

A hereditary aristocracy was slow to develop in Byzantium. The names of noble families do not appear in the histories until the ninth century. Traditionally, it was education rather than birth that was the key to advancement, and there was considerable upward mobility. Nevertheless, by the time the Tokali frescoes were painted aristocratic clans were firmly entrenched in Anatolia. Their estates were expanding at the expense of the freeholdings of the peasantry, and they took on increasingly independent airs. According to an Arab chronicler the estates of the Maleinos family extended for over a hundred miles from end to end. Although it would be premature to speak of feudalism in the western sense (even the most illustrious noble was still, in theory, an imperial functionary who could be dismissed, dispossessed or exiled at any moment), they presented an obvious threat to the authority of the central government, which repeatedly issued edicts that were supposed to protect the poor (i.e., the free peasants) but were, in reality, chiefly aimed at curbing the power and acquisitiveness of the landed aristocracy. For all that, there can be no denying the talents of the Anatolians or the glory they brought to the empire. Over a period of two centuries this small group of families produced men of tremendous energy and courage, and the greatest of them all were the Phocades, who possessed more military genius, generation after generation, than any other family in Byzantine history. When he was crowned emperor in 963, Nicephorus II Phocas must have thought it no more than just reward for the conquest of Crete, Cyprus, Cilicia and Aleppo. The conquests of Tarsus and Antioch soon followed, and Nicephorus' nephew and successor, John Tzimiskes, was to bring his armies almost within sight of Jerusalem.

The epic of Digenis Akritas gives full expression to the heroic ideals of the Anatolian nobles and of the Comnenian emperors who were their true descendants. He was a soldier, a hunter and a lover, and his appearance was magnificent: "His hair was blond and curly; his eyebrows contrastingly black; his complexion ruddy; and his chest broad and white as crystal. He was clothed in a red tunic, embroidered with pearls and fastened with golden buttons. Round his neck hung a collar of amber and pearls. His boots were embroidered with gold, his spurs inset with stones. Holding a green Arab lance written over with golden characters, he sat a white horse, bridled in enamelled gold, upon a saddle-cloth of green and rose. The mane of his horse was powdered with turquoises . . ."

Digenis began his career as a child by slaying wild beasts and soon moved on to brigands, monsters and Arab armies. He also found time to elope with a high-born wife (of the Ducas family), who was his cousin, and have affairs with an abandoned Arab princess and an Amazon queen, whom he had defeated in battle. This picaresque farrago is lent some air of reality by the appearance of historical figures, including Nicephorus Phocas, who came to visit the hero and was rewarded with a platitudinous lecture on the duties of an emperor. Eventually Digenis retired to his palace on the Euphrates with his beloved wife Eudokia (who apparently remained faithful to him in spite of his infidelity), and she sang to him while dancing on a silk carpet as he accompanied her on a lute. Then, at the age of thirty-three, he died.

The epic contains an elaborate description of Digenis' palace, which, while fanciful in many respects, is one of the few insights into the living conditions of the Anatolian magnates offered by Byzantine literature. The palace was surrounded by gardens filled with songbirds and at its center was a three-story ashlar structure containing a cruciform hall with vaults that gleamed with gold. This was flanked by two banqueting halls, and at the center of the courtyard thus formed stood a church dedicated to a suitably militant saint. The description also speaks of "stately columns," floors of pebble mosaic (an ancient Anatolian art that can be traced back to the Phrygians) and others paved with onyx so highly polished that they resembled sheets of ice. But it is the palace's wall mosaics that are given the most detailed attention. They illustrate the extraordinary eclecticism of Byzantine secular art, for here Samson's destruction of the temple, David's defeat of Goliath and the plagues of Egypt were depicted next to the exploits of Achilles, Agamemnon, Odysseus and Alexander.

Cappadocia must have contained several country mansions but none have been located, let alone excavated. Robert Bryon, in *The Byzantine Achievement*, suggests that they may have resembled the castles of Moorish Spain, but it is more likely that they were related to the sixth-century fortified palaces that can still be seen along the western fringes of the Syrian desert. It may be doubted whether these mansions ever achieved the fabulous splendor of Digenis' riverside palace, but they could still be magnificent enough to arouse the envy and suspicion of emperors, as the case of the unfortunate Eustathios Maleinos makes plain.

On his way back from a brief Syrian campaign in 996, the Emperor Basil II was entertained by this nobleman at his Cappadocian estate. Hoping to demonstrate his loyalty—which was decidedly suspect—Eustathios prepared an extravagant banquet, but he had misjudged his man. Basil was impressed, but not in the way his host would have liked. The severe and unforgiving emperor observed the grandeur of the Maleinos mansion, the number of armed retainers and the vast extent of the estate, and he concluded that such men lived too much like kings. He had reason enough to detest the Anatolians, having spent the first thirteen years of his reign struggling to suppress rebellions by the Phocas and Scleros families and, immediately on his return to the capital, he issued an edict with the resounding title *New Constitution of the pious Emperor Basil the Young, by which are Condemned those Rich Men who Amass their Wealth at the Expense of the Poor.* Throughout Anatolia the blood of nobles ran cold, particularly that of the Maleinoi and Phocades, who were mentioned specifically in the document: neither family, according to Basil, had legal rights to the estates they had possessed for more than a century.

Eustathios was deprived of all his property and spent the remainder of his life a virtual prisoner in Constantinople; the Phocades also lost the vast proportion of their property, and never again did either family play a significant part in history. This decimation of the military aristocracy enhanced Basil's personal power enormously, but it cannot be said to have benefited the empire in the long term. While Basil was alive the ill-effects were not felt: he held the empire in an iron grip and was almost as great a warrior as Nicephorus Phocas, but he was succeeded on his death in 1025 by a gaggle of bureaucrats and courtiers who inherited nothing from him but a determination to undermine the power and fighting ability of the Anatolian nobility by any means possible. In the process they fatally undermined the empire's defenses and the result was the calamitous defeat at Manzikert in 1071. In the decade that followed, the empire seemed close to extinction. It was saved when Alexius Comnenus seized the throne in 1081. The Comneni were a military family from Kastamon in northern Anatolia, and for a century they ruled the empire as if it were one vast family estate, but when they fell from power (in part as a result of family feuds) the processes of disintegration reasserted themselves. If the central government could not live with the Anatolian nobility, the empire evidently could not live without them, and it is fitting that memories of their exploits should have lingered in Cappadocian folklore down to our own century. A more concrete reminder of their days of greatness is to be found just outside the village of Çavuşin.

THE JUDGMENT OF HISTORY

If reports say true, she was a very bad woman indeed.
But report is not always just.
—ROMILLY JENKINS, *Byzantium: The Imperial Centuries*

The church of Çavuşin is a monument to the glory of God
and the Phocas family. From a distance it appears to have
a painted façade, but in fact the original façade has sheered
away and what is visible today is the exposed interior of
the narthex. To the right of the door stand the archangels
Michael and Gabriel, both almost as tall as a man,
stretching out their long red wings against a pale-blue
ground. The entire interior is painted but it is the figures in
the northern apse that make the church unique, for here
stand the Emperor Nicephorus II Phocas, his wife, the
Empress Theophano, his father, Bardas, and his brother
Leo. This group portrait represents the apogee of the
Anatolian aristocracy, commemorating a visit Nicephorus
made to Cappadocia in 964, shortly before his victorious
campaign against Tarsus. An image of the angel appearing
to Joshua on the eve of the fall of Jericho may allude to the
capture of this last Arab stronghold in Cilicia.

The style of the paintings is delicate and mannered,
quite without the sculptural solidity of the Tokali frescoes.

The colors are mostly pale reds, greens and blues, and the figures are noticeably attenuated. It is an oddly inappropriate style with which to honor a warrior and ascetic like Nicephorus Phocas, but the artist was probably wise to avoid any trace of naturalism: even Byzantine chroniclers admit that Nicephorus was squat and ill-favored, and in the account of Liutprand of Cremona—who loathed him— he appears as "a monstrosity of a man, a dwarf with a broad, flat head and tiny eyes like a mole; disfigured by a short, thick, grizzled beard; disgraced by a neck scarcely an inch long; piglike by reason of the big close bristles on his head; in colour an Ethiopian. As the poet says, 'you would not like to meet him in the dark.' "

There is an equestrian figure in the church of Çavuşin which some have identified as a portrait of Nicephorus' nephew John Tzimiskes. If this is true, the painter of Çavuşin has unwittingly preserved for us an echo of one of the most luridly operatic dramas in Byzantine history. The protagonists are all before us: the lovely but ruthless Theophano, the heroic but hideous Nicephorus and the gallant but murderous John. The story is a complicated one and it is best to begin with Theophano, a dazzling figure wrapped in the smoke of rumor and slander.

Theophano was a wine-merchant's daughter, and for this reason alone the more snobbish Byzantine commentators have hated her, but even her worst detractors do not attempt to deny that she was beautiful, so beautiful and so beguiling that Romanus II, while still heir to the throne, insisted on marrying her over the strong objections of his father, Constantine VII. Beauty was not Theophano's only asset; she was also fiercely intelligent, strong-willed and politically astute. Events soon combined to consolidate her position: in 957 she gave birth to a son and two years later the old emperor died. Thus she became empress at the age of eighteen and like many of her predecessors was, from the first, determined to play an active role in politics. Her pliable and adoring husband would deny her nothing, and she immediately demanded that her five sisters-in-law be banished to convents. This does not show her personality in an attractive light, but it should perhaps be remembered that teenage girls are rarely tolerant of female rivals. She was also acting within her rights as empress. A Byzantine empress was much more than a bejeweled figurehead. Since her authority descended directly from God, she was not dependent on her spouse and maintained her own court in her separate quarters within the palace precincts. It was her right to summon the highest ministers of state whenever she wished and confer titles as she saw fit. She could come and go as she pleased, but no one, not even the emperor, could enter her apartments without her express permission.

In 959 Theophano's position seemed secure for many years to come, but in 963 her young and handsome husband died quite unexpectedly. At once the rumors began to spread throughout the city. Theophano was already suspected—without foundation—of poisoning her father-in-law; now she was accused of poisoning her husband. The charge is patently false: Theophano had everything to lose by Romanus' death and at the time news of it was brought to her she lay in childbed, having given birth to a daughter only forty-eight hours before. This should excite sympathy, not suspicion. No one disputed her legal right to rule as regent on behalf of her sons, but she was very young and alone and her sons were respectively six and three years old. The lack of an adult male heir was an open invitation to usurpation and rebellion. At the court she was surrounded by unscrupulous politicians; in Anatolia the nobles, full of pride for their victories over the Arabs, thought it high time one of their number was rewarded with the imperial throne, and Nicephorus Phocas was the obvious candidate. A lesser woman might have given in, allowing herself to be pulled this way and that by contending political forces, but Theophano acted boldly and decisively, opening negotiations with Nicephorus and offering him her hand in marriage on condition that he swear a solemn oath to protect her sons.

If any of the Byzantine chroniclers had been inclined to take the charitable view (and none were) they might have seen something heroic in Theophano's actions. She cannot have relished the prospect of marriage to a confirmed ascetic of repellent aspect more than twice her age, who habitually wore a verminous hair shirt and preferred to sleep on the floor, the better to mortify his flesh.

As a political alliance the "white marriage" of Theophano and Nicephorus began well. When the new emperor entered the capital, the populace set aside its customary distrust of Anatolian warlords and jubilantly acclaimed the hero of Crete and Syria. The ambitious officers of the court were cowed and the Anatolians were unlikely to rebel against one of their own. It seemed that Theophano and her children had found the strong and upright protector they needed, but Nicephorus was as uncouth in manner as he was in appearance, and, while this was a matter of small consequence on the eastern frontier, in Constantinople, at the center of the delicate web of Byzantine diplomacy, it was disastrous. He took to abusing the ambassadors of foreign potentates as if they were common foot-soldiers and within a very brief period had involved the empire in wars on three fronts. The sophisticated diplomats of the Byzantine court were horrified and the people groaned under the weight of the extraordinary taxes that were imposed to support the war effort. To make matters worse, a series of bad harvests reduced thousands to near starvation and Nicephorus did nothing to alleviate their suffering. Most remarkably, for a man of such ostentatious piety, he managed to alienate the Church by attempting to restrict the wealth of monasteries. By 968 the conquering hero of 963 was no longer welcome in his capital. All sections of society were united against him and for the first time in his life Nicephorus went in fear.

His worst mistake was to quarrel with his brilliant and popular nephew John Tzimiskes. Uncle and nephew shared military genius and shortness of stature, but were otherwise as different as night and day. John was irresistibly charming, generous, pleasure-loving and exceptionally handsome. He had been numbered among his uncle's most trusted commanders, but suddenly he had fallen from favor. We do not know the reason for this: it may have been a family quarrel of some kind, or Nicephorus (who was notoriously ungenerous) may simply have grown jealous of his nephew's growing fame. However that may be, Tzimiskes was relieved of his command and exiled to his estates in Anatolia; he never forgot the insult. He soon became the focus for the opposition to his uncle's oppressive rule.

Theophano cannot have been unaware of these developments, but the extent of her involvement remains a matter of conjecture. According to legend, she had fallen passionately in love with Tzimiskes and was motivated entirely by a desire to rid herself of a burdensome elderly husband and place her dashing lover on the throne. This version of events has a strong odor of palatine gossip. Malice and a willingness to believe the worst of anyone were the besetting vices of Byzantine historians and perhaps of Byzantines in general, and if we accept this account, we must find Theophano guilty not only of adultery and complicity in murder, but also of banality. Theophano is not a figure from a soap opera. Everything we know about her suggests that she was not the sort of woman to lose her head over a man: her motives were complex and her actions carefully considered.

She must have observed with alarm Nicephorus' growing isolation. She saw that his fall was inevitable. If she was to maintain her own position and ensure the safety of her sons she had no choice but to abandon him to his fate. She probably did so without too much regret, but it is absurd to suggest that the murder of Nicephorus was plotted within the women's quarters of the palace. The conspiracy was very widespread, and even the Church might be said to have given its tacit approval. Nevertheless the empress and the nephew reached an understanding, and on the evening of 10 December 969 Theophano showed that she knew what was about to happen by tactfully absenting herself from the imperial bedchamber, leaving the door ajar.

As the night wore on, a violent snowstorm blew in from the Black Sea and the conspirators in the palace began to worry that Tzimiskes would not be able to make his way across the Bosphorus, but he arrived according to plan and, having been hauled by ropes up onto the roof of the palace, descended into his uncle's private apartments. The conspirators found the emperor asleep on the floor and, having kicked him awake, brutally cut him down while he called on the Virgin for mercy. His dismembered corpse was thrown from a balcony.

As dawn broke, John Tzimiskes sat enthroned in the Chrysotriklinos and at his side stood Theophano and her sons. Snow had given way to fog, and as this fog spread through the city streets, gathering in hollows and curling up alleyways, so did news of the murder. There were neither protests nor acclamations. A profound silence settled over the city, and this we may guess to be the result of mingled feelings of relief and shame—relief that the tyrant was dead and shame that the man whose martial exploits had brought such glory to the empire had met such a dishonorable end. Yet if the emperor was dead it was God's will, and no one disputed Tzimiskes' right to the throne. Theophano confidently expected to marry him, and whether or not they were already lovers, this third marriage must have been a much more appealing prospect than her second: here was a man who combined the charm and good looks of her first husband with the courage and fighting ability of her second. But Theophano was to be bitterly disappointed. Scandal and rumor had done their work and the Patriarch Polyeuctus (an elderly bigot more than willing to believe the worst of a beautiful and ambitious young woman) flatly refused to perform the coronation while the "scarlet empress" still resided in the palace. Tzimiskes made no attempt to defend his benefactress. Enraged and humiliated, she was immediately bundled off to a convent on the island of Proté. She was not yet thirty and her life was effectively over.

Historians have been harsh in their judgment of Theophano, but to John Tzimiskes they have extended a truly astonishing generosity. Byzantine chroniclers tirelessly extol his virtues, and yet this paragon, this "new paradise from which flowed the four rivers of justice, wisdom, prudence and courage," was responsible for the murder of his uncle, and Theophano murdered no one. Historiography affords no more striking example of the double standard in action. The worst that can be said of Theophano, with any certainty, is that she acted ruthlessly in her own interests, but she was also a mother defending her children and her self-interest had a way of coinciding with the best interests of the state. At the very least she deserves to be honored for giving the empire one of its greatest rulers in the person of her eldest son, Basil II. There can be no doubt that this remarkable man inherited his fierce and unyielding strength of character from his mother. It was unfortunate for Theophano's reputation that what was considered a sign of greatness in the son was deemed "vicious" and "unnatural" in the mother.

THREE GRACES, FORTY MARTYRS

The village of Sinassos lies a few miles south of Ürgüp in the broad, fertile Damsa valley. Its official name is now Mustafapaşa, but this is so commonplace that local people prefer to use its old Greek name. This was a predominantly Greek community until the 1920s and its wealth is demonstrated by a large nineteenth-century church that stands next to the main square. The interior is dim and desolate, with ranks of graceless columns that show no loyalty to Byzantine tradition, but the door is framed by a charming relief carving of vines picked out in green and yellow paint. The village is best known to Turks, however, as the site of one of the many miracles credited to the great dervish leader Haci Bektaş.

As he was making his way from Kayseri to Ürgüp (so the story goes), Haci Bektaş encountered a Christian woman on the outskirts of Sinassos. She was carrying a tray of rye loaves on her head and at once began to complain loudly about the poor quality of the bread and begged him to help her. This was a small matter for a man who was capable of turning himself into a dove, a falcon or a stag as the need arose and Haci Bektaş said to her, "Henceforth you will plant rye, but you will harvest wheat and from small portions of flour you will make large loaves." Naturally everything turned out as he had promised and the people of Sinassos built a shrine in the place where Haci Bektaş had met the woman. This admirably practical miracle is an indication of the friendly relations that existed between the major dervish sects and the Christians of Anatolia.

Like Ürgüp, Sinassos is full of fine stone-built houses, some of them slowly falling into ruin. While we were admiring one of these, three exquisite girls, all about ten or eleven years old, emerged from its weathered gateway and, seeing our interest, beckoned us inside. Beyond the gateway was a small courtyard half-filled with unkempt masses of roses and oleanders. The family of one of the girls lived on the ground floor of the house, but the upper story was abandoned. We were gracefully conducted up an external staircase and into a large, sun-filled room decorated with niches, trompe l'oeil drapes and perspective views of imaginary cities. The long streets of these cities were bordered by columned buildings and clipped trees, but peopled by only a few rudimentary, doll-like figures, some of them riding in horse-drawn carriages. Haunted by enigma and absence, these oddly bleak attempts to portray the metropolitan splendors of a Europe the painter had never seen reminded me strongly of De Chirico.

As we were about to leave I paused to photograph the Three Graces of Sinassos standing against a hedge of roses. The girl on the right has a serious expression enhanced by large glasses and a bulky sweater, but even her slightly downturned mouth cannot conceal the fact that she will soon be very lovely. The girl in the middle has small, fine features and seems to have the lightest spirit; her smile sparkles and she wears a red headband and tiny pearl-drop earrings. The girl on the left is a tall, fair-haired beauty with large, luminous gray-blue eyes; her slight, serene smile seems to exude an understanding far beyond her years. I imagine them as participants in some Mozartian or Straussian trio for mezzo, coloratura and lyric sopranos.

Not far south of Sinassos, and close by the road, we came to the Keşlik Monastery, its churches and chambers carved out of a cluster of pinnacles that rises from an apple orchard. In October the trees are heavy with fruit as bright as lanterns, but the place casts its enchantment in any season. As we approached, our way was barred by a vigilant donkey that trotted toward us, braying cacophonously to alert the custodian, who was asleep in the shade of a tree. This gentleman took his job very seriously, and having calmed the donkey by patting it affectionately on the nose, ushered us into the Church of the Archangel. It was a double-vaulted church, but its extensive frescoes were so blackened by candle smoke that we would not have been able to recognize any of the scenes without the custodian's guidance, and it was the little Chapel of Saint Stephen that proved to be the real glory of Keşlik.

Its flat ceiling was painted with a jeweled crucifix surrounded by curling vines executed with delightful spontaneity on a pale yellow ground. Around this central motif there were simple, tilelike geometric patterns and more complex interlacing designs painted in red, yellow and black on white. With a restricted palette and vocabulary of forms the painter had created an effect of wonderful richness and exuberance, and it was hard to understand why some authorities had dismissed his work as mediocre. The same authorities have not been able to agree on a date for these frescoes. Since they are largely nonfigurative, it is often claimed that they must date from the iconoclast period, but a nonfigurative decorative scheme could be as much a matter of personal taste as of imperial edict; furthermore the frescoes are not *entirely* nonfigurative: there are angels and busts of saints in medallions. In view of the fact that these elements are used somewhat tentatively, a date shortly after the restoration of images in 843 seems most likely: portrayal of the human figure was once again permitted in church decoration, but perhaps the painter of Keşlik did not yet feel confident of his ability to use this new resource effectively. However that may be, it is clear that he took joy in his work. His jeweled cross amid its vines is a hymn of praise unshadowed by doubt or the fear of death.

The road continued on its gentle course southward between orchards and groves of poplars, passing a mausoleum like a pleasure pavilion and the ruins of a Seljuk medrese with an elegant doorway wreathed in stone lacework, until it turned west and began to climb into arid hills. As we were approaching Şahineffendi (the former bishopric of Suves), I noticed a fragment of pilastered façade carved halfway up a hillside on the edge of the village, and we turned off on to a track that seemed to lead toward it. The lower slopes of the hill were white but liberally scattered with sharply pointed black cones, in one

of which was a large doorway. There was nothing remarkable about this doorway and I was not aware that anything
of particular interest lay in the immediate vicinity of
Şahineffendi, but I walked through the door and what I
saw astonished me.

Overhead were two parallel vaults completely covered
with frescoes. On the more northerly of the vaults was a
depiction of the forty martyrs of Sebasteia. These were
early Christians who were forced to spend a night standing
naked on the frozen surface of an Anatolian lake. The
subject was popular with Byzantine painters, perhaps
because it provided them with a unique opportunity to
depict the naked human form en masse. In this case there
seemed to be considerably more than forty martyrs huddled
together on the ceiling, their modesty protected by white
loincloths that reached almost to their knees. All of them
seemed old. Their skin was yellowish. Their gestures were
appropriately agonized, but their faces expressed nothing
beyond a formalized sadness, typical of the faces of all
Byzantine saints: this generic expression tells us, with
regret but absolute certainty, that happiness is only to be
found in eternity. A more festive atmosphere prevailed in
the southern vault: figures were clad in clinging robes of
pink, blue-gray, pale yellow, pale green and deep purplish
red; the Nativity was set in a nearly abstract expressionist
landscape of red and green; in the Annunciation, Gabriel's
robes billowed out before him in blithe defiance of the
laws of gravity and aerodynamics.

I was to learn later that these frescoes were the work of
the monk Aetios, who completed them in 1216, more
than a hundred and forty years after the Turkish conquest.
They are by no means the best of the Cappadocian frescoes, but their isolation and the fact that I discovered them
entirely by chance greatly enhanced their value in my eyes.

Many more such discoveries can be made in the regions that lie in the shadow of Mount Hasan, some seventy-five kilometers to the southwest of Ürgüp.

THE RED CHURCH/THE SECOND LIZARD

The road is lovely
As if there is no death
—MELIH CEVDET ANDAY, *"One Moment" (trans. Talat S. Halman)*

West of Ürgüp lies Nevşehir, the largest town in central Cappadocia, and west of Nevşehir the modern road merges with the *Uzun Yol,* the "Long Road" of the Seljuk sultans that stretches in a straight line to Konya. Marco Polo traveled this road and must have spent the night in one of the three great caravansarays that lie between Nevşehir and Aksaray. To drive from one caravansaray to the other across the vast rolling plain is to experience a rising sense of exhilaration. They form a kind of suite in which the last movement combines the contrasted themes of the previous two: the first of them retains most of its exterior walls and a fine gateway, but the interior has gone; the second reverses this pattern, being a mass of arches and vaults, while the third, the Ağzikara Han, is equally well preserved internally and externally, looking much as it must have done in 1238. A tall honeycombed portal leads into a courtyard, at the center of which is an arched pavilion surmounted by a small mosque. On the east side of this courtyard another magnificent portal with a high, fretted arch leads into a vaulted hall like a cathedral, where travelers and their pack animals could seek refuge in the winter months. Under the arches of the pavilion kilims were spread out and in the entrance passageway a grizzled tradesman sold packets of turmeric and red saffron.

Shortly beyond Ağzikara we turned off to the southeast, crossing the turbulent waters of the river Melendiz. We ignored the turning for the Ihlara valley and drove straight on until we came to a crossroads, miles from any habitation, where there was a makeshift arch with a sign: WELCOME TO GÜZELYURT. Like most Turkish toponyms that do not derive from Greek (as even Istanbul does), the name Güzelyurt is translatable: *güzel* means beautiful or good; a *yurt* is a kind of circular tent that is still used in parts of Central Asia and Siberia, but since the majority of Turks have abandoned their nomadic ways it has come to stand for "home" or "homeland." As we approached the village, the name seemed entirely appropriate. To our right the land fell away gently toward a broad green basin that concealed the ravine of Ihlara; in the foreground the dome of a monastery rose from a pillar of rock and in the distance the peaks of Mount Hasan filled the horizon, their long gullies streaked with vestigial snows. It was easy to understand how such a landscape should have attracted anchorites and mystics.

Until 1922 Güzelyurt was known as Gelvere. In a narrow defile below the main square of the modern village lies the old Greek quarter, complete with nineteenth-century cave-monasteries, a stygian eighteenth-century laundry that is still very much in use, and a large and handsome eleventh-century church, so perfectly preserved that it would be easy to imagine that you were in Greece. This was the first freestanding masonry church that I had seen in Cappadocia (which is to say, the first church that was *built*, not carved out of the rock). It stood serenely among long grass and fruit trees, its dome carried on a high drum, its walls enlivened with niches and recessed moldings. It was also locked, and this was one of the few occasions on which I was unable to find an obliging person with a key, but as it had been converted to a mosque after the expulsion of the Greeks, it was unlikely that its interior decoration would have survived. So, at least, I attempted to console myself.

The church of Gelvere was dedicated to Saint Gregory of Nazianzos, who was born and died only a few miles away. Gregory was one of the three Cappadocian Fathers, the other two being his close friend Saint Basil, bishop of Caesarea, and Basil's younger brother, Gregory of Nyssa. Born in 330, Gregory of Nazianzos was extremely devout and a staunch defender of orthodoxy, but there was nothing rigid or narrow-minded about his way of thinking. He received an excellent classical education in Alexandria and Athens and was well acquainted with the work of Plato. Like Basil and the younger Gregory, he believed religious dogma should be supported by reason, and to this end advocated continued study of the pagan philosophers. Although he bore the official title of theologian, he was, in reality, more of a poet and a man of letters who considered the writing of poetry to be a prophetic vocation sanctioned by God. His style is elegant and highly artificial, often making use of archaic meters and richly encrusted with classical allusions, and in this he set the tone for all later Byzantine litterateurs. It seems likely, for example, that

Gregory would have approved of the sentiments expressed in an oddly touching epigram, written some seven centuries later by the courtier John Mauropous, which begins "If perchance you wish to exempt certain pagans from punishment, my Christ / May you for my sake spare Plato and Plutarch . . ."

For a brief period Gregory was patriarch of Constantinople, but he could not endure the continual disputes that poisoned the air of the capital—remarking that it was impossible to buy a loaf of bread without being engaged in a discussion on the nature of the Trinity—and soon returned to his native Cappadocia, where he spent his last years praising the virtues of solitude and simplicity:

Blessed is he who lives the solitary life and keeps apart
From those who walk the earth, but lifts his thoughts always
    towards God.

Even for the modern traveler solitude is not hard to come by in this region of Cappadocia. Beyond Güzelyurt the road climbed to a high pass and then descended, close by the dusty and impoverished troglodytic village of Sivri-hisar, toward a small plateau covered with a lake of yellow and white flowers, ringed by low, crumbling hills. And at the center of this plateau, in complete isolation, stood the Red Church (Kizil Kilise). My response was no different from that of the traveler and scholar W. F. Ainsworth, who visited the same place in 1840: "The ascent over the next low range of hills brought us to another of these secluded and rocky spots, but what surprised us not a little was a rather elegantly built Greek church standing in its centre, with no habitations near it, and gradually falling into ruins. So regular and handsome an edifice, isolated in the midst of savage scenery, naturally interested our feelings very much."

Interested as our feeling may be, we do not know much

about this church. It is a modified domed cross with a single aisle attached somewhat eccentrically to the north side of the nave. (Gertrude Bell reports a church with a similar plan farther to the west on the lower slopes of Mount Hasan.) Low mounds in the fields surrounding it suggest that it must have been part of a monastic complex—there could be no other reason for building a church at a height of well over four thousand feet in the middle of nowhere—but the site has not been excavated and there is no inscription giving a date or the name of a donor. As soon as I caught sight of the Red Church I assumed, on the basis of its silhouette alone, that it must be a product of the middle-Byzantine period, but it is only fair to mention that others have placed it as early as the fifth century.

What is most surprising about the Red Church is the fact that its condition has hardly altered since Ainsworth's visit: the dome still rides atop its tall octagonal drum; the walls of its handsome polygonal apse still stand, pierced by three generously proportioned windows. Unlike a number of other Byzantine masonry structures in Cappadocia, that were intact in 1910 and have now vanished without a trace, it has survived the twentieth century's repetitive cycles of destruction with remarkable aplomb, to bear witness to Byzantium's civilizing mission. Despite its extremely remote location there is nothing awkward or rustic about its construction: its red trachyte masonry is of the highest quality and its proportions are finely calcu-lated, giving it an air of monumentality that belies its comparatively small scale.

As I was about to leave, a sudden flashing movement caught my attention. An emerald-green lizard was skit-tering about on the stones of the apse—a lizard exactly similar to the one I had seen in the church at Ayazin.

Could it be that this spectacularly decorative breed of lizard was naturally attracted to the interiors of Byzantine churches? I had the curious sensation that I was being followed and observed. But perhaps "watched over" would be a better term, since I had no doubt that this was a creature of good omen.

INVISIBLE FAÇADES

This is a region of beautiful names. The Ihlara valley was known to the Greeks as Peristrema. Today, for better or worse, it is in the process of becoming a major tourist destination, but driving from Güzelyurt toward Mount Hasan we did not see it until we were directly above it. Its cliffs descended sheer for many hundreds of feet to the river Melendiz, which bustled ceaselessly along its stony bed between willows and poplars. In the midst of a nearly treeless and waterless plateau this linear oasis is a welcome sight, but this is not how Saint Gregory of Nazianzos saw it.

In a letter he wrote to Saint Basil, Gregory gives an ironic description of his native Cappadocia. It is, he says, a fearsome place

For all that is not rock is gullies and all that is not gullies is bramble, and what is not bramble is precipice. And the road above all this, craggy and tortuous, boggles the mind of the traveller and for safety's sake makes an acrobat of him. Down below roars a river . . . teaming less with fish than rocks and instead of running into a lake it plunges into the abyss. It is huge, this river, and terrible and its reverberations drown out the psalmody of the brethren who live above it. The cataracts of the Nile are nothing to it, so it rages day and night against you. Being unruly it is unnavigable: being murky, undrinkable. You are lucky if your cell doesn't get swept away when torrents and winter storms set it going.

It might be objected that Gregory cannot be referring to Ihlara-Peristrema since the Melendiz is a small river, but it is surely obvious that he is exaggerating for comic effect, a fact of which Basil, as a fellow Cappadocian, would have been well aware. The Melendiz is the *only* river in western Cappadocia and by comparing it to the Nile, Gregory intended to make his old friend laugh. His reference to monks being swept from their cells reveals that the valley was already a major center of monasticism before the fourth century had entered its last decade (Gregory died in 390), and today its cliffs still conceal more than a hundred churches. The whole valley is a paradise for walkers, but there remains the problem of where to begin and what to see. A mile or so to the north of Ihlara village, a parking lot and a huge restaurant (complete with a poetry-quoting waiter) are perched on the lip of the chasm, and from here you can descend by hundreds of steps to the river, but the churches in the immediate vicinity of the steps—which are all that most visitors see—are, in general, extremely small and the frescoes sometimes crude to the point of ugliness. The best paintings are to be found several miles downstream at Belisirma, and the most interesting architecture is even further away at Yaprakhisar and Selime at the point where the gorge comes to an end.

The village of Selime stands directly by the Ihlara road, its houses scattered amid a massive cluster of cones at the foot of a flat-topped hill. Concerning it, the guidebooks maintain a unanimous silence, so when a teenage boy offered to show me the *kalesi* (castle) I had no idea what he was referring to, but I had already concluded that the rock-carvers of Cappadocia would not have been able to resist so inviting a group of pinnacles. We set off at once along a winding track leading up into the rocks. It soon became apparent that this "track" was in fact a carefully graded Byzantine road or street. Chambers had been carved out on either side, one of which our guide identified as a stable. Soon the road looped back on itself and entered a spacious tunnel, at least twelve feet high. I might have guessed from this that whatever lay ahead of us would be designed on the grandest scale, but nothing could have prepared me for what we found on emerging from the tunnel. We were standing on a terrace high above the village; to our left was an enormous kitchen with a pyramidal roof, pierced at its apex by a chimney; ahead of us was a barrel-vaulted porch and beyond that was the largest and most elaborate rock-cut hall I had yet seen in Cappadocia. It was two stories high, had a flat ceiling and was surrounded on three sides by galleries. At its far end we entered a narrow curving corridor that debouched into a second great hall, this one vaulted and adorned with blind arcades; at its rear was a square chamber with a massive cross carved in high relief on its flat ceiling. Passing under a lintel carved with a pattern of vines, we emerged onto a second terrace. On every side were doorways, windows and shattered vestibules. It was becoming apparent that we had stumbled, quite by chance, on the most architecturally ambitious of all the Cappadocian cave-monasteries.

I felt as if I had just discovered Machu Picchu. Ibsen's Hall of the Mountain King and sundry dimly remembered scenes from Tolkien also came to mind. But we had not yet reached the end of the monastery's astonishing sequence of more than twenty-five halls and chambers. At the eastern edge of the terrace, steps led up to the church; it had been carved through a spur of the mountain so that it received light both from its western door and from a window in the central apse. For all that it had a very gloomy aspect, its walls and vaults being covered with obscure masses of black or reddish figures—all that remained of frescoes that appeared to have been scorched by fire. This could have been the result of pure accident, especially if the church had been used as a dwelling or storeroom after the monks abandoned the monastery, but there is also the grim possibility that Selime Kalesi was sacked in the anarchic years that followed Manzikert. In the vestibule of the church was a painted inscription of which I later obtained a translation. It consisted of an incomplete, dodecasyllabic poem with a stern, moralizing tone: "Let no one be misled by the desire for wealth, / For the love of money has destroyed many, / For this flesh is earth, clay and . . ."

The Oxford Dictionary of Byzantium has nothing to say about this remarkable monument, but a detailed scholarly account (with plan) can be found in Lynn Rodley's *The Cave Monasteries of Byzantine Cappadocia*. Ms. Rodley is thorough, but she is no Gertrude Bell and in her version a visit to Selime is apt to sound hardly more exciting than a tour of a parking lot. Even she has nothing to say about Yaprakhisar other than that she has not been there and that it is reported to have "a façade." In fact, the numerous and monumental façades of Yaprakhisar are to be found no more than a mile and a half from Selime, and they are clearly visible from the road. I had glimpsed them on an earlier visit and was now determined to investigate.

We had not gone very far into the village before the customary small boy attached himself to us. The façades loomed behind the straggling modern village like a petrified theatrical backdrop. There were perhaps half a dozen of them, mostly between twenty and forty feet high. The grandest and best-preserved had four stories of horseshoe-arched niches framed by plain pilasters and entablatures. It bore a curious resemblance to the façades of Parthian and Sassanian palaces: like the architecture of those palaces, the architecture of Yaprakhisar seems to preserve a dim, orientalized memory of the public buildings of the great Hellenistic cities—Pergamum, Antioch and Seleucia ad Tigris.

I was not able to penetrate beyond this façade. Both the charm and the difficulty of Yaprakhisar reside in the fact that the Byzantine chambers are still used by the villagers as barns and storerooms. Arched doorways and windows were blocked with crude masonry or wooden slats. Ladders and frail flights of stairs led up into mysterious eroded apertures, and the many low doors were kept firmly locked. But there was one point where the cliff face had collapsed, revealing a finely carved church in dramatic cross-section. Its three apses and two of the original four piers remained in place, but arches were broken off and the dome was suspended above us like a dark tent. At the far end of the complex our young guide led us up into the chambers inside the rock: this chamber, he confidently asserted, was a wine-press and that a kitchen, and this again was a laundry, although it was hard to know how he had come by this information. Finally, he led us down a curving corridor that led into the heart of the mountain and ended in a vertical shaft with hand-holds and foot-holds. He vanished upward into pitch darkness, bringing a shower of loose stones down on my head. Even with a flashlight I could not see the end of this shaft, and despite his echoing insistence that there was "a very good church" somewhere above me, I adamantly refused to follow.

AS IF DARKENED BY THICK SMOKE

. . . the emir Samuh and other emirs suddenly appeared before the unwalled city [of Sebasteia], but initially they hesitated to attack, mistaking the domes of the many churches for the tents of a defending army. They soon realised that the city was defenseless, and so massacred pitilessly large numbers of the inhabitants.
—SPEROS VRYONIS, JR., *The Decline of Medieval Hellenism*

The village of Belisirma appears to have been tipped over the edge of the Ihlara ravine, its houses tumbling down to the Melendiz, its streets like streambeds. Its people are robust and cheerful, and the women dress magnificently: across the river I saw a woman in her fifties who was working in a vegetable garden clad in incandescent shades of purple and lime green; a friend who was working beside her wore a violet bodice over sky-blue pants, and a young woman with a noble profile and the bearing of an empress strode across a bridge dressed, from her headscarf to the hem of her skirt, in the same shade of deep burgundy.

High above the river and the vegetable gardens we could see the windows and doorways of the Direkli Kilise (the Church with Columns). As we made our way toward it we were joined by an entourage of four boys, all of them about eight or nine years old. Like most of the children I encountered in rural Turkey they were charming, courteous and helpful, and seemed delighted to be in the company of foreigners. Since the landscape and architecture of Cappadocia are a child's paradise, it is children who are the most reliable guides: it is they who know every nook and cranny of the rocks.

The Direkli Kilise is carved into rock that is like soft white cheese. We entered a lofty vaulted hall and turned toward the narthex, stepping carefully to avoid slipping into one of the narrow graves set in its floor. To our right chambers receded into the rock, but ahead of us lay the church, which is the finest in all of Ihlara. On the surface of a square pier stood a tall and graceful Virgin holding the Christ child in her arms. As we moved in deeper, we encountered a bulky, muscular Saint George and the patron saints of Justinian I, Saints Sergius and Bacchus, dressed in the patterned silk robes of courtiers. In the central apse, Christ sat on a jeweled throne shaped like a lyre. On the north wall there had been a painting of Saint George defeating the dragon: George had vanished, but his vermilion stallion still pranced on a dragon like a two-headed snake, and the stallion's genitals were portrayed with a loving attention to detail.

Unlike the majority of Ihlara painters, the painter of the Direkli Kilise was no naïve provincial. He was well acquainted with the fashions of the Byzantine court and must have worked for a wealthy patron, yet his decorative scheme remained incomplete: the dome and the southern apse, though covered with plaster, are devoid of images, and this, together with an inscription, gives us a good indication of the frescoes' date. The inscription tells us that the church was built during the reign of the Emperors Basil II and Constantine VIII, that is to say, between 976 and 1025, and other factors tell us that it must have been completed toward the end of that period. Like Yaprakhisar and Selime Kalesi, the Direkli Kilise could only have been created after a long period of security and prosperity (all three complexes are lavish in scale and advertise themselves with monumental façades) but by the late 1050s this security was seriously threatened. In 1059 the Emir Samuh and his allies spent more than a week burning and looting Sebasteia (modern Sivas) at their leisure, and, as ill-luck would have it, in that same year Constantine X Ducas came to the throne.

This prodigiously shortsighted and irresponsible ruler came from an old Anatolian aristocratic family, but he was a traitor to his class who pursued a virulently antimilitary policy. Even the sack of Sebasteia could not persuade him that the army was anything more than an unnecessary expense and a threat to his power. Consequently, the best troops were withdrawn from Anatolia and disbanded, and the few that remained went without pay or supplies. Demoralization was general and the historian John Skylitzes, who wrote not long after these events, observed that "The very standards spoke out taciturnly, having a squalid appearance as if darkened by thick smoke." The army that only forty years previously had been an invincible military machine before which the potentates of Islam trembled was reduced to a shadow, its soldiers "bowed down with poverty and ill-health." Indeed, every decision made by

Ducas and his self-satisfied coterie of advisers (Michael Psellus prominent among them) might have been calculated to ensure the destruction of the empire, and if blame is due in the context of this immense tragedy, then it is they rather than the Turks who must be judged guilty, for it was they who had read all the books and understood nothing. It is true that nomads who could mistake domes for tents were incapable of appreciating the value of the civilization on which they had so violently intruded, but (to use Jeffersonian terms) Turkish "ignorance" seems less reprehensible than the "error" of Byzantine bureaucrats and intellectuals. While the empire fell to pieces as a result of policies he had advocated, Michael Psellus—arch-bureaucrat of the eleventh century—continued to maintain that a good command of rhetoric was the principal qualification for an emperor.

Constantine X died in 1067, which was much too late for it to do any good. In that year the Turks captured Caesarea, the chief city of eastern Cappadocia, burnt it to the ground, massacred its inhabitants and desecrated the great shrine of Saint Basil. So complete was the destruction that the city remained uninhabited for half a century. The shock was sufficient to produce a change of policy in the capital, and the widow of the late emperor was hastily married to Romanus Diogenes. Romanus came from a distinguished Cappadocian family and remained true to the martial traditions of his class. He may not have been the inspired leader that the empire needed, but he was at least brave and honorable and at once set about the arduous task of rebuilding a ruined army. If he had been given time he might have succeeded, but there was no time, his efforts were undermined by the treachery of the Ducas faction, and at Manzikert he met with disaster.

Turkmen tribes now flooded into Anatolia unchecked.

It is no longer sufficient to speak of "raids" or even of "invasion," what was taking place was a full-scale migration of entire tribes numbering in the tens of thousands, whose women—to the horror of the Christians—fought alongside their men and thought nothing of nursing a child while managing a horse. They were a poor people who saw Anatolia as a rich source of plunder, and were quick to realize that its high central plains were ideally suited to a pastoral and nomadic way of life: Anatolia reminded them of home. Furthermore, the Byzantine government had all but invited them into the empire, hoping to use them as a counterweight to the military magnates who were now in full revolt. So it came about that a peaceful population of villagers and townsfolk for whom the Arab raids were a fading memory was plunged into a nightmare, and the distant emperor, secure in his God-guarded city, was apparently incapable of coming to their aid.

The emperor in question was Michael VII Ducas, the son of Constantine X and the pupil of Michael Psellus, according to whom he was "a prodigy of our generation and a most beloved character," but John Skylitzes tears this veil of flattery asunder: "While he spent his time in the useless pursuit of eloquence and wasted his energy on the composition of iambic and anapestic verse (and they were poor efforts indeed) he brought his empire to ruin, led astray by his mentor, the philosopher Psellus." Within a few years the people of Cappadocia found themselves completely cut off from the capital. The monasteries at Belisirma, Yaprakhisar and Selime may have been in use for forty years or as little as ten before destruction fell upon them. All artistic production ceased abruptly. Anatolia had been Hellenized since the time of Alexander's successors and Christian since the time of the first Constantine. Now everything was in doubt.

THE LADY THAMAR
AND HER EMIR

The Church of Bahattin is named for a local eccentric who used it to store hay. Concealed amid fallen rocks less than a hundred yards from the Direkli Kilise, it is hardly more than a chapel but is richly endowed with frescoes, among them a Crucifixion painted in delicate pastel tones in which the figures seem frozen with grief, and a dramatic Raising of Lazarus in which Christ's robes fly out behind him as he reaches powerfully forward and down to haul the dead man from his grave.

Bahattin's church is so inconspicuous externally that we would have missed it altogether without our troupe of guides. I now asked them if they could take us to the Church of Saint George (Kirkdamalti Kilise), which I had been unable to find on an earlier visit. They at once set off down the hillside and along the left bank of the Melendiz, heading upstream. Willows and wild olives shaded the path, which swerved aside from time to time to avoid gigantic boulders that had fallen from the cliffs above. The animadversions of Saint Gregory notwithstanding, the waters of the Melendiz were very clear and edged with scarlet weeds, trailing like ribbons. Evening was drawing in, and the valley was sunk in shadow and silence. High above, the summits of the cliffs, still drenched in sunlight, resembled gilded cornices. To our right rose a mass of angular boulders, and it was into these boulders that the four boys suddenly turned. There was no path, only a maze of goat tracks. After we had climbed steeply for more than a hundred and fifty feet I glimpsed traces of bright paint in a crudely carved niche. When we emerged onto a narrow grassy ledge (our party having now grown to seven by the addition of a diminutive, fair-haired goatherd) I saw that the niche contained another portrait of Saint George in monster-slaying mode. The saint's white charger pranced gracefully, its plump tail intricately braided, its arched neck recalling equine figurines of the T'ang dynasty, but the saint himself had been reduced to fragments of an orange tunic, a green boot, a shield and a billowing dark-brown cloak. To the left of the niche was the church, exposed by the collapse of its northern wall, and here was the single fresco in all of Cappadocia that I most wanted to see.

It was not an exceptionally beautiful painting and it was severely damaged: Muslims had gouged out the faces of the figures and it was covered with lengthy Greek graffiti, one of which was clearly dated 1826. The fresco shows Saint George holding a spear and a shield, flanked by portraits of the church's donors: to the left is a bearded man dressed in the Turkish style in turban and caftan, and to the right is a woman in Byzantine court dress who proffers a model of the church. It is a faint and strangely transformed echo of the imperial portraits in the south gallery of Hagia Sophia.

The fresco is accompanied by a painted inscription

which has survived in full, and opens a wide window on the past. It reads: "This most venerable church dedicated to the holy and great martyr Saint George was magnificently decorated through the assistance, the high wish and care of the Lady Thamar, here pictured, and of her Emir Basil Giagoupes, under his high majesty the most noble and great Sultan Masud at the time when Sire Andronikos reigned over the Romans." A number of facts follow immediately from this: Thamar, judging by her name, was a Georgian, and since the inscription refers to Basil as "her Emir," she was probably his wife; Basil was a high-ranking officer in the Seljuk army; Sultan Masud is Masud II who came to the throne in 1282; "Sire Andronikos" is the Emperor Andronicus II Palaeologus, who came to the throne in the same year, and from these two last facts we know that the church was cut out of the rock between the years 1282 and 1304. Thus, the frescoes were painted more than two centuries after the Turkish conquest and bear moving testimony to the tenacity of Byzantine artistic traditions and the wisdom of the Seljuks.

Cappadocian Christians of the late eleventh century had every excuse for pessimism, but over the course of the next century their circumstances gradually improved. As the sultans of Konya consolidated their hold on Central Anatolia they came to appreciate the skills of their Christian subjects (who still constituted the majority of the population), and did all they could to protect them from the depredations of the Turkmens. Regions that had been abandoned during the first period of invasions and migrations were resettled with Christians. If the Seljuks had not been inclined by temperament to tolerance it would have been forced upon them, for without it their state would have been torn apart. Governmental tolerance had its counterpart at the lower levels of society in exotic and transitory syncretisms: Turks and Greeks revered the same saints; the practice of baptism became common among the Anatolian Muslims, who believed that their children would be ill-favored and evil-smelling if they had not been anointed by a Christian priest; the customs of the Bektaşi dervishes were an amalgam of elements derived from Islam, Central Asiatic Shamanism, Judaism and Christianity. In these fluid circumstances it was not hard for Cappadocian Christians to come to terms with their new masters, and by the early thirteenth century the construction of churches and the painting of frescoes had resumed. By the end of that century certain upper-class Christians—Basil Giagoupes among them—had come to identify their own interests with those of the declining Seljuk royal house.

But how sad, how sheerly wistful this inscription is! "The most noble and great Sultan Masud" exercised little real power; his realm was divided and he was unable to control the continued influx of new hordes of Turkmens. The proud sultanate of Rum ceased to exist only four years after his death. As for "Sire Andronikos," his reign is a catalogue of disasters. He was devout, intelligent and cultivated, and his ministers were men of the highest intellectual caliber. Under their enlightened patronage Byzantine art enjoyed its last great flowering, but neither Andronicus nor his ministers were able to halt the empire's inexorable and alarmingly rapid decline. When he came to the throne Andronicus still possessed extensive Anatolian provinces, stretching from Bithynia to the Maeander valley, but when he died in 1332, nothing remained except the cities of Nikomedia and Philadelphia. The Byzantines held Constantinople and some small provinces in Europe, but without Anatolia their empire was an empire only in name, and to talk of Andronicus II as "Emperor of the Romans" was to perpetuate a nostalgic fiction. In the capital, intellectuals pondered the inscrutable workings of Tyche. The devout and the simple clung to the belief that God would restore the empire and bring peace to the world, but it was not to be: no angel descended in glory to drive back the Turks at the eleventh hour. The inscription in the Church of Saint George reveals a world that was on the point of vanishing.

The sky was still blue above the valley but the light had withdrawn from the tops of the precipices. The boys scattered to their homes and herds. Beyond Mount Hasan a huge sun sank through banded air. We drove back to Ürgüp through Derinkuyu, where all the lights had failed and people wandering in the streets seemed drained of color like ghosts.

VI

EPILOGUE

And the entire wealth of the city and its people were to be seen in the tents of the Turkish camp, the city deserted, lying lifeless, naked, soundless, without either form or beauty. O City, City, head of all cities! O City, City, center of the four corners of the world! O City, City, pride of the Romans, civilizer of the barbarians! O City, second paradise planted toward the west, possessing every kind of vegetation, laden with spiritual fruits . . . Where is your beauty? Where are the bodies of the Apostles? Where the purple cloak, the lance, the sponge, the reed? . . . Where are the relics of the saints, where the body of the first Constantine and the bodies of his successors? O roads, courtyards, crossroads, fields and vineyards! . . . O temple! O earthly heaven! . . . O sacred and divine places! O ancient and modern laws! O magnificence of the churches! O tablets inscribed by the finger of God! O commonwealth! O citizens! O army, formerly beyond number, now removed from our sight like a ship sunk in the sea! O houses and palaces of every imaginable type! O sacred walls! Today I invoke you all and, as if you were incarnate beings, I mourn with you, for surely there must be a new Jeremiah to lead the chorus of this lamentable tragedy . . .

—THE HISTORIAN DUCAS

THE GOLDEN GATE

The bus from Ürgüp to Istanbul takes a full twelve hours. It leaves in the early evening and arrives in the early morning. The usual civilities are observed—travelers are liberally splashed with lemon-scented cologne, and iced water is provided whenever you might need it—but the journey cannot be recommended. Despite their reputation for toughness, the Turks are morbidly sensitive to drafts and the driver will turn off the air-conditioning whenever your vigilance slackens. Since the majority of Turkish males seem to consider it their patriotic duty to smoke heavily, the air soon becomes asphyxiating. I slept and dreamt fitfully. I dreamt that I slept in a richly carpeted chamber of the Hotel Asia Minor. The figure of a small boy kept coming and going. The room was decorated with paper bouquets, streamers and cellophane curtains. The boy was dressed for his circumcision in a cape and a cap of midnight blue scattered with silver stars. I woke briefly to find the light of a full moon pouring down onto the surface of the great salt lake that lies at the center of the Anatolian plateau.

Beyond Ankara the road began to climb into the mountains. This puzzled me. Why had we not taken the easier route, along the northern edge of the plateau and down the valley of the Sangarius? I slept again but if I dreamt I do not remember it. In the mountains it began to rain. It was still raining when a gray dawn broke over the dismal outskirts of Izmit, the ancient Nikomedia. The coastline between Izmit and Istanbul must once have been very beautiful, but it has been ruined beyond recovery. It was here that the Emperor Theophilus chose to build his Arabian Nights palace of Bryas, and there were other palaces, small walled cities and famous monasteries. In those days the sea was clear and the hills were thickly wooded. Now the sea is a toxic soup and the vast majority of the trees have been cut down. Appalled but unable to look away, I stared out blankly at eroded hillsides and piles of logs as high as five-story apartment buildings. Refineries flared by the shore; chemical plants spewed out yellow smoke; cement factories, quarries and open-cast mines covered everything with dust. The earthly paradise invoked by Byzantine poets and historians had been converted into a close approximation of hell. After weeks spent amid the empty spaces of the plateau, this teeming, disorderly and despoiled landscape was hard to believe: I felt that it might all disappear if only I blinked hard enough, but it persisted obstinately, like a migraine.

The highway veered north into the hills, emerging suddenly on a bridge high above the Bosphorus, and almost before we had time to register the fact, we had crossed from Asia into Europe and plunged into the high-rise suburbs that encircled Pera. We were deposited in a bus station that sprawled across the valley of the little river Lykos, close to the gate of Saint Romanus. No memorial marks the spot, but it was here on the morning of 29 May 1453, after a siege nearly two months long, that the Turks finally broke through the walls and the last emperor, Constantine XI Palaeologus, not wishing to survive the loss of his city, plunged into the midst of the struggle and disappeared. His body was never identified with any certainty and this circumstance allowed a wistful legend to take shape, according to which an angel snatched Constantine from the battle and laid him to rest (either asleep or turned to stone) beneath the Golden Gate, the great triumphal arch that stands at the southern end of the land walls. From here, on the appointed day, he would rise to reclaim the city for Christendom and reestablish the empire of the Romans. The legend was widely believed among the Greeks of Istanbul, and among the Turks the Golden Gate became a place of ill-omen.

In the late afternoon we made our way to the gate, catching the dilapidated commuter train that runs along the Marmaran shore. The Golden Gate is little visited today but it was one of the principal wonders of the city and was imitated in distant Kiev and Vladimir. It was decorated with gilded statues of emperors and elephants, of Nike (Victory) and Tyche (Fate), and it was through it that emperors made their ceremonial entrances on the occasion of their triumphs. Under the Ottomans it was incorporated into a fortress known as Yedikule—the Seven Towers—but even before the conquest two of its three great arches had been walled up and most of its statuary had disappeared: in the last century and a half of the empire's existence, when rival members of the Palaeologus dynasty squabbled among themselves and the Turks steadily tightened the noose, there were no triumphs to celebrate. Viewed from the interior of the Ottoman fortress, the Golden Gate was a blank wall of white marble, pierced by only one arch, and that arch was obstructed by a wrecked car (a Renault, if I remember correctly). Simple neglect I could understand—it is preferable to insensitive restoration—but this was a gratuitous insult. Someone must have gone to considerable trouble to drive the dying car across the broad quadrangle of the fortress and abandon it in just this place. The iron gate beyond the car was locked and so, in a mood of mounting fury, I retreated to the summit of a nearby tower to survey what remained of the great walls built by Theodosius II in the fifth century and brood on the mutual hostility of nations and religions. I had hardly had time to lean on the parapet when I saw a workman enter the gate. I knew at once that this was our chance. We ran down the steps and across the courtyard, found the gate unlocked and surprised the workman urinating on a block of white marble. He zipped up hastily and told us by gestures that we should leave, but we smiled innocently, produced our cameras and stayed where we were. Now we could appreciate the full grandeur of the gate. Its arches were unusually high—high enough to accomodate a parade of elephants, as they had done in 628, when the Emperor Heraclius had celebrated his triumph over the Persians. They were flanked by massive square towers, imposing as the pylons of an Egyptian temple, and clad in marble, which, by some miracle, had retained the dazzling white of compacted snow. It is an appropriate resting place for the last emperor, a man who had redeemed the tarnished reputation of his dynasty by choosing to die a hero's death, and perhaps the legend of his return still causes unease in some quarters, for it is clear that the Turks would prefer you to stay away.

THE PANTOKRATOR

The domes of the Pantokrator Monastery rise grandly from the summit of a hill overlooking the Golden Horn. On all my previous trips to Istanbul I had avoided the place, even though I knew that it contained the mausoleum of the Emperors John II Comnenus, Manuel I Comnenus and Manuel II Palaeologus—men for whom I entertained the highest admiration. It was this admiration that accounted for my reluctance, for I had heard that the Pantokrator was in an advanced state of dereliction and saw no point in courting disappointment. But on the afternoon of 28 June I decided that a visit could no longer be postponed: my journey was almost over and it was time to pay my respects.

We approached along a lane that climbed steeply through an arch of the aqueduct of Valens. The district was poor. Everything seemed to be the color of mud and dust and rotten wood; here and there were lines of crumbling walls and fragments of arches that I took to be remnants of the monastery's outlying buildings. People in the twisting streets pointed out the way for us, and at last we broke free of the crush of houses and the three interlinked churches of the Pantokrator stood before us. There were signs of mutilation—windows bricked up, marble colonettes torn out and replaced by crude struts—but the seven apses of the churches, decorated with niches and blind arcading, produced a delightful effect of undulation. Brick and masonry were colored a soft red. I was glad I had come.

Concerning the Pantokrator, there is, for once, no need to resort to conjecture, since the text of the monastery's *typikon* or foundation charter has come down to us. Drawn up in 1136 under the guidance of John II, the *typikon* is a meticulously detailed document. From it we learn what the monks wore and ate, how much wine they drank, exactly where they were supposed to stand during services and how the churches were to be lighted. The prayers to be recited and the hymns to be sung for the salvation of the imperial family are also specified, but it is the practical and charitable provisions of the *typikon* that are most likely to impress the modern reader. The monastery included a hospital of fifty beds, an old peoples' home of twenty-four beds, a leprosarium and a bath that could be used on certain days by the public. Patients in the hospital were provided with mattresses, carpets, pillows, blankets, shirts and coats. Women were attended by female doctors; inspectors toured the wards each day to listen to the complaints of the patients; there were machines for the cleaning and sharpening of surgical instruments (of which there were well over two hundred, many of highly sophisticated design), and sound regulations governed every aspect of diet, hygiene, heating and ventilation.

Robert Byron does not exaggerate when he declares that "no comparison reveals the West of Europe, right up to the nineteenth century, in so unprogressive a light as that of its charitable organizations with those of the Greek East." John II was only following the example of his father, who had built a complex known as the Orphanage which, if Anna Comnena can be believed, was the size of a small town and could accommodate several thousand inmates— the sick, the orphaned, the blind and handicapped war veterans. John's younger brother, Isaac, also built a hospital, and other members of the family, notably Anna herself and Manuel I, did not consider it beneath their dignity to acquire and apply a practical knowledge of medical matters. Since they also took an intense interest in literature, art, theology, scholarship, philosophy and (of necessity) military strategy, the Comneni deserve to be recognized as renaissance men—and women—ahead of their time.

It is a curious fact that, although the Comnenian emperors assiduously cultivated the martial virtues of their Anatolian forbears and devoted their leisure time to such traditional masculine pursuits as hunting, under their rule women enjoyed an unusual degree of independence and influence. Not far from the Pantokrator, but hard to find in a tangle of narrow lanes, is the exquisite little church of the Pantepoptes Monastery, founded by Anna Dalassena, the remarkable mother of Alexius I. Her granddaughter, Anna Comnena, describes her as a woman of "surpassing virtue, intelligence and energy" who "had an exceptional grasp of public affairs, with a genius for organization and government; she was capable, in fact, of managing not only the Roman Empire, but every other empire under the sun as well." In the early years of his reign Alexius depended on her advice, and when he was away from the capital, as was often the case, he placed the government entirely in her hands. Her word was law and there is some reason to regard her as the true founder of the Comnenian dynasty. Anna Comnena remarks that although Alexius "was in theory the emperor . . . she had the real power." Anna's eulogy of her grandmother is militantly feminist in tone; it is also self-serving, since she herself hoped to rule the empire through her pliable husband, who had once been promised the throne. It was only when her political ambitions were thwarted that she turned to the great history of her father's reign that was to ensure her lasting fame. In it she displays a compendious knowledge of classical Greek literature, a firm grasp of politics, and a surprising expertise in matters of seigecraft. *The Alexiad* is, without doubt, one of the masterpieces of medieval literature.

The two Annas (Dalassena and Comnena) set the tone: the women of the Comnenus clan were notably learned and ambitious. It is typical of them that, when the political activities of the Sebastocratorissa Irene led the Emperor Manuel to question her loyalty, she should have responded indignantly, commissioning a leading poet to defend her reputation in verse. After her father's death, Manuel's spirited daughter, Maria, resorted to direct political action, leading a revolt against the unpopular regency of her stepmother. None of these women allowed their interests or actions to be constrained by narrow definitions of appropriate womanly behavior. As highly educated members of the upper class, they considered it their right to assume a leading role in society. This would be a rich field of exploration for feminist historians.

I approached the Pantokrator with circumspection. I did and did not want to see its interior. Little could have withstood fifty years of Venetian depredation and five centuries of neglect. The doors were locked, which seemed to solve the problem, but a boy appeared and ran off in search of a key. From contemporary accounts and archaeological evidence we know that the interior of the Pantokrator was especially lavish. The dome of the southern church was originally supported by four great porphyry columns; there were mosaics, frescoes, marble revetments, brilliantly colored enamels and vessels and furnishings of gold and silver. What is more surprising—since we think of it as a western invention—is the fact that the windows were filled with figural stained glass. The whole interior must have been saturated in color and refracted light, but the prospect that opened before us, once the door was unlocked, was grim and dark in the extreme. Apart from the rose and green marble frames of the doorways, the broad expanses of the double narthex had been stripped of every trace of ornamentation: even the brick of the vaults was exposed.

I hoped for better things in the south church. I had seen photographs of a superb marble floor with designs of roundels bordered by interlaces, and corner panels filled with vines and mysterious figurative elements, which had been variously identified as depictions of the Labors of Hercules or astrological signs—both of which would have been highly peculiar in a church. I was unable to solve the mystery: the floor was completely covered by a wooden deck. The pleasant woman who had unlocked the place for us pulled aside a rug and opened a miniature trap door in the deck so that we could see the image of a man on horseback surrounded by formalized vines, executed in deep red and pale yellow stone. The south church retains some of its marble paneling, but the mosaics have gone, the enamels are lost or in Venice, and the four porphyry columns have been replaced by ugly baroque piers. The condition of the north church is worse, the only remnants of its original decoration being a cornice ornamented with a vine and a very small fragment of red and gold mosaic in the arch of a window. Its columns of Theban marble have been replaced by crude square piers; most of the windows are broken and pigeons come and go as they please, roosting on the high sills: in the weeks that followed I found it hard to forget the echoes set up by the monotonous clapping of their wings.

Between the two main churches is a domed chapel dedicated to the Archangel Michael, the angel believed to be present at the moment of death. This was the mausoleum of the Comneni and in the *typikon* it is referred to as a *heroön*, an archaic term meaning the tomb of a hero. The term is entirely appropriate, for Alexius I, John II and Manuel I were men of valor, intelligence and stupendous energy. Hindsight tells us that their shared vision of a restored Empire of New Rome could never have been realized—it was too late, and the world was changing too quickly—yet for the better part of a century the Comneni held the empire back from the brink of disaster. After they fell from power the decline was rapid and catastrophic. And Manuel II, who was laid to rest beside them in 1425, was a man who might have achieved great things had the times been more propitious, but as it was, he behaved with dignity and fortitude in impossible circumstances. We do not remember him as a statesman or a soldier, but as a representative of all that is admirable in the Byzantine intellectual tradition, whose erudition enchanted the professors of the Sorbonne when he toured the West vainly pleading for help against the Turks.

The tombs have vanished and the empty shell of the *heroön* is presently used as a dump for broken furniture. I recalled the words with which Anna Comnena concludes *The Alexiad:* "Let this be the end of my history, then, lest as I write of these sad events I become more embittered."

THE CHORA/IMPLICATIONS OF A SHAWL

... Owing to the absence of a strong well-spring of native energy, Byzantine civilisation, considered as a whole, cannot remotely rank with the great civilisations of which history bears record, and which at the slightest touch and at the remove of centuries quicken our spirit and excite our admiration. It is by reason of this meager harvest that we yield the Byzantine empire at best a distant homage and remain unmoved before the storms which gathered round it in its old age and swept it, an enfeebled despotism content to eke out a bare existence and incapable of a single generous thought, into outer darkness and oblivion.

—FERDINAND SCHEVILL, *A History of the Balkans*

After the gloom of the Pantokrator a visit to the Kariye Cami is an absolute necessity. To go from the one to the other is to pass from a wasteland to a garden in full bloom, for the Kariye Cami, which stands on the edge of the city close to the Adrianople Gate, is the former church of the Monastery of Saint Savior in Chora, and it contains mosaics and frescoes commissioned in the early fourteenth century by Theodore Metochites. Taken together they constitute one of the supreme masterpieces of European art, and deserve to be placed on a level with the nearly contemporary work of Giotto or the greatest achievements of the High Renaissance. At the time they were commissioned, the empire was beset with troubles: the Anatolian provinces were all but lost and the Italian maritime republics were draining the state of what little wealth it retained, but none of this is reflected in the art of the Chora. Here there is nothing tired or formulaic, nothing remotely decadent or pessimistic. Any unprejudiced observer who steps into the Chora today is likely to be overwhelmed by the brilliance and freshness of the vitrified colors, the shimmering fields of gold, the grace of the figures, the harmony of the compositions and the wealth of picturesque detail. There are peacocks and pheasants, groups of children at play, crags and windswept trees, fantastic architectural backdrops, billowing awnings and nearly cubist views of towns and cities. In John the Baptist Bearing Witness of Christ, a waterfowl grabs at a snake in a pool; in the Annunciation to Saint Anne, a bird flies toward a nest of squawking fledglings high in a tree. There is sorrow in the world of the Chora—mothers lament the deaths of their children, the blind, the crippled and the sick are very much with us—but there is also an intense delight in existence.

Not the least remarkable of the mosaics is the portrait of Theodore Metochites in a lunette above the door that leads into the main sanctuary. He is shown in the typical attitude of a donor, kneeling at the side of an enthroned Christ, offering a model of the church he has restored. His costume is rich and exotic—almost Turkish in style—consisting of a kind of caftan colored a deep turquoise, patterned with leaves and edged in gold and red; and on his head sits one of the most prodigious pieces of headgear ever represented in a work of art. At first glance it resembles a voluminous turban fitting tightly around the wearer's brow and swelling out to a high, flat, circular crown, but closer examination suggests that it consisted of

silk stretched over a light armature—white silk horizon-
tally pleated and crossed by vertical bands of red and gold
brocade. Scholarly attempts to classify Metochites' hat (is
it or is it not a *skiadion*?) are unconvincing, but what is
immediately apparent is that late Byzantine milliners
borrowed from the Turks and gave to the Italians.

The hat may be a unique creation, but it is certain that,
in the Byzantium of the fourteenth century, only a very
high-ranking official would have been permitted to wear
it. Theodore Metochites was a close friend and confidant
of the Emperor Andronicus II Palaeologus and rose to be
his Grand Logothete. He was also one of the preeminent
litterateurs of the period and an ardent classical scholar.
His voluminous writings included commentaries on Aristotle, an *Introduction to Astronomy* and essays on ancient
Greek history, as well as a poem describing his restoration
of the Chora monastery. Although he was proud of his
literary efforts and hoped that his name would live
through them, they nevertheless have an air of futility.
Their style is described in the *Oxford Dictionary of Byzantium* as "notoriously obscure" and, like many a Byzantine
before him, Metochites often felt so overwhelmed by the
glorious achievements of the ancients that he wondered if
there was anything left for him to say.

The anonymous master painter of the Chora clearly had
no such doubts, yet his patron's veneration of the past is
reflected in the strong classicizing tendencies of his work.
This is most evident in the picturesque elements, which
have no explicit religious connotations, and in groups of
luxuriously coiffed and robed maidens who might be
strolling in the gardens of Hellenistic Alexandria. Even
when we look in from the margins to the central figures of
the Christian drama there is no trace of the stiff, hieratic
formality commonly associated with Byzantine art: figures
are animated and expressive and their humanity is never in

doubt. In scenes from the Infancy of the Virgin, the master of the Chora creates images of simple domestic tenderness that have few clear precedents in the Byzantine tradition, yet his approach remains sophisticated and without sentimentality. In the First Seven Steps of the Virgin he cunningly nods toward the erudite tastes of his patron without failing to engage the emotions of the common worshiper. At the center of the composition the charming figure of the infant Virgin totters toward her mother with arms outstretched, but behind her stands the strange and marvelous figure of a tall handmaiden, who bends protectively toward her. The handmaiden wears a long blue classical robe hemmed with gold and her head is encircled by a flying shawl colored a light red. In a tenth-century miniature, now in Paris, a figure personifying night has a similar shawl arching over her head. She is undoubtedly copied from a Hellenistic original. The handmaiden of the Chora is thus an elegantly nostalgic allusion of the kind that Theodore Metochites and his learned friends could be expected to appreciate. But she is much more than that. She may be only the echo of a personification, but she is also a poignant symbol of the intense pride in the achievements of Hellenism that characterized late-Byzantine intellectual circles, a pride that led to an increased tolerance of pagan concepts. Metochites resorted to the concept of tyche to account for the empire's decline; Gemistus Plethon, the last and most original of Byzantine Neoplatonists, went much further, spending his last years writing hymns to Zeus and Apollo. Metochites felt that Christ had abandoned the empire; Plethon abandoned Christ.

The scenes of Christ's Passion that would have decorated the main sanctuary of the Chora have been lost, and most of the surviving mosaics are to be found in the outer and inner narthexes. All the important frescoes are located in the *parecclesion* or side chapel, to the south of the sanctuary. Here the artist was less concerned to charm with detail and allusion. The background tone is a deep blue, the compositions are monumental and dramatic, the themes eschatological. It seems that, from the first, Metochites planned to be buried here in sight of the great *Anastasis* or Resurrection scene that fills the eastern apse. At its center, Christ stands in a luminous white robe, against a mandorla that shades outward from very pale blue to white scattered with gold stars; beneath his widely spread feet, Satan lies manacled amid the remnants of the shattered gates of Hell; to left and right are the companies of the righteous posed against shelving rock formations that lean in toward the center of the composition. The Christ of the *Anastasis* is dynamic beyond anything in earlier Byzantine art: his robe is stretched taut between his right knee and his left calf; he grasps Adam and Eve by their wrists and pulls them, robes flying, from their tombs. It is an image that burns itself into the mind of anyone who has seen it. The emotional intensity of the scene and the elongation of certain of the figures (especially the elegantly despondent, red-robed Eve) have reminded commentators of El Greco, whose real name was Domenico Theotocopuli and whose early training was in the Byzantine tradition, which still survived in his native Crete a century after the fall of Constantinople.

In 1332 Theodore Metochites had his wish and was buried in his beloved Chora, but not before his life had taken a tragic turn. The restoration of the Chora was completed in 1321, but that year saw the beginning of a disastrous civil war between Andronicus II and his grandson, Andronicus III. At a time when the empire should have been mustering all its resources to stem the Turkish advance in Anatolia, it was torn apart from within. When, seven years later, the struggle was decided in favor of the younger Andronicus, Metochites suffered the consequences of his long and close association with the old emperor. His palace was torn down by a mob—perhaps inspired by envy of his great wealth as much as any political antipathy to the old regime—and he was exiled for several dismal years to western Thrace. In 1330 the new regime relented and allowed him to return to the capital, where he retired, as the humble monk Theoleptos, to the monastery on which he had lavished so much of his now-vanished wealth. It is to be hoped that his assiduous studies of the Hellenic philosophers enabled him to bear these changes of fortune with composure, for we owe him a great debt: without the art of the Chora the world would be an impoverished place.

THE LOST PALACE

Exhausted from five weeks of travel and the lingering effects of a virus acquired in Cappadocia, I spent my last day quietly in the Sultan Ahmet district, where our modest hotel lay huddled in the shadow of Hagia Sophia and the Blue Mosque. It was time to visit the Church of Saints Sergius and Bacchus, one of the loveliest of all

Justinian's buildings, which lies on the southern edge of the district, just inside the sea walls. It is now a mosque, little-used and generally locked, but if you wait a while in its tree-shaded forecourt someone will unlock it for you. The interior is essentially an octagon set at a slight angle within a square, but the arcades between the eight piers that support the dome are alternately straight and curved, and this gives the whole space a marvelous feeling of fluidity and lightness. Its mosaics are long gone or hidden under plaster, but its marble columns with their delicately undercut capitals still support a magnificent entablature inscribed with a long epigram praising the imperial patrons Justinian and Theodora. Complex, harmonious and eminently human in scale, it does not look like a place that could ever have fostered mere superstition. Perhaps, if Voltaire had seen it, he might have revised his opinion of a culture he dismissed as "a worthless collection of orations and miracles."

Between Saints Sergius and Bacchus and Hagia Sophia, the twisting lanes of Sultan Ahmet slope steeply down toward the Sea of Marmara lined with small hotels and Ottoman houses, but in among the hotels and houses are mysterious decayed structures of brick and masonry—the ruins of bastions, massive substructures and terraces that are among the little that remains of the Great Palace of the emperors. If Constantinople was the greatest city of medieval Europe, it follows that its Great Palace should have been by far the largest and most richly decorated: since it was the residence of God's vice-regent on earth, sole emperor of the sole, legitimate empire, nothing less would do. It was bounded on the west by the Hippodrome (which still exists as a long dusty park punctuated by obelisks), on the north by Hagia Sophia and on the east and south by the sea, and at the time of its heyday in the tenth century, it covered a wider area than most contemporary western European towns.

Constructed at intervals over a period of eight hundred years, the Great Palace was in reality an agglomeration of many palaces or palatial complexes—The Daphne, the Magnaura, the Boukoleon and so on. There were great halls, private apartments and churches as well as innumerable more mundane structures such as barracks, eunuchs' quarters, kitchens, baths and workshops. This longest of all building projects was begun by Constantine the Great, whose palace was largely confined to the high ground close to the Hippodrome. It was entered from the north through a monumental gateway named the Chalke because of its great bronze doors. Beyond the Chalke was the Delphax, a colonnaded courtyard around which were arranged the main public areas—the barracks of the imperial guard, the imperial treasury and the Hall of the Nineteen Couches, where, in later centuries, the bodies of the emperors lay in state prior to their burial. Farther south, approximately where the Blue Mosque is today, was the Daphne. Named after a statue of the nymph that had been brought from Rome, it contained the private apartments of the emperor and was linked to the imperial box in the Hippodrome. To the southeast of the Daphne, on lower ground, were the apartments of the empress, including her birthing room, the famous Purple Chamber: it is from this room that the term *porphyrogenitus* (born in the purple) derives. From the first the palace had a private harbor with an adjacent pharos (or lighthouse) and close to it was the Boukoleon, so named because of the statues of bulls and lions that adorned the steps that led up to it.

Some churches were added during the fifth century, but it was not until the reign of Justinian I that the next major building phase began. The northern area of the palace had been damaged by the fires that swept through the city during the Nika riots, and Justinian's restorations easily surpassed what had gone before. The Chalke was rebuilt as a massive domed structure decorated with mosaics and statues. But it was Justinian's nephew and successor, Justin II, who made what is perhaps the single most important contribution to the fabric of the palace, namely the Chrysotriklinos or Golden Hall, which was to become the chief center of court ceremonial.

Conceived on the grandest scale and not completed until the reign of Justin's successor, the Chrysotriklinos was entered from the west through doors of solid silver. It took the form of a domed octagon with apses radiating like the petals of a rose. On walls and ceilings there were mosaics of flowers. In the eastern apse stood the emperor's throne and on the half-dome above it was a mosaic image of Christ seated on a similar throne, while in the apses to the north and south were golden organs set with precious stones. The Chrysotriklinos has entirely vanished, but it is not hard to imagine how it must have looked, since the Church of Saints Sergius and Bacchus, and the Church of San Vitale in Ravenna have survived. Both are domed octagons with multiple apses dating from the sixth century, and the latter has imperial portraits in mosaic of a kind that must have been very common in the public spaces of the Great Palace.

Justin II came to the throne determined to restore the Roman virtues, but even as the Chrysotriklinos started to rise his ears were battered with news of defeats and he succumbed to the violent madness for which he is chiefly remembered. The hard-pressed emperors of the seventh and eighth centuries had neither the time nor the resources for major building schemes. The notable exception was Justinian II, whose reign began in 685 when he was a mere sixteen years old and full of fiery ambition. Having proved his valor by defeating the Slavs, he turned his attention to the construction of enduring monuments to his fame. The result was two vast, mosaiced halls lying to the west of the Chrysotriklinos, known respectively as the Lausiakos and the Triklinos of Justinian.

Some one hundred and thirty years later the equally youthful Theophilus adorned Justinian's triklinos with new mosaics and to its south, on a steeply sloping site between the Chrysotriklinos and the Daphne, commenced work on a complex of buildings so exquisite that even the most sophisticated members of his court were dazzled: the pavilions known as the Pearl, the Camilas and the Carianos (see pp. 127–128) were arranged symmetrically around two linked halls called the Sigma and the Triconchos. The first of these was shaped like the letter C and its roof was supported by fifteen marble columns; its curving arms embraced a forecourt in which stood a golden throne flanked by bronze lions spouting water into a semicircular pool. There was also a graceful arch raised on a stage and a second fountain in the form of a golden pinecone rising from a bronze basin rimmed with silver. The overall effect was intentionally theatrical, since this was the setting for performances of the Saximodeximum, a kind of ballet with horses, during which the pinecone would spurt spiced wine. From this forecourt one passed through the Sigma, then through doors of silver to the Triconchos, which, as its name suggests, had three apses (or "conches") radiating from a central dome raised on porphyry columns. Its ceiling was gilded. The whole complex represents a clear attempt to revive the late-antique style that had prevailed during the fourth and fifth centuries: such a revival of, or reversion to, earlier forms was perhaps intended to indicate that the empire had entered on a new period of prosperity and greatness, as indeed it had.

Theophilus' son Michael III took little interest in art and

architecture, but his successor and murderer, Basil I, although the illiterate son of peasants, brought the palace to the height of its glory. The Chalke was once more restored, but Basil's chief contribution was the church he built to the east of the Chrysotriklinos. There were several other churches inside the palace precincts, but Basil's Nea Ekklesia, as it was universally known, easily surpassed them and set the model for all later imperial foundations. Since it stood on sloping ground it was probably raised on a high terrace. Approached through an atrium with two marble fountains, it was cruciform in plan and had five domes clad in polished bronze; in the central dome was a mosaic of Christ Pantokrator, while in the eastern apse the Virgin extended her protection to the emperor and his empire; the floor was of varicolored polished marble arranged in elaborate designs and the iconostasis was made of gilded silver inlaid with precious stones. Here, for the first time, the classic middle-Byzantine style appeared fully formed: architecture and image were fused to produce an overwhelming effect of luxury and refinement—a great chorus of colors and stones and precious metals hymning the mystery of Christ's incarnation. For the remaining five-and-a-half centuries of the empire's existence the Nea continued to be regarded as one of the principal marvels of the capital. Even so it was not enough for Basil, who also built a polo court known as the Tzykanisterion, a new triklinos with columns of verd antique and red onyx, and a suite of apartments decorated with mosaics of peacocks.

The Palace as it stood at the time of Basil's death in 886 is best imagined as a vast stage set designed to accommodate the ceaseless rituals of the court. Although it had been built piecemeal, its plan was far from haphazard: throne rooms, like churches, had an east-west orientation, symbolizing the sacred character of the imperial office, and many of the major structures were aligned according to a series of "processional routes." One of the most important of these began at the Gate of Skylax, which opened into the palace from the Hippodrome. To the east of the gate there would have been a courtyard from which one would have continued eastward, passing under the gilded ceilings and between the mosaiced walls of the Triklinos of Justinian II and the Lausiakos, perhaps descending broad flights of marble steps between the halls. Beyond the Lausiakos was the grand vestibule called the Tripeton, on the far side of which were the silver doors leading into the Chrysotriklinos. At the approach of a procession these doors would have swung open and the two golden organs would have begun to play.

The emperors of the tenth and eleventh century added little to the Great Palace. This was not the result of any lack of enthusiasm for building; rather it seems to have been generally agreed that the palace was now complete. Over the years some parts of it may have fallen into disuse, but there is no truth to the oft-repeated assertion that the Comnenian emperors abandoned it in favor of the Blachernae. Abandonment of the very seat and symbol of imperial authority would have been an act of despair and the Comneni were not much given to despair. The Blachernae, with its proximity to the open country, may have been their preferred residence, but the old palace of the emperors remained the center of official business and ceremonial. It is clear from *The Alexiad* that it was still in use during the final years of Alexius I's reign, and his grandson, Manuel I, while adding greatly to the splendor of the Blachernae, did not neglect the older foundation. In a complex act of architectural symbolism he restored and redecorated the Lausiakos of Justinian II and built, close by, his famous hall in the Seljuk style—the so called

Persian House or Mouchroutas. By restoring a structure more than five centuries old he signaled his determination to restore the empire; by the construction of the Persian House, with its *muqarnas* ceiling, he indicated his openness to the idea of rapprochement with the Turks, and presumably Turkish or other Muslim craftsmen must have collaborated on its construction.

No trace of the Mouchroutas remains, but the Zisa Palace, which can still be seen on the outskirts of Palermo, offers strong clues as to its appearance. Built for the Norman King William I of Sicily in 1162, the Zisa is roughly contemporary with the Mouchroutas. Both names derive from Arabic and in both structures Islamic and Byzantine styles were combined. In the lovely central hall of the Zisa, stalactites and honeycombs are suspended above mosaic medallions of archers shooting birds and peacocks pecking at dates, and the floor is paved with polychrome marble. Manuel's new hall cannot have been any less magnificent or fanciful.

Manuel was the last emperor to undertake significant building activity within the old palace, but it remained largely intact until 1204 and even in that terrible year it escaped the worst effects of the sack due to the fact that the leaders of the Fourth Crusade chose it as their headquarters. They were dumbfounded; the chronicler Robert de Clari counted "fully five hundred halls, all connected with one another and all made with gold mosaic" and remarked that even the hinges of the doors were made of silver, where one might expect iron. When the Byzantines reentered the city in 1261, the palace was still in sufficiently good repair to serve a ceremonial function, but during the Latin occupation it had been looted of most of its movable treasures and its structure had suffered seriously from neglect. The Palaeologan emperors did not have the means to embark on the vast campaign of restoration that was needed, and so it came about that the Constantinople of their "restored" empire had at its heart the inexorably decaying mass of the edifice that was the chief symbol of its former power and glory. When the Turks entered the city the palace lay in ruins, amid which the conquering sultan is supposed to have wandered quoting Persian verses on the theme of mutability: "Now the spider weaves the curtains in the palace of the Caesars."

It is sometimes argued that because of its overwhelmingly religious nature our understanding of Byzantine civilization is not substantially altered by the loss of the Great Palace, but one could equally well argue that Byzantine civilization would seem less religious if we knew more of its secular art and architecture. Consider how much our knowledge of French culture would be impoverished if Versailles, Fontainebleau and all the great chateaux had been destroyed, leaving only a few moldering walls and pilasters. The palace was the center of the Byzantine world and the treasure-house of its secular art: its disappearance is a major tragedy. There is no reason to believe that the many mosaic scenes of triumphs, of hunting, of birds, animals and flowers referred to in the sources were any less fine than the Nativities and Crucifixions that have survived.

All that remains today are some floor mosaics hidden under a new shopping mall behind the Blue Mosque. Although they are thought to date from the sixth century, they are purely classical in style. Since they are not mentioned in any of the Byzantine sources they must have been considered unremarkable, yet their technique is superb: images of hunting and combat between animals have an almost alarming naturalism (the claws tear, the wounds gape and bleed), while landscapes and views of towns have a delicate Theocritan charm, as do certain genre scenes—one of two boys riding a camel and another of a mare suckling a foal. Byzantium could not escape the influence of Asia, but its interest in the classical past never lapsed, as the mosaics of the Chora prove. From the Justinianic age onward, the Oriental and the classical (peacocks and centaurs) coexisted and commingled with ever-varying results: the same emperor could build palaces in imitation of late-Roman and Arab models, and the same glass bowl that was decorated with Greek ephebes had a rim bearing designs derived from Arabic script.

There is only one substantial architectural fragment that can give us some idea (it is really no more than a hint) of how the palace looked during its heyday. It is sometimes referred to as the House of Justinian, but it must have formed part of the Boukoleon. To reach it you must descend through a warren of narrow lanes lined with old wooden houses. Some of these are abandoned; others, still inhabited, sag and lean so much that they seem about to submit gracefully to gravity and time. Upper stories project out over the streets, in the manner of the old *heliaka* of Byzantium, their fretted window frames underlined with neat rows of flowerpots.

On emerging from these streets, you must pass under the railway line and through a gap in the sea walls and walk along the broad highway that follows the Marmaran shore. After a time you will come upon the low arch of a water gate that bears a fluid design of curling vines, but it is filled with trash and scorched by fires. Walk a little farther, and you come upon a massive projecting bastion; just beyond that is the ruinous but still-handsome façade that is your destination. High above you and surmounted by brick arches are three nobly proportioned marble window frames that once opened out onto balconies overlooking a narrow sandy beach and the sea. Old photographs show fishing boats drawn up on this beach, and fishermen's shacks lean against the ancient walls.

When William of Tyre visited Constantinople in the twelfth century he was enraptured by the approach to the Great Palace from the sea, speaking of "Marble steps descending to the water's edge, and statues of lions and columns, also of marble, adorning the place with royal splendour." Today the only extant façade of the Boukoleon is suspended like a motheaten curtain between the highway and the railway, and its windows are stacked with splintered wooden crates. Nevertheless couples like to sit in the evening on the benches of the small park that lies in front of it, and as the sun begins to set over the Sea of Marmara the walls turn a deep shade of rose, and in October the long strands of creeper that drape the whole structure resemble a great plait of red hair that has unraveled. But wait a little longer and as the light fades the bats of the Boukoleon will emerge, dancing through its windows and arches. They are now its sole possessors.

A LAST ENCOUNTER

It was in the streets of Sultan Ahmet that I encountered an American woman called Mrs. Davis. We sat down at a café table and she told me her life story:

Mrs. Davis is a small woman with violet hair. She moves easily about the tea garden of the Hotel Side, imparting episodes of her life story to parties of disoriented New Zealanders who hardly seem to know they are in Istanbul. Mrs. Davis knows that. She knows she is in Istanbul. Each time she sits down at a table the whole garden seems to sigh a little. Mrs. Davis worries about the climbing roses, which, to the manager's sorrow, have not flowered this year. She gives advice to the best of her ability, but cheerfully confesses that she is "no gardener." The rose leaves are covered with a dusty gray blight. At midday, when the reflected light from the garden's white pebble floor becomes too glaring, Mrs. Davis vanishes.

Mrs. Davis is a trained nurse and a native of Columbus, Ohio. She is divorced. She is always brightly and neatly

dressed. She must be at least sixty-five, but could be considerably older. Her manner of storytelling seems to suggest as
much. She will remember the twenty-two-room guesthouse she
once owned in the Berkshires, how during the Tanglewood
season it would be full to bursting so that whole families
camped out on the back lawn, and they came back year after
year; she will remember the concerts (how she had to slip
away before the final chord, so as to be home before her music-
loving guests); she will remember the colors of the fall, and you
will agree that they are beautiful, so beautiful there, and then
she will say, "That was the year my mother died," and a new,
darker episode begins to grow, threatening to obliterate the
story of the house and the paying guests, the music and the
autumn foliage: "It wouldn't have been fair to her. It wouldn't
have been fair to my children—they were still teenagers—but
I never should have put her on that plane at Albany. She died
of total renal failure."

Buying that house in the Berkshires, Mrs. Davis considers,
was the best thing she ever did, selling it the worst thing. "On
my way to Lenox to sign the papers I nearly turned back. I
turned the car around but it was too late." Mrs. Davis's
digressions can be fatiguing, but impatience is something to be
avoided. After a time a pattern emerges: the themes of the lost
house and the dying mother are inseparably linked, and both
prepare us for the fateful, casual journey.

One year at the end of a tour of Greece Mrs. Davis decided
to spend a few days in Istanbul. She remembered the name
Constantinople from geography lessons or history lessons and,
though she could not recall why, she knew it was a magical
name. At first she was afraid. The weather was overcast and
humid as it often is in Istanbul in the summer. The city
seemed gloomy, tangled, chaotic, full of strange cries and
laments. She was a woman alone and a long way from Ohio,
but when she stepped out on the street and began to walk

about, with no particular aim in view, she felt immediately at home. She was safe, she knew this place, she had been here before. *She greeted each new maze of streets, each handsome mosque or neglected church as a friend, a friend who had perhaps been wondering why she had been away for so long. Of course, she had not been here before. Mrs. Davis is not of a mystical bent. She does not believe in reincarnation or former lives, but she can't think of any other way to explain it. This old, wild, messy, occidental-oriental city fit like a glove—a perfumed glove such as Mrs. Davis might have worn to a dance in her youth. She couldn't understand it, yet it all seemed to make perfect sense.* "Perhaps you were a Byzantine," *we suggest.* "Perhaps you were a princess like Anna Comnena." *Mrs. Davis's cheeks dimple.* "Well, I don't know about that, but I love beautiful old buildings, always have." *She pauses reflectively, then—*"I think I must've been an artist."

Mrs. Davis has her anxieties. She knows three different ways to get to the American consulate. She must have free access to a phone late at night. The phone at the Hotel Side is kept locked and international calls by ladies from Ohio or suddenly homesick New Zealanders are not permitted at any time. Mrs. Davis frets about this. How will she keep in touch with her children? Typically, she will come for a two- or three-week tour, and just stay and stay. Last year her daughter asked, "Mom, are you ever coming home?" *That time she stayed for six months. Nor did she stay timidly within the confines of some convenient, consular radius. Mrs. Davis has seen the towers of Trebizond (though, in truth, they aren't much to see); she has been to Artvin and Ani, and to Hopa, so close to the Russian border; she has walked in the lands of the Laz, she has seen the great church at Vank. But mostly she stays in Istanbul, exploring the different quarters alone and on foot. When asked to name her favorite place—Zeyrek*

*or Fener, Balat or Yedikule?—her eyes go momentarily blank.
She looks almost panicked, as if she were being asked to prove
something. She recovers and remarks blandly, "Oh, I don't
know that I have a favorite place. I just like it all." Mrs. Davis
knows she is in Istanbul, but one begins to wonder if she
knows where Istanbul is. She feels she has found her way
home, yet it still seems as if she is looking for a coin or a
kerchief that she dropped in the dust of a back street.*

*One time Mrs. Davis took a room on the top floor of the
Hotel Populër. She loved the view of the Sea of Marmara and
the moon, but after a while she began to feel that the management wanted to get rid of her. A family needed her large room.
She became friends with a young Kurd named Ahmet. How
Ahmet hated the silly fez—the fez that Atatürk had banned—
that the management made him wear, and what a wonderful
smile he had—like the sun coming up. Once Ahmet fell ill and
Mrs. Davis prescribed a course of aspirin and water. He got
better and was grateful ever after to "the American doctor."
He would kiss her hand and press it to his forehead.*

*Mrs. Davis moved into an apartment, and the hotel soon
went to the dogs. The staff drank raki day and night; wall-
paper peeled from the walls, and desperate women from disin-
tegrating Romania—who had only themselves to sell—began
taking in customers. Mrs. Davis shivers. "You should see the
place now."*

*Her apartment, meanwhile, turned out to be waterless—
that is to say, there was water but only on certain days, at
certain times, times when Mrs. Davis was invariably out on
one of her walks. Where was the apartment, we ask. "Oh,
way over there," she says, gesturing vaguely toward the
Golden Horn and beyond. As if five days without water
wasn't enough, on the sixth day she found that she was locked
out. As she had no place to go and very little ready cash, she
began to walk down the hill from her apartment building with*

no clear idea of what she would do. The steep street had no sidewalk. It was late at night, but luckily she was carrying a flashlight, so she was not too badly afraid, besides in Turkey women of a certain age, especially lone foreign women of a certain age, are treated with respect. Don't they kiss your hand here? She would be all right. A door opened and Mrs. Davis stepped into an oblong of light. A woman's voice out of the light asked her where she was going. Although she had acquired no Turkish beyond polite greetings, Mrs. Davis managed to explain that she had nowhere to sleep. She slept two nights at the woman's house. After that she had had it with apartments.

We tell Mrs. Davis how brave she is, but wonder privately what it is that drives her to do these things. She smiles and says, "Why, thank you, I think I was *very brave," and adds by way of explanation that she likes "a challenge." This does not satisfy us, and there are many questions we would still like to ask, but it is long past breakfast and the sun is getting strong: it is time for Mrs. Davis to disappear.*

In the early evening we see her again, sitting outside a storefront deep in conversation with a tradesman, or rather, she is talking and he is listening. Her story has not ended. It wanders and divides and doubles back. It is like the street plan of old Istanbul, and there is no map that can help you find your way through that maze. All are incomplete, misleading, laughably schematic. The year may come when— as her daughter fears—Mrs. Davis does not come home.

BYZANTINE EMPERORS

324–37 Constantine I
337–61 Constantius
361–3 Julian
363–4 Jovian
364–78 Valens
379–95 Theodosius I
395–408 Arcadius
408–450 Theodosius II
450–7 Marcian
457–74 Leo I
474 Leo II
474–5 Zeno
475–6 Basiliscus
476–91 Zeno (again)
491–518 Anastasius I
518–27 Justin I
527–65 Justinian I
565–78 Justin II
578–82 Tiberius I
   Constantine

582–602 Maurice
602–10 Phocas
610–41 Heraclius
641 Constantine III and
   Heraclonas
641 Heraclonas
641–68 Constans II
668–85 Constantine IV
685–95 Justinian II
695–8 Leontius
698–705 Tiberius II
705–11 Justinian II (again)
711–13 Philippicus
713–15 Anastasius II
715–17 Theodosius III
717–41 Leo III
741–75 Constantine V
775–80 Leo IV
780–97 Constantine VI
797–802 Irene

802–11 Nicephorus I
811 Stauracius
811–13 Michael I Rangabe
813–20 Leo V
820–9 Michael II
829–42 Theophilus
842–67 Michael III
867–86 Basil I
886–912 Leo VI
912–13 Alexander
913–59 Constantine VII
920–44 Romanus I Lecapenus
959–63 Romanus II
963–9 Nicephorus II Phocas
969–76 John I Tzimiskes
976–1025 Basil II
1025–28 Constantine VIII
1028–34 Romanus III Argyrus
1034–41 Michael IV
1041–2 Michael V
1042 Zoë and Theodora
1042–55 Constantine IX
Monomachus
1055–6 Theodora (again)
1056–7 Michael VI
1057–9 Isaac I Comnenus
1059–67 Constantine X
Ducas
1068–71 Romanus IV
Diogenes
1071–8 Michael VII Ducas
1078–81 Nicephorus III
Botaneiates
1081–1118 Alexius I
Comnenus
1118–43 John II Comnenus

1143–80 Manuel I Comnenus
1180–3 Alexius II Comnenus
1183–5 Andronicus I
Comnenus
1185–95 Isaac II Angelus
1195–1203 Alexius III
Angelus
1203–4 Isaac II (again) and
Alexius IV Angeli
1204 Alexius V Murtzuphlus
1204–22 Theodore I Lascaris
1222–54 John III Ducas
Vatatzes
1254–8 Theodore II Lascaris
1258–61 John IV Lascaris
1259–82 Michael VIII Palaeologus
1282–1328 Andronicus II
Palaeologus
1328–41 Andronicus III
Palaeologus
1341–91 John V Palaeologus
1347–54 John VI
Cantacuzenus
1376–9 Andronicus IV Palaeologus
1390 John VII Palaeologus
1391–1425 Manuel II Palaeologus
1425–48 John VIII Palaeo-
logus
1449–53 Constantine XI
Palaeologus

CHRONOLOGY

286 Diocletian divides the Roman Empire into eastern and western halves, each with its own emperor. It is the Eastern Empire that will evolve into the Byzantine Empire.

313 Constantine the Great issues Edict of Milan, extending to Christianity the toleration enjoyed by other religions.

324 Constantine unites the Eastern and Western Empires, but acknowledges the much greater importance of the Eastern by establishing his capital in the old Greek city of Byzantium, which is renamed Nea Roma (New Rome) or Constantinople (City of Constantine). It expands rapidly.

379–95 Reign of Theodosius I, the last emperor to rule both East and West. Makes Christianity the state religion. Suppresses paganism.

406 A confederation of German tribes crosses the frozen Rhine near Mainz. The break-up of the Western Empire has begun.

410 Visigoths sack Rome.

413 Construction of the great land walls of Constantinople. Until the thirteenth century they defeat all of Byzantium's enemies and, because of them, the barbarian invaders of the fifth century are unable to penetrate the Asian provinces. By contrast, no part of the West is safe.

452 Attila invades Italy. Five years later Vandals sack Rome.

476 The barbarian Odoacer forces the last Western emperor to abdicate. Eastern Empire retains control of Anatolia, Syria, Egypt, Greece and the Balkans.

476–527 Period of consolidation in the East. Art and architecture begin to take on the hybrid characteristics we think of as Byzantine. Population of Constantinople rises to half a million.

527–65 Reign of Justinian I. Reconquest of North Africa, Sicily, Italy and southern Spain. Laws codified. Period of great artistic and literary activity. Construction of Hagia Sophia.

542 The plague arrives in Constantinople and recurs at intervals for the next century, accompanied by earthquakes, famines, civil disturbances. Sharp demographic decline. Slavs invade the Balkans.

602 Murder of Emperor Maurice. Persians invade, conquering Syria and Egypt, and causing widespread devastation in Anatolia. The Avars beseige Constantinople. The Lombards press down into Italy.

610 Heraclius seizes the throne. Embarks on restoration of the empire. By 628 his victory over the Persians is complete.

636 Battle of Yarmuk (in modern Jordan). Byzantine army annihilated by the Arabs. Syria and Egypt are abandoned, but the Byzantines hold the line at the Taurus Mountains. This much-reduced and Greek-speaking empire is very different from the empire of Constantine, and it is at this point that most historians abandon the term "Eastern Roman" in favor of the term "Byzantine."

674–78 First Arab siege of Constantinople defeated, thanks in part to the invention of Greek fire—the "Byzantine secret weapon." This was a liquid that burnt on water. It was propeled from long tubes or syphons attached to the prows of battleships. Its chemical composition remains a mystery.

717–18 Second Arab siege of Constantinople defeated.

726 Leo III issues his Iconoclast Edict banning all representation of Christ, His Mother or the saints in human form. A long and bitter controversy results.

747 Last major outbreak of the plague before the fourteenth century. To make up for the population loss Constantine V transports large numbers of Slavs into Anatolia.

811 Emperor Nicephorus I defeated and killed by the Bulgars. From this point on the Bulgarian Empire is periodically a major threat to Byzantium.

825 Arabs capture Crete.

829–42 Reign of Theophilus. Beginnings of demographic and economic recovery. First major building program since the seventh century.

838 Sack of Amorion by the Arabs, followed by reforms in Byzantine military system.

842–867 Victories over the Arabs. Period of great intellectual brilliance. University of Constantinople refounded. Icons restored (843).

867 Basil I founds Macedonian dynasty, which rules the empire for nearly two centuries. Much building activity. Byzantine authority reestablished in southern Italy. Despite setbacks the Byzantine recovery is sustained into the next century.

934 Capture of Melitene (Malatya), an important Arab stronghold in eastern Anatolia.

961 Nicephorus II Phocas captures Crete.

962 Phocas invades Syria, sacks Aleppo. Much of Cilicia is also recovered, and in the following year Phocas marries the Empress Theophano, and becomes emperor.

965 Conquests of Tarsus and Cyprus.

969 Recapture of Antioch, ancient capital of Syria. In the same year Phocas is murdered by his nephew, John I Tzimiskes, who claims the throne.

975 Tzimiskes leads a brilliant campaign into Syria and Palestine. Apogee of Byzantium.

976–1025 Reign of Basil II. Suppresses rebellions by the Anatolian magnates and crushes the last vestiges of Bulgarian independence. The empire now extends from the Crimea to Cyprus, and from Calabria to Armenia, but on Basil's death a rapid decline sets in—a decline that coincides with the mobilization of the Turks under the energetic Seljuk dynasty.

1056 Having conquered Iran, the Seljuks establish themselves in Baghdad. Raids into Anatolia soon follow.

1059 Turks sack Sebasteia (Sivas), but the central government is dominated by bureaucrats hostile to the military, and the warning goes unheeded.

1068 Turks sack Caesarea (Kayseri).

1071 Battle of Manzikert. Emperor Romanus IV Diogenes defeated and captured by Seljuks. Chaos in Anatolia. Influx of Turkmen tribes.

1080 Seljuks take Nicaea and make it the capital of their western territories.

1081 Alexius I, Comnenus seizes the throne, grants trading privileges to the Venetians in return for help against a Norman invasion. Beginning of a period of increasing tension between Byzantium and the West.

1095 Alexius appeals to the West for help against the Turks. The alarming result is the First Crusade.

1097 Crusaders besiege Nicaea and the Turks surrender to Alexius. Reconquest of western Anatolia follows, but relations with the crusaders soon deteriorate.

1118-76 Alexius' son and grandson (John II and Manuel I) continue his work of restoration, gaining control in all the coastal regions of Anatolia, but the Seljuks remain firmly entrenched on the central plateau.

1176 Battle of Myriocephalon. Seljuks defeat Manuel I. Comnenian reconquest is halted.

1180 Death of Manuel. Second period of sharp decline. Rebellions and raids in Anatolia. Mutual contempt of Byzantium and the West exacerbated by trade disputes and acts of violence. Massacre of Westerners in Constantinople (1182), Norman invasion and sack of Thessalonica (1185).

1204 The Fourth Crusade, diverted by the Venetians from its original goal (an attack on Muslim Egypt), captures Constantinople and subjects it to a brutal sack. Much of the city is destroyed by fire.

1205 Theodore I Lascaris establishes an empire-in-exile in Nicaea.

1220-37 Reign of Alaeddin Kaykobad. Apogee of the Seljuk sultanate of Konya.

1243 Battle of Köse Dağ. Mongols defeat Seljuks.

1261 Emperor Michael VIII Palaeologus recaptures Constantinople.

1288-1321 Establishment of the Ottoman (Osmanli) state on the borders of Bithynia. Collapse of Byzantine defences in Asia. Last flowering of art in Constantinople.

1321-28 First Palaeologan civil war.

1331 Loss of Nicaea to the Ottomans.

1341-47 Second civil war. Turks enter Europe for the first time. Black Death.

1390 Turks capture Philadelphia, the last Byzantine outpost in western Asia.

1394 Sultan Beyazid I blockades Constantinople. After 1396 this becomes a full-scale siege.

1402 Battle of Ankara. Timur defeats and captures Beyazid. Siege of Constantinople is lifted and a civil war breaks out among the Ottoman princes, allowing the empire to survive for another half-century.

1453 Fall of Constantinople.

SELECTED READING

Angold, Michael, *The Byzantine Empire 1025–1204*, Longman, London/New York, N.Y., 1984.

Arnott Hamilton, J., *Byzantine Architecture and Decoration*, B. T. Batsford, London, 1933.

Byron, Robert, *The Byzantine Achievement*, Routledge & Kegan Paul, London, 1929, 1987.

Cahen, C., *Pre-Ottoman Turkey*, trans. J. Jones Williams, New York, N. Y., 1968.

Comnena, Anna, *The Alexiad*, trans. E.R.A. Sewter, Penguin Books, New York, N.Y., 1969.

Cormack, Robin, *Writing in Gold: Byzantine Society and Its Icons*, George Philip, London, 1985.

Diehl, Charles, *Byzantium: Greatness and Decline*, Rutgers University Press, New Brunswick, N.J., 1957.

Geanakoplos, D. John, ed., *Byzantium: Church, Society and Civilisation Seen Through Contemporary Eyes*, Chicago University Press, Chicago, Ill., 1984.

Gough, Michael, *Alahan, An Early Christian Monastery in Southern Turkey*, The Pontifical Institute of Medieval Studies, Toronto, 1985.

Haussig, H. W., *History of Byzantine Civilisation*, trans. J. M. Hussey, Praeger London, 1971.

Hourani, Albert, *A History of the Arab Peoples*, Harvard University Press, Boston, Mass., 1991.

Housepian Dobkin, Marjorie, *Smyrna 1922: The Destruction of a City*, Kent State University Press, Kent, Ohio, 1988.

Hussey, J. M., ed., *Cambridge Medieval History*, Vol. IV, Cambridge University Press, England, 1966–76.

Jenkins, R., *Byzantium: The Imperial Centuries 610–1071*, Weidenfeld & Nicolson, London, 1966.

Kazhdan, Alexander P., ed., *The Oxford Dictionary of Byzantium*, 3 vols., Oxford University Press, Oxford/New York, N.Y., 1991.

———, and Ann Epstein Wharton, *Change in Byzantine Culture in the 11th and 12th Centuries*, University of California Press, Berkeley and Los Angeles, Calif., and London, 1985.

Kinross, Lord, *The Ottoman Centuries*, Morrow Quill Paperbacks, New York, N.Y., 1977.

Kostof, Spiro, *Caves of God: Cappadocia and Its Churches*, Oxford University Press, Oxford/New York, N.Y., 1972.

Krautheimer, Richard, *Early Christian and Byzantine Architecture*, Yale University Press, New Haven, Conn., 1986.

McDonagh, Bernard, *Blue Guide: Turkey, the Aegean and Mediterranean Coasts*, Norton, New York, N.Y., 1989.

McEvedy, Colin, *The Penguin Atlas of Medieval History*, Penguin Books, New York, N.Y., 1987.

Mango, Cyril, *Byzantine Architecture*, Academy Editions, London, 1979.

———, *Byzantium: The Empire of New Rome*, Charles Scribner's Sons, New York, N.Y., 1980.

Matthew, Gervase, *Byzantine Aesthetics*, Viking Books, New York, N.Y., 1964.

Mehling, Marianne, ed., *Turkey: A Phaidon Cultural Guide*, Phaidon Press, Oxford, 1989.

Nicol, Donald M., *The Last Centuries of Byzantium, 1261–1453*, Hart-Davis, London, 1972.

———, *The Immortal Emperor*, Cambridge University Press, England, 1992.

Norwich, John Julius, *Byzantium, The Early Centuries*, Knopf, New York, N.Y., 1989.

——, *Byzantium, The Apogee*, Knopf, New York, N.Y., 1992.

Ostrogorsky, George, *History of the Byzantine State*, Rutgers University Press, New Brunswick, N.J., 1969.

Payne, Robert, *The History of Islam*, Dorset Press, New York, N.Y., 1990.

Psellus, Michael, *Fourteen Byzantine Rulers*, trans. E.R.A. Sewter, Yale University Press, New Haven, Conn., 1953.

Ramsay, William, and Gertrude Bell, *The Thousand and One Churches*, London, 1909.

Rodley, L., *Cave Monasteries of Byzantine Cappadocia*, Cambridge University Press, England, 1985.

Runciman, Steven, *The Emperor Romanus Lecapenus and His Reign*, Cambridge University Press, England, 1929.

——, *A History of the Crusades*, 3 vols., Cambridge University Press, England, 1954.

——, *Byzantine Style and Civilisation*, Cambridge University Press, England, 1965.

——, *The Fall of Constantinople, 1453*, Cambridge University Press, England, 1965.

Stark, Freya, *Alexander's Path*, Overlook Press, London, 1958.

Talbot Rice, David, *Art of the Byzantine Era*, Thames & Hudson, London, 1963.

Treadgold, Warren, *The Byzantine Revival*, Stanford University Press, Stanford, Calif., 1988.

Vasiliev, A. A., *History of the Byzantine Empire*, 2 vols., University of Wisconsin Press, Madison, Wisc., 1958.

Veyne, Paul, ed., *A History of Private Life: From Pagan Rome to Byzantium*, Harvard University Press, Cambridge, Mass., 1987.

Vronis, Jr., Speros, *The Decline of Medieval Hellenism in Asia Minor and the Process of Islamization from the Eleventh Through the Fifteenth Century*, University of California Press, Berkeley and Los Angeles, Calif., and London, 1971.

Wharton, Annabel Jane, *Art of Empire: Painting and Architecture of the Byzantine Periphery*, Pennsylvania University Press, University Park, Penn., 1988.

A NOTE ON SPELLING
AND PRONUNCIATION

Turkish names can look alarming, but in fact the rules of spelling and pronunciation are completely logical and consistent. The principal stumbling blocks for non-Turks are *c* and the accented *g* (*ğ*).

c is pronounced like the English *j* as in *jar*, e.g., *cami* (mosque) is pronounced *jahmi*.

ğ is silent, but lengthens the preceding vowel, thus *dağ* (mountain) is pronounced *dah*, and *Niğde* is pronounced *Needay*.

Umlauts have much the same function they have in German, thus *göl* (lake) is very close in sound to *girl*.

ç is pronounced like *ch* in *charm*, and *ş* like *sh* in *shout*.

With regard to Byzantine names: I have reluctantly opted for the Latinized spelling, since this is what is used by Runciman and Norwich, and will be more familiar to readers. It should be borne in mind that *c* is invariably hard, as in *cat*, never soft, as in *ceremony*. Thus a more accurate spelling of Nicephorus Phocas would be Nikephorus Phokas.

ACKNOWLEDGMENTS

I would like to thank the following people for their encouragement and comments: Susan Bell, Anne Borchardt, Roberta Allen, Andrew Moore, Maggie Paley, Ted Mooney, April Bernhard, Joel Agee, Asher Paul Eden, Peter Hristoff, Lawrence LaRose, Jean-Isabel McNutt, Mona Amer, Marjorie Housepian Dobkin and Speros Vryonis, Jr.

INDEX

ABOUT THE AUTHOR

JOHN ASH, who was born in Manchester, England, in 1948, graduated from the University of Birmingham. He taught for a year in Cyprus, and for the last ten years has made his home in New York City. He has won a Guggenheim Fellowship, an Ingram Merrill Grant, a Whiting Foundation Writers Award, and an Anne and Erlo Van Waveren Foundation Award.

ABOUT THE TYPE

This book was set in Berling. Designed in 1951 by Karl Erik Forsberg for the Typefoundry Berlingska Stilgjuteri AB in Lund, Sweden, it was released the same year in foundry type by H. Berthold AG. A classic oldface design, its generous proportions and inclined serifs make it highly legible.